ONCE UPON A TIME IN LA LIGA

'A meticulously researched work that gets to the heart of some of the lesser-known corners of Spanish football.'

Jonathan Wilson — *The Guardian*; editor *The Blizzard*

'If you love football, you'll NEVER regret buying this book. Packed full of extraordinary stories from Spanish football - uplifting, idiosyncratic, passionate, mad, sad, bad and brilliant - almost all of which you've never read before.'

Graham Hunter — ESPN & *Revista de La Liga*

'These are the stories about the people you haven't heard about or, if you have, not like this.'

Sid Lowe — *The Guardian* & *The Spanish Football Podcast*

'Brendan Madden is such an atmospheric writer who transports you to the heart of these enthralling tales, which are an absolute treat for any fan of Spanish football.'

Tim Lee — commentator and analyst, LaLiga TV

'Extraordinary stories brilliantly told — a fresh, beautiful take on Spanish football's past.'

Phil Kitromilides — presenter, LaLiga TV & *The Spanish Football Podcast*

'Brendan Madden is a gifted writer with a deep knowledge of Spanish football and its culture, and an eye for an untold, absurd story, told with real flair. I love reading his work and I'd recommend it to anyone with even a passing interest in La Liga.'

Alex Kirkland — Madrid correspondent ESPN FC; producer, *The Spanish Football Podcast*

BRENDAN MADDEN

ONCE UPON A TIME IN LA LIGA

SPANISH FOOTBALL'S FORGOTTEN TALES

FOREWORD BY
SID LOWE

First published by Pitch Publishing, 2025

1

Pitch Publishing
9 Donnington Park,
85 Birdham Road,
Chichester, West Sussex,
PO20 7AJ
www.pitchpublishing.co.uk
info@pitchpublishing.co.uk

© 2025, Brendan Madden

Every effort has been made to trace the copyright. Any oversight will be rectified in future editions at the earliest opportunity by the publisher.

All rights reserved. No part of this book may be reproduced, sold or utilised in any form or transmitted in any form or by any means, electronic or mechanical, including photocopying, recording or by any information storage and retrieval system, without prior permission in writing from the publisher.

A CIP catalogue record is available for this book from the British Library.

ISBN 978 1 83680 168 9

Typesetting and origination by Pitch Publishing

Printed and bound on FSC® certified paper in line with our continuing commitment to ethical business practices, sustainability and the environment.

Printed and bound in India by Replika Press Pvt. Ltd.

Contents

Foreword 11
Introduction 15
Author's note 16

El Vestuario: The Players 17
  1. Black Armbands 18
  2. Canito: Once Barça, Forever Espanyol. 40
  3. Apocalypse in Aragón 60
  4. Levante's Cruyff Turn 74
  5. The Spy That Wouldn't Break 86
  6. The Saviour of Mauthausen 103
  7. *El Valladolid de los Colombianos* 113
  8. Quini: Bound to Forgive 126
  9. Once Upon a Time in the Desert 137

La Sala de Prensa: The Media 145
  10. The Prince of the Night 146
  11. They All Have Their Idols 160
  12. Tell Me a Story 176

El Palco: The Directors 195
  13. Carmen: Celta Vigo's Wonder Woman 196
  14. The Man Who Could Organise Anything 212
  15. You Will See Me at Atotxa Applauding *la Real* . . *230*
  16. The Night Barcelona Shook 240

La Grada: The Fans 253
  17. The Derby Like No Other 254
  18. They Tell Me Yellow is Cursed 266

Acknowledgements 284

To Sinéad, Malachy & Róisín for everything.

To Shane forever.

Foreword

SOME TIME in the spring of 2020, an article appeared online about Juan Alcorta, a Real Sociedad director who defied ETA. The story told how one day in April 1980 Alcorta received the letter that people in the Basque Country dreaded the most. Stamped with the frighteningly familiar image of a snake wrapped around an axe, inside the envelope was a demand for what the terrorist organisation always described as a revolutionary tax, raised to support the armed struggle for independence against the Spanish state.

The way Alcorta saw it, the way everyone did, there were three choices: pay in full, negotiate or flee. Instead, he chose a fourth: he said no. He did so publicly too, writing an open letter in the region's press refusing to collaborate and insisting that he was not going to hide. If they wanted to hunt him down and kidnap or kill him, which is what normally happened to those who refused, he was going to make it easy for them. You'll find me at Atotxa supporting *la Real*, he said. His team were top of the league, after all.

This was a fascinating, mostly unknown chapter from Spanish football which had appeared unannounced but was soon passed around. It was also only the first. Over time, other pieces followed, something very different to the usual stuff. Like the story about the two Racing Santander players, friends who had dared to challenge the Franco regime together, wearing black armbands in protest at its repression.

There was the story of the devastating fire which, as fate and stubbornness would have it, Jorge Valdano escaped but

José Ramón Badiola, forcing his way through the smoke and jumping from the second floor, never truly could: although he was found unconscious, charred and presumed dead, Badiola was not among the 83 people who died that night but his career, his life, was never the same again.

There was the one about the Celta Vigo director who took on the traffickers when Spain's north-west Galician coast became cocaine's gateway to Europe, flushing football with cash and destroying communities. And about the Barcelona player, the country's best striker, who was bundled into a van and kept in a tiny hole but still forgave his kidnappers.

'In a saloon bar on the edge of the desert, a man strides in, tosses his dusty Stetson on the counter and orders a beer to slake his high noon thirst,' another begins. The cowboy demands another, putting it down in front of a Real Oviedo winger, turning him into an Oscar-winning movie star. Then there was the deeply troubled talent brought up in an orphanage who celebrated a goal scored by Espanyol – while on the pitch playing for their rivals Barcelona. Or the tale of the most famous testicle-touching in Spanish football history.

None of the stories appeared in the press to start with, not in those early days. Instead they were published on a blog called *Fútbol es la leche:* football is the milk. In Spain, *la leche*, the milk, is the dog's bollocks, the business, and in these stories it was too.

Every Monday night for two decades, the whole of Spain would come together to watch *El Día Después*. Directed and presented by the former Liverpool striker Michael Robinson – whose unique place in Spain appears on these pages too – *El Día Después* was a TV show, Michael always liked to say, that was 'offside free'. He understood that the best football stories were very often not really about football at all. Instead, they were about people, humanity, and that is reflected in this collection, many of the chapters of which started in the blog. Others have been added since, written specially: some deadly serious, deeply moving, others silly. Read all about

Ronaldinho out scoring in the small hours and the club that's a carnival, piss-taking as a way of life. About the footballer who became a Nazi spy and the player who rescued a small boy from Mauthausen concentration camp, inventing an entire identity for him.

These are the stories about the people you haven't heard about or, if you have, not like this. In some cases, they are not so much about *a* person as an entire community, society through sport. And nothing provides a better portrait of Spain than football. In some cases, they are about the storytellers too, the people who kept those tales alive, celebrating their dedication to something different, to a passion, a feeling, a history, a *meaning*. And they are really, really good.

When the first of these stories came out, they were unattributed. There was a blog, a Twitter account too, but *Fútbol es la leche* had no author; instead there was anonymity. Which, although unintended, created a kind of intrigue. It also gave a purity to its discovery and enjoyment. Who was *Fútbol es la leche*? Speculation started. Perhaps it was someone we knew, maybe it was a secret side project, a writer satisfying themselves with the kind of stories that, alas, most media wouldn't run.

We wouldn't have bothered wondering if we hadn't liked them. Whoever was doing this *got it*. They were good: too good, too knowledgeable, to be just anyone. They knew Spain and Spanish football; they told stories we hadn't heard in ways we didn't expect. There were clues, or so we thought, but no confirmation. As it happened, we were even closer than we thought. Just not the *way* we thought.

One October morning – at 11.47am, it says here – my colleague Phil Kitromilides, handsome host of the Spanish Football Podcast, decided to ask. So he sent a direct message on Twitter – and it *was* direct. 'Hello, who are you?' it asked. 'We're keen to know. Thanks.'

The reply didn't take long. 'Basically I'm a guy called Brendan who lives not far from the Broadway Hair Stylist,' Brendan who lives not far from the Broadway Hair Stylist replied. Now, 'Broadway Hair Stylist' was the absurdly overblown name of a legendary (to us) old school barber's run for 40-odd years by a Greek Cypriot called Michael for whom every cut was 'a trendy cut'. On his wall was a faded, curled postcard of Camp Nou. All that speculation and Brendan lived within five minutes of both me and Phil in north London. Even if, to use his own words, he was originally from the Spanish football hotbed that is Luton.

Brendan had spent two decades analysing the game here in what he called 'excruciating detail', but his thing had been stats, not stories. Fortunately he had got a bit tired of that and tried something else. He hadn't intended to be anonymous, but nor was he sure this was for him just yet. He may not thank me for reminding him of this, or for telling you either, but at least now he knows and so do you. 'I started writing to see if I could string two sentences together and put out something worth reading,' he replied. He could and he has. It is called *Once Upon a Time in La Liga* and it is the *milk*. Enjoy.

Sid Lowe
Oviedo, June 2025.

Introduction

SOMEHOW, IT was always exactly 5.22am when I'd glance at the bedside clock and my mind began to whir – wondering again, how to structure this book. The brain can be a mutinous place at that hour, and for a long time it was a riot of contrived concepts and questionable titles.

In the end, it felt more honest – and more natural – to put the people who were so generous and candid front and centre. It's their lives and experiences that drive this book. The structure, such as it is, came second.

What you have in your hands is an anthology of stories from Spanish football. Each chapter stands alone, and although an obsessive amount of time was spent deciding the order, the truth is it can be read in any sequence you like.

We're fortunate to have a growing body of excellent writing on Spanish football in English – covering the national team, the big clubs, the underdogs, the regions, the rivalries. This isn't a comprehensive history, and it doesn't pretend to be. But it is an attempt to wander a little off the beaten track to uncover or delve deeper into episodes and characters that have been shaped by Spain's unique history and culture.

Putting this book together and giving voice to these stories has been a privilege. I hope you enjoy discovering them as much as I did – hopefully without the 5.22am wake-ups.

Author's note

Place names are given in Castilian Spanish, except where a widely accepted English equivalent exists – such as *Seville*, which helpfully distinguishes the city from the football club.

The names of buildings, streets, and stadiums appear in their local languages.

After their first mention, individuals are generally referred to by their first surname. Footballers are referred to as they were commonly known during their playing careers – whether by first name, surname, or nickname.

El Vestuario

The Players

1.
Black Armbands

AMID THE clatter of studs and the shouts of encouragement, the players of Racing Santander filed out of the home dressing room and into the tunnel to face their opponents. All of them, that was, except two.

'We said that if we could do something, we should. We were the ones who could do the most damage to this military regime. But it had to be subtle – if they noticed, they wouldn't let us onto the pitch. So, just before we went out, we slipped into the toilets with a pair of bootlaces. I tied one onto Sergio, and he tied one onto me. We wrapped them around our arms a few times, so they'd look like armbands.'

The pair exchanged one last glance before swiftly rejoining their team-mates, leaving an empty changing room behind. A very different scene would greet them on their return at half-time, the narrow corridors stuffed with armed police officers after their humble gesture of defiance had not gone unnoticed by the authorities. Repercussions began.

What followed was swift and severe: judicial proceedings, death threats, public condemnation. Yet the experience would only serve to forge an emerging friendship into a unique, lifelong bond.

* * *

It was 1975, and while Spanish society was nervously sensing that the sands of history were about to shift again, life in the elegant seaside city of Santander was good. Racing had returned to the first division, powered by the goals of Aitor Aguirre, who, after an itinerant start to life as a professional had finally found a home in Cantabria.

'In Santander, they called me *El Madero*,' smiles Aguirre on the terrace of the traditional *asador* in Getxo, where he manned the grill for decades and now leases it out. Even into his 70s, he carries the broad shoulders of a traditional Basque number nine, and it's easy to see why his nickname was essentially 'The Log'.

'I was tough, strong, tall, and when I entered the penalty area, even if they tried to hit me and stop me, my strength allowed me to push through and take a few players with me.

'The pitches back then were completely different from today. In those days, you could only play on the wings; it was the only place there was grass. You couldn't play through the middle without the ball getting stuck. It was OK at the start of the season but then just mud. So, we had to play with wingers delivering good crosses and then get up for the headers.

'At that time, we had an Argentinian on the right called Zuviría. Then, on the left, we had Ufarte, the one from Atlético Madrid, Armando Ufarte. He was great; his crosses were a joy and we had a really good understanding.'

Brought in to provide more ammunition for Aguirre was winger Sergio Manzanera, who was moving north after five successful seasons with his hometown club, Valencia. His acquisition as a teenager from city rivals Levante had been a specific request from incoming manager Alfredo Di Stéfano, even before he'd taken up his new post.

'He told me that he went to see a game or two and asked them to sign me,' recalls Sergio in a hotel lounge just a leisurely stroll away from the Estadio de Mestalla. 'I signed, but I was very young. I arrived at Valencia when I was 19 years old. He renewed the team a lot. He brought in some youngsters, not many, but some from the youth academy.'

Di Stéfano's refresh proved stunningly effective as Valencia emerged on top of an epic four-way fight to earn their first league title in 24 years. A double was denied to them only by an agonising extra time defeat to Barcelona in the final of the Copa del Generalísimo.

Far from simply adapting to the sudden leap from *Tercera* to *Primera*, Sergio flourished, playing every single game in all competitions and starting in all but one. Remarkably, he managed all that while also studying for a chemistry degree.

'I would train in the mornings, and at times, I'd leave running to go down to a laboratory here in the port to do the practical work. Organic chemistry it was. I was in there with the professor all year.'

That breakthrough season wasn't entirely without its challenges, though. 'We were pretty poor, so my mother couldn't always make me enough food at home. So, I'd eat a little with the family, then I'd go and eat at a bar or eat at another place. Then I was perhaps getting a bit overweight, maybe just a kilo or two, but I didn't feel great. They'd put a detective on me – I didn't know that, but they wanted to see where I was going and what I was doing. So, when I told Di Stéfano I felt tired and so on, he said: "How do you expect to feel if you're eating in those places?"

'So, he sent me to eat in a *pensión* here in Valencia where all the players went when they wanted to eat healthier. It was a lot healthier, a lot of Basque food – meat and fish.'

That episode was typical of the avuncular relationship that developed between Sergio and Di Stéfano in their four seasons together and endured until Di Stéfano's death in 2014. 'One of the times he had a heart attack was here in Valencia, and I went to see him in the main hospital, La Fe. But the same morning I went, they'd taken him to Madrid, so I never got to see him.

'I loved him dearly. The truth is you only realise how much you love someone when they die, right? There's a saying that goes: "The person who loves you the most will make you cry."

His death really shook me because I had become so fond of him. He was so very good to me.'

Becoming the protégé of one of Spanish football's most emblematic figures and delivering a long-awaited league title to your home city would ordinarily be enough to go to a young man's head. But while the newspapers of that season fizzed with headlines such as 'Sergio: The Revelation of Valencia' and 'Sergio: The Lightning Bolt of Valencia', the interviews beneath revealed a player uncommonly circumspect about his own abilities.

Looking back over his achievements years later, his self-appraisal is still strikingly humble. 'I was 100 per cent professional. I looked after myself as well as I could; I didn't like to go out partying or anything like that. I trained very conscientiously. Physically, I was very well prepared, and I had a lot of pace; I was very fast.

'The thing was that I wasn't a technically great player, and I didn't score many goals. If I had scored just 30 per cent of the chances I had, I would have been such a better player. I finished a season and scored four or five goals, but I had 27 chances to score because I was very nervous in front of goal.

'You can't train for that – you either have it or you don't. There are things that you can improve because they tell you when you get to this situation, "do this" or "do that", and you try. But the decision has to be instinctive because you don't have time to think about anything. If you are born like that, you solve it straight away.'

With Di Stéfano departed, Sergio sensed he needed a change. 'I had been there for five years and reached my ceiling. I was stuck at a level. In the first year, I played all the games; in the second year, I played maybe 90 per cent of the games; and in the third year, I played 80 per cent. I was starting less and less, but I was still good.'

A transfer to Racing provided a fresh challenge, and his new colleagues, including the man he was brought in to supply, would prove to be delighted with him. But before a productive relationship began on the field, Aguirre and Sergio struck up an instant friendship off it.

'Straight away,' remembers Aguirre, 'when Sergio arrived, it was just that thing where you immediately hit it off with someone. And look, when someone arrives in a new city, they need to find a house. So, I gave him a hand with an estate agent I knew, and he got a flat right next to the stadium at El Sardinero.'

'We became very, very close friends,' says Sergio. 'We always roomed together. I met his kids; he had a daughter and a son then, and we went out a lot. I went out with him and his wife; we'd go out to dinner, to lunch, to the cinema and see each other a lot.'

That instant friendship was underpinned by a shared political persuasion. 'Aitor was left-wing. You could classify him as a [Basque] nationalist. I was also left-wing but not a nationalist. He's very much from the Basque Country.'

Those beliefs had been shaped by their respective upbringings in Franco's Spain.

Aguirre was born in Sondika, just outside Bilbao, and raised in a family of strong Basque convictions. 'It was something that came from when I was very young. In my family, Basque nationalism has always been in the air. And, well, as you know, Franco was in power back then, and anyone who breathed that way was dealt with harshly.

'The Basque language has always been important. That was another thing where they would shake you down if they heard you speaking Basque. We spoke it at home, we spoke it among friends, but that was it. In public? No! Nowadays, that's changed, thank God. Now we can speak Basque, but before, it was tough. Really, really tough.

'The political atmosphere here... well, you can imagine during the Franco era. It was like this: we were always running from the police. Any protest, anything at all, would be met with gunfire and beatings. I remember being at a dance in Erandio as a kid. Some *ikurriñas* [the then outlawed Basque flag] were put up on the mountain, and because of that, the police came in with full force. There were two deaths near the slopes of Arriaga, a mountain just over there. That's where they found two bodies.'

When more *ikurriñas* appeared on the route of the Spanish Cycling Championship when it came through Vizcaya, a teenage Aguirre found himself directly targeted by police.

'That happened at the church in Erandio, but it wasn't me. What happened was that the ones they arrested, they took to the barracks and roughed up, ended up saying that a third person was involved, called Aitor. But obviously, there are plenty of Aitors around here!

'So, when they were told it was Aitor, what did they do? Naturally, they thought to go to my house in Sondika. I was leaving the house to go training with Sestao, and they arrested me. My parents saw as they took me to La Salve, a barracks in Bilbao, and, of course, the lads who said it was Aitor were bruised all over – they had been given a beating.

'Well, from there, my parents came to the barracks, confronted the sergeant, and told him, "My son didn't leave the house all night. So, it would have been impossible for him to be involved."'

Aguirre was released, but the experience only served to deepen his distrust of those in authority.

Although his new room-mate's upbringing was less spectacular, it was, in its own way, indelibly marked by the regime's vindictiveness.

'My father was a Republican, and so was my mother,' says Sergio. 'My mother was a teacher, what, in those days, was called a national teacher, working in villages and educating young children.

'There are things about my father's life that I don't know – probably because, in those times, people were afraid to talk. If someone had been a Republican [during the Civil War], they didn't want their children to face any repercussions from Franco or the regime.'

'As a result, they wouldn't share much. So, there are things I know about my father, but I'm also aware that there are many interesting aspects of his life that he never told me because of those circumstances.'

One thing Sergio did know was that his father had been stripped of a career and well-paid employment because of his beliefs. 'My father was a postal officer. He took his exams in 1916 when he was 16 years old and passed a really competitive exam. He worked as a supervisor on trains, guarding the mail and all that.

'Then, during the war, he was in prison for a short time. Just a few days, until a friend of his who was aligned with Franco's regime helped him. This friend was a well-known doctor, and he went to the prison, spoke with the authorities there, and got my father released. However, they took away his job. He was no longer a postal official and had to make a living however he could. Since he knew how to write, read, and do numbers – he was pretty intelligent – he worked for many years at some company.

'So, we were a very humble family. I used to go with my mother to the villages when I was little – this village, that village, another one. We'd come back to Valencia to reunite with my father at the weekends.

'I never felt I lacked anything because I was able to go to school. Still, we were a poor family. We lived in a very modest ground-floor flat, very basic, until finally, we were able to buy an apartment. That only happened when I signed for Valencia in 1970, when I was 19 years old. Then I began earning a little money, and our economic situation improved slightly.'

So imbued was the pair's mistrust of the regime that they rarely took their news from Spanish-based outlets. Instead on nights when they roomed together, they would switch on the radio, surfing the waves of static until they picked up the ever-changing frequency of *La Pirenaica* – Radio España Independiente, a station founded by Dolores Ibárruri, the exiled leader of the Spanish Communist Party to broadcast unfiltered news to Spaniards at home and abroad.

What they heard on those evening bulletins began to increasingly disturb them.

***

By 1975, Franco's failing health and the regime's deepening vulnerability were encouraging those who hoped for change to escalate activity and challenge the constraints on expression. Franco himself had spent much of the previous decade absorbed in succession planning.

His regime had exerted an iron grip on the country, but its institutions were heavily reliant on Franco's personal power and patronage.

The solution came in two stages. In 1969, Franco anointed Juan Carlos as his successor as head of state, by-passing the prince's exiled father, the moderate Juan de Borbon, as the legitimate heir to the Spanish throne. Still, while Juan Carlos was involved in much Francoist pomp over the proceeding years, there appeared a reluctance to grant him any meaningful power.

The second part of the strategy was unveiled in 1973 when Franco appointed Admiral Luis Carrero Blanco as Prime Minister, an office that had laid in dormant irrelevance since 1937. As Franco's staunchest acolyte, Carrero was deemed of sufficient conviction that the continuation of authoritarianism beyond the Caudillo's death was guaranteed. The partnership with Juan Carlos had the benefit of offering an arrangement agreeable to the regime's jostling factions.

The plan lasted precisely 195 days.

On 20 December 1973, on his way from morning Mass in the Salamanca district of Madrid, Carrero's car was blown 20 metres into the air over San Francisco de Borja church and into the courtyard of a neighbouring Jesuit college.

The assassination was the result of a meticulously planned operation by the Basque separatist group ETA, who had tunnelled for months to place 80kg of explosives in the optimum spot to target Carrero's government vehicle.

The continuation of Francoism after Franco suddenly seemed doubtful, and the regime was plunged into crisis. A swell of civil unrest that had begun the decade became a tide. With Spain left increasingly isolated after the toppling of Portugal's military dictatorship, authorities became ever more reactive in their attempts to suppress dissent.

In August 1975, Franco signed Decree No. 10/1975 into law. The hastily enshrined anti-terrorist powers compelled military tribunals to automatically impose the death sentence for those convicted of killing police, military or government officials. The decree also extended the definitions of terror offences while ramping up penal tariffs.

The new law was retrospectively applied to existing cases. Over four tribunals, 11 suspects were convicted of the murders of police and civil guards and handed down death sentences – three members of ETA and eight of the Revolutionary Antifascist Patriotic Front (FRAP). Observers noted a procedure so swift that defence lawyers struggled to read the accusations against their clients and were expelled from the room when they protested.

The sentences sparked international demonstrations and protests at countless Spanish embassies. There was also petitioning at the very highest levels. The Swedish Prime Minister, Olof Palme, led a march in Stockholm while Mexico motioned that Spain be dismissed from the UN Security Council. Pope Paul VI publicly called for clemency and privately telephoned *El Pardo* – only to be told that Franco was sleeping and would not be woken.

Nicolás Franco had even appealed to his younger brother in a letter pleading, 'Dear Paco, Don't sign this sentence… You're a good Christian; you'll regret it later. We're old now – listen to my advice.'

It was all to no avail. On Friday, 26 September 1975, a Franco-led cabinet meeting confirmed five of the death penalties for two members of ETA and three of FRAP. Seemingly the only concession to international pressure was the replacement of the regime's preferred method of execution – the garrotte – with firing squads.

One of the five condemned was José Humberto Baena, a bespectacled 24-year-old who spoke French, Latin and Greek, who was active in anti-regime protests and FRAP activity in his native city of Vigo. He was convicted of murdering policeman Lucio Rodríguez Martínez in Madrid two months earlier; despite presenting passport stamps apparently proving he was in Portugal at the time as part of 194 pieces of evidence submitted by the defence.

Instead, the tribunal ruled on the strength of a confession obtained by police including Juan Antonio González Pacheco – known as 'Billy the Kid' for the notorious interrogation techniques that saw him posthumously stripped of his service medals. That Friday evening, Baena wrote a farewell letter to his parents from his cell in Carabanchel, Madrid.

> *Mamá, Papá,* They will execute me tomorrow morning. I want to encourage you. You know that I will die, but life goes on.
>
> On your last visit, *Papá*, I remember you told me to be brave, like a good Galician. I have been, I assure you. When they shoot me tomorrow, I will ask them not to blindfold me, so I can face death head-on.
>
> Do you remember what I said at the trial? That my death be the last one pronounced by a military court.
>
> That was my wish, but I am sure there will be many more. Bad luck!'
>
> A huge hug, the last one.
> *Adiós papá, adiós mamá.*
> Your son,
> José Humberto.

The following morning, Saturday, 27 September, over the course of an hour and three-quarters, the five men were executed. Àngel Otaegui, in Burgos at 8.30am, followed by fellow ETA member Juan Paredes Manot in Barcelona at 8.35am. In Madrid, Ramón Garcia Sanz faced the firing squad at 9.20am, followed by José Luis Sánchez Bravo at 9.40am.

Finally, Baena was shot dead at 10.15am.

That night, the Racing players gathered to spend the night before the following day's game against Elche at the Hotel Rhin on Santander's seafront promenade. In their room, Aguirre and Sergio listened solemnly as the news of the executions was relayed on the radio. They decided that they needed to do something to mark what they had just heard.

They opted for that most simple gesture of mourning – the black armband.

* * *

'That night, we listened to *La Pirenaica* and heard the details of the executions,' recalls Sergio. 'My heart was pounding, and we said, "Hey, we have to do something."'

Aguirre remembers the conversation, 'That night, Sergio was saying, "This can't be. Everyone was against the death penalty, or at least a large part of Europe. And this backwards country, still with the death penalty, decides to execute whoever. It's unbelievable."'

'I used to read a lot,' says Sergio, 'and I read a lot about the death penalty, and I was very against it. These people were being executed in 1975 – this wasn't 1936, or 1940, or 1945, or even 1950. Democracy was on the verge of arriving. There was a certain social awareness already.

'Executing five people like that... because those on the right will say, "Well, they killed people, so they have to be punished." Nobody is saying they shouldn't be punished, and what they did was very wrong, but you imprison them, and that's it. You don't have to kill them; you don't have to execute them.

'I've never remembered who suggested the armbands because there were three of us in the room.'

Another forward, José María Errandonea, was also in on the plan.

'So, there was Errandonea, Aitor, and me. The thing is, Errandonea wasn't a starter, so he didn't play that Sunday. I don't know which of us said, "We could wear armbands?" Someone did, and we all agreed, "Well, let's do it."

'The next morning, when Aitor and I woke up to go to breakfast, we asked each other, "Hey, that thing we talked about last night, is it still on?" And Aitor told me, "For my part, yes." And I said: "Me too." So that's how it was decided.'

In the dressing room before the game, the plan was put into action – as inconspicuously as possible.

'Nobody knew anything at all,' says Sergio. 'Errandonea ducked into a room for a moment, grabbed some bootlaces and cut them for us.

'Then, when they told us it was time to go out onto the field, I quickly tied one on Aitor, and Aitor tied one on me, and that was it – we went out.

'Almost nobody noticed as everyone was focused on the match, but there was a player who said to me, "What's that?" and I told him, "Nothing, just a thing of ours." He didn't know why we were wearing it or anything, but he said, "I'm not wearing one, so why are you? Take it off." I just told him I wasn't taking it off, and that was that.'

It was business as usual in the first half, with Sergio and Aguirre linking up at what they did best. 'I made a very good play down the left side and Aitor headed it in. Thank goodness, really, because whatever you do in a match, no matter how bad things are, if you win the match, the repercussions are cut in half compared to what they could be.'

As for the armbands, it seemed that no one had noticed. 'We couldn't hear much,' says Sergio. 'At least I didn't. You're playing and hear a *runrún* [a grumble from the crowd], but you don't know if someone lost the ball or something else.' But when the teams returned to the dressing rooms during the break, it soon became apparent that their gesture had very much been noted.

'Well, they were there,' says Aguirre, 'in the tunnel. There must have been about 20 police officers there or maybe more.'

The distinctive grey uniforms of the *Policia Armada* packed the narrow corridors. *Los Grises,* as they were more colloquially known, were the feared national police force and a key facilitator of the regime's repression.

'So, a bunch of them came in and told us to take the armbands off,' says Sergio. 'Aitor and I didn't know what to do, and then they said, "If you don't take them off, you won't play the second half, and you'll be arrested."'

The pair quickly came to a decision, says Aguirre, 'Sergio and I talked about what we wanted. We had already achieved it. They had fallen into the trap – this would be in all the newspapers tomorrow. The whole world was going to find out, which was exactly what we wanted.'

With the start of the second half delayed, causing rumours to begin circulating in the crowd, Aguirre and Sergio untied the makeshift armbands and prepared to take the field again. The fact that they avoided arrest would prove to be a determining factor in what was to follow, as Sergio, with his keen eye for nuance, explains.

'That was crucial, that detail. The difference between being arrested or not was significant because it determined whether they could apply an article of the anti-terrorism law.

'The law stated that if you disrupted public order, you could go to jail, but you had to be arrested first. If you weren't, it was up to the judge to decide, but if you were arrested, you could be automatically sent to prison.

'Of course, we would've been taken directly to the station, jail, or wherever, but we weren't arrested. Instead, they told us that in the morning, we had to come to the police station in the centre of Santander, in Plaza Porticada.'

Back out on the field, matters also began to get complicated. Having dominated the first half, Racing lost their way in the second, allowing Elche to equalise just after the hour. But with two minutes remaining, when, as *Mundo Deportivo* put it, 'Nobody would give five *centimos* for a Racing win,' Aguirre crashed in a trademark header from a corner to ensure his name would appear in bold in both the sports and news headlines the following morning.

'The last moment was good,' says Aguirre. 'We won the match, and everyone was really happy. And the president started saying: "Don't worry, we'll take care of this." And so, they started pulling strings. The president must have had some contacts with people in the regime. He had quite a bit of influence, you know how club presidents always have connections. In the VIP box, the so-called powers that be would sit together. Even today, they still do.'

The pair went home uncertain whether that night's sleep might be their last in their own beds for some time.

* * *

'So, the next morning, we went,' says Sergio. 'We could've chosen not to go, run away, or stay put and see what happened. But we went, both of us.'

At the police station, the pair were split into different rooms, where they had two distinct experiences. 'For me, I didn't even feel like they wanted to hit me. I just walked in, greeted them with, "Hello, good morning, here I am," and answered their questions. It took a while, but everything was calm.'

In the other room, Aguirre was living in a very different encounter.

'Hostile, very hostile,' grimaces Aguirre. 'You could see how much they wanted to beat us black and blue, but on the other hand, they would have had orders to be careful – not to hit us. If it had come out in the press that they'd given us a beating, that wouldn't have helped them. They were smart individuals.'

Sergio believes the contrasting approach was a function of where the two were from. 'With me, they couldn't work out an explanation. With Aitor, they could say, "Well, you're Basque, so we understand." For me, they were like, "Why did you do it?"

'What was I supposed to say? They could easily throw you in jail if you said the wrong thing. In those moments, your imagination runs at 100 miles per hour. Everything is happening quickly.'

Sergio laughs as he recounts one explanation he gave, plucking the memory of a newspaper obituary to claim it was the anniversary of an old Racing president. His interrogators were unconvinced. 'But it plants a doubt in the minds of the police, and they start to think, "Is this guy just so stupid that he wears an armband every year?"

'After that, they told us we had to go to court in the afternoon. The courts in Santander are up in the higher part of the city. So, Aitor and I arrived, and the police vans were there outside, ready for whatever the judge decided. If the judge had said, "Yes, to jail," then they would've taken us straight to prison.'

Prosecutors asked for a custodial sentence of five years and a day, a term that would have certainly finished their careers.

'We were lucky because the judge could have said it qualified as a public disturbance. In the end, it wasn't because no one did anything – no protests, no objects thrown onto the field, no assaults, nothing. There was still a provision in the law, but for that to apply, you had to have been arrested.

'Aitor and I were sitting outside, waiting to see what would happen. Then the club's lawyer came out and told us that since we hadn't been arrested, the judge had decided to impose a very large fine, but we could go home.'

The fines were reported as 100,000 pesetas, though Aguirre remembers a figure five times that amount. Either way, it was a significant amount of money and almost comically difficult to pay.

'At that time, payments to the state were done through something called *papel del estado* (state paper). Every tobacconist and most post offices had this. So, you'd go and say, "I want to enrol in university, and I need to pay a fee." They would give you a little stamp, maybe worth one peseta, 50 cents, 20 cents, 10, whatever, and you'd stick all those stamps onto the paper and then hand it in.

'So, we'd go to a tobacconist and say, "Give us 100,000 pesetas in *papel del estado*." They'd say, "What are you talking about? I don't have that much." Man, we had to go to so many tobacconists!'

While their judicial issues were abated, an even more malevolent threat was about to emerge.

'About a week later, a newspaper reported that in a meeting of what was the *Guerrilleros de Cristo Rey* (Warriors of Christ the King), which was like *Fuerza Nueva*, the equivalent of today's Vox only worse – because they carried guns and murdered people – they had sentenced us to death; Aitor Aguirre, me... and the president of Racing.'

Sergio laughs at the memory of Racing's usually urbane, unruffled president, José Manuel López-Alonso Polvorinos, absolutely horrified that he'd been included. 'The president was like, "I haven't done anything, I didn't know anything," he was terrified by that!'

While Sergio finds humour in it now, the threat was all too credible at the time. A year later, the group murdered 21-year-old student Carlos González Martínez for attending an anniversary vigil for the very same executions Sergio and Aguirre had protested.

Aguirre, for his part, was livid with the local media. 'The regime controlled the press – there was *El Alerta* and the other one. The issue was, and I told this to one of the newspapers years later when I was in Santander with them, I said, "With Sergio and me, you didn't do anything right, absolutely nothing right." I mean, how can you publish that the *Guerrilleros de Cristo Rey* have decided to execute so-and-so? Why put that in the press? You essentially painted a target on Sergio and me for so many people.

'After that, we had to live cautiously, leaving the house carefully. We even had someone check under the cars for us just to make sure nothing was placed there. When you're under death threats, you have to see if they've planted a bomb or something. You had to be careful. That lasted for a while.'

Aguirre took the precaution of sending his family home. 'I had two small children, one around two or three and the other just a year old. My wife had to leave and come here to Sestao, to her mother's house, because I didn't want her to stay. We lived apart for that season.'

Sergio recalls many sleepless nights: 'Of course, it left me shaken. I lived alone in an apartment near El Sardinero, in a building with maybe 30 or 40 apartments. In winter, only two or three of us lived there. I lived there on the top floor, and every night after that, when I heard the elevator coming up at 2am, I would think, "What's going on here?" At the time, I liked hunting, so I had a shotgun, and I slept with that gun next to my bed.'

Even going about their daily business became hostile in a city that traditionally leans to the right.

'Some people didn't like what we did. Maybe you'd be walking down the street, and they'd insult you or say something. I remember one person – he wasn't exactly a close friend, but I always went to a workshop in Santander to wash and fix my car. A few days after it happened, I went there, and the guy told me he thought what I had done was very wrong. He said that Aitor and I should go out on the pitch on Sunday, kneel down at the centre with our arms outstretched in a cross, and ask for forgiveness. I never took my car there again.'

Training became complicated, with newspapers reporting that Aguirre was the target of heckling from his own supporters. 'At El Sardinero, people could come to watch the training sessions, but for a while, they had to stop letting anyone in because some people would come just to cause trouble, disrupting the session.'

Though there was some support, as Aguirre recounts, 'A priest from the fishing neighbourhood sent us a letter. He knew he couldn't send it by post because they confiscated all our letters – any mail for me or Sergio never reached us.

'But this priest passed a letter via a boy named Luis. Poor kid, he had mobility issues – we used to take him to training sessions. One day, he came to me with this letter which said, "You might think the whole world is against you, but that's not true. There are many more of us who are with you." It was a heartfelt letter. It really boosted our spirits.'

The pair continued training and playing and perhaps felt more comfortable away from El Sardinero, where Aguirre was on the scoresheet at Camp Nou and the Vicente Calderón to add to his burgeoning reputation.

More permanent relief was to arrive in the form of four simple words spoken at 10am on 20 November 1975.

* * *

'*Españoles… Franco ha muerto.*'

The trembling voice of Prime Minister Carlos Arias Navarro announced Franco's death to a nation. Arias had taken office after Carrero's assassination but had proven too politically enfeebled to deliver continuity for the regime. Two days later, Juan Carlos was proclaimed King of Spain and though a guarded coronation speech disappointed those impatient for change, he proved adept at unpicking Franco's institutions and steering Spain towards democracy.

Arias's attempts at obstructing reform soon saw him removed by Juan Carlos and replaced by the surprising choice of Adolfo Suárez, a Falangist bureaucrat. Within a year, Suárez helped deliver Spain's first free general election for four decades, setting the country on a fragile road to transition.

An amnesty relieved Aguirre and Sergio of any lingering legal process, and their fines were returned. 'In theory,' says

Sergio, 'But I don't remember if they ever gave it back. Aitor says they did, but I don't remember receiving it!'

Groups from all sides of the political spectrum continued their bloody violence, but the specific threat from the *Guerrilleros de Cristo Rey* faded, and the pair's lives returned to relative normality.

Though the straight-spoken Aguirre maintained a testy relationship with the Santander public, as exemplified by one famous incident.

Trailing at home after Mario Kempes had struck twice for Valencia, Aguirre rescued the situation, levelling the game with two goals in the final ten minutes. Rather than celebrate the goals, Aguirre delivered a message to the hitherto disgruntled home support.

The scene was observed by his injured room-mate, 'I was behind the goal where he scored. Then he gave a *corte de mangas* [a "sleeve-cutter" a kind of all-arm "Up Yours"] – it wasn't just a quick one, and that's it. No, he turned to one stand, then to another, and to everyone – to all four sides.'

'I didn't handle it very well,' laments Aguirre. 'It hurt to score two goals, and instead of cheering for you, they're booing and saying things. Not the whole crowd, not everyone in the stadium, but a part of it.

'That was all a consequence of the armbands. Everything stemmed from that; some people still held grudges. The tension lingered.'

As Spaniards excitedly went to the polls, Aguirre's own future was at stake in the summer of 1977 as Racing's economic situation forced them to sell their most influential players. Barcelona appeared the most likely destination, but Racing's indecisiveness saw their interest fade. Aguirre was left disappointed, but soon, the dream solution arrived.

'The president told me, "Aitor, the next chance you get, you'll leave. Don't worry." That's when I came to Athletic. Of course, coming to Athletic was what I had wanted from the very beginning.'

Aguirre spent two seasons playing out his childhood dreams at San Mamés, rounding off his career with another spell in the south with Recreativo de Huelva, and finally returning to Sestao, where it all began.

With his ally departed, Sergio played on for one more season in Santander before coming to a surprise decision.

'At the end of the third year, when I still had one year left on my contract, I decided to quit football. This was before the season ended. I thought about it a lot, reflected deeply, and realised I didn't want to play anymore. I was tired.

'Mentally, I was tired of football. I loved football, but there's a saying, "Football would be wonderful if Sundays didn't exist." You train in the morning, you're with your mates on the field, you all go out to eat – it's incredible.

'Then Sunday comes, and so does the stress. You lose a match, and the press are all on top of you. The tension… I couldn't handle it anymore and was exhausted. I wanted to study medicine. I had already done my first year, and I thought, "I want to keep studying, I don't want to play anymore."'

Racing reluctantly agreed to rescind his contract, and Sergio retired at just 27 years of age. He moved to Málaga, the home city of his newly married wife, and started a new life.

'It was a leap into the unknown. Back then, you didn't earn as much money as you do now, where you can quit football at 27 and have €10m in the bank, but I ran the numbers, *pum, pum, pum,* and said, "I have enough money to move to Málaga, buy a house, and live there with my wife and my son for six or seven years." I figured that's how long it would take me to finish my medical degree.

'So, I moved there, lived off that money, passed all my courses in June, didn't fail a single assignment throughout the entire degree, and finished in five years.'

Medicine became a specialism in dentistry, and Sergio returned to his native city, where he built up two successful and innovative practices.

* * *

Despite the often-turbulent relationship, Aguirre shared with the Racing fans, looking back now, he holds no ill feeling. In fact, he speaks as excitedly about the club's recent resurgence as he does his beloved Athletic's historic achievements.

'The only problem I had was the one Sergio and I had. Racing are on a roll right now, and they'll call me, "Aitor, are you coming to El Sardinero?" I'm a *socio* of Racing and part of their Association of Former Players. I'm also registered with Athletic's association, so I'm part of both.'

Though many years have passed and hundreds of miles separate them, a special connection remains between the pair.

'Those kinds of things bring you very close together,' explains Sergio. 'It's the same as when people share stories about their adventures in prison. Those bonds you create... when you come out, there's an intimate connection. That's very hard to break – especially if you continue to think the same way.

'Because life can change; it can take you in one direction or another. I could have ended up supporting Vox, for example, and Aitor could have become far-left. In that case, we'd still have a relationship, but it wouldn't be the same.'

'I see his daughter, who was four or five years old back then – now she's in her 50s, and it brings me so much joy to see them. It's the same with Aitor and me. Even though we don't see each other often, that bond is always there.'

As for the decision they came to after listening to the news over those faint radio waves in a seaside hotel room in a very different Spain, there's only pride, as they both explain in their own distinct way.

'It gives me great satisfaction to know that I've contributed my tiny grain of sand, the little I was able to contribute, to democracy, to trying to change something,' Sergio eruditely explains.

'They often say to groups of youngsters that we must leave the world a little better than we found it. That's a phrase everyone knows. I believe I've done that. I've done other things, too, because, in medicine, you have many opportunities to help people and do things for others that also change the world a little – but that's something personal.'

'But doing something like this – a significant gesture, where you're taking a risk – because if you risk nothing, there's no merit. If all you're doing is signing a petition for democracy, that's easy, but if someone says, "Hey, you need to go there and do this," that's another thing. If it goes well, that's great, but if it had gone badly, I might've been sent to jail, my football career could have ended, or something could have happened to me in jail.

'I'm happy I did it. If we hadn't have done it, I think it would've left a thorn in my side, which would've felt like we didn't have the courage to do it. When you do it, you take a risk, but the satisfaction is infinitely greater than if you hadn't done it.'

As for Aguirre, 'Would I do it again?' he asks himself. 'The same circumstances would have to exist. I was young. At this age, maybe I would've thought about it more, but I'm almost certain I'd do it again.

'It was an important milestone. A significant moment in my life, and I'll carry that with me until they take me to the cemetery.'

2.

Canito: Once Barça, Forever Espanyol

ESPANYOL BREAK nearly an hour's worth of nervous deadlock to take the lead in their pivotal relegation clash against Hércules in Alicante. On the halfway line, two fists pump the air in delight, an instinctive reaction to a goal that will almost certainly ensure Espanyol's top-flight survival. And there's nobody it matters as much to. For him, Espanyol is like family – certainly, the closest thing to it for somebody abandoned to an orphanage as a young boy. It was Espanyol that had offered opportunity when a lifetime of lonely struggle seemed his destiny. It was the club where every staff member held tales of his charm and generosity.

And it was Espanyol where decades later, years after his tragically young death, he would be remembered as an icon. Where his handsome likeness and easy smile would ripple across the stands, the rebellious personification of the struggle of a club forever in the shadows of their city rivals.

For José Cano López – the generational talent known as Canito – Espanyol was everything, and his joy was understandable.

There was only one problem. He was 400km away from Alicante – and playing for Barcelona at Camp Nou.

* * *

'The frustrating thing is that no images of the incident have ever been found,' says Jesús Beltrán, who, as a youngster, watched Canito playing for Espanyol and wrote a book entitled *Canito: El Gesto de un Rebelde* (The Gesture of a Rebel), that was made into a compelling documentary.

Beltrán has certainly looked, 'For years, and even with Movistar while making the documentary, we combed through everything – archives, libraries, even old radio recordings. Newspapers from that time that no longer exist… we contacted photographers and sports journalists of that era. Despite all efforts, no one has been able to find an image.'

Don Balon produced a cartoon of a deed that has, over time, taken on an almost mythical quality. But contemporary reports and Canito's unguarded nature allow the confident conclusion that it definitely happened. The moment came an hour into Barcelona's game with Athletic Club when the Camp Nou scoreboard relayed news of Espanyol's goal at Hércules.

'Canito applauded, raised his arms, and celebrated. Naturally, he was booed by the Barcelona crowd, which wasn't uncommon, but, even then, there were some little doubts. After all, a gesture like that from a player in the middle of the field could have been misinterpreted. Let's be clear, celebrating a city rival's goal in your home stadium isn't exactly normal, right?

'Then after, in the mixed zone with journalists, he says, "Yes, I celebrated because I'm happy Espanyol scored." He is smiling and says, "Why wouldn't I celebrate?" He didn't try to deny it or make excuses. He admitted it outright.

'Then later they interviewed him on the radio programme that practically all of Spain listened to, the Cadena Ser show hosted by José María García, a legendary journalist. He admitted it again and criticised his club, Barça, on the radio. That sullied his relationship with the fans, and that had never been great.'

Canito arrived at Camp Nou in the previous summer of 1979, with Barcelona in the middle of a post-Cruyff rebuild. With their talisman having departed a year previously and then been followed Stateside by compatriot Johan Neeskens, the focus fell on adding younger talent to the squad.

Having outlasted Real Madrid in pursuit of Canito, Barcelona matched Espanyol's 40m peseta asking price. It was a significant fee, but for a proven *Primera* talent and a rising star of the Spanish national team, one the board felt represented value. Questions about the player's free-spirited nature were deflected away.

'I was lucky enough to spend the afternoon with him, and he seems to be a phenomenal person. They say he's hot-headed, but with some love, the boy will fit in well with us,' declared Barcelona director Albert Parera as camera lenses snapped and handshakes were posed in the boardroom.

The 23-year-old in question stood smiling in an immaculate white jacket with plunging open-necked shirt. He cut a figure that somehow managed to embody two very different icons of the 1970s. On the field, his composed defending and ability to smoothly bring the ball forward from the back drew discerning comparisons to Franz Beckenbauer. Off it, his telegenic looks, love of fashion and of the city's nightclubs were such that public and press couldn't resist the similarities with John Travolta.

The following day's front covers heaved with Canito's image alongside headlines heralding the transfer. Though it was a few pages back, in the scarce column inches afforded to Espanyol in that morning's *Mundo Deportivo* that held the biggest clue to how matters would fare for Canito on the other side of the city's Avinguida Diagonal.

The Espanyol correspondent detailed Canito's farewell to the club that had plucked him from the lower reaches of Catalan football. The player had gathered together every single employee for a farewell to thank them for what they had done for him. 'Rarely has there been such a gesture in the Espanyol family.'

It was a line that proved prescient. More than that, it was a sentiment that was, quite simply, the key to everything, because for Canito, Espanyol really was the closest thing to family.

CANITO: ONCE BARÇA, FOREVER ESPANYOL

***

Born in the Pyrenees, Canito lost his father at an early age and with his mother struggling to cope, he was left in the reception of La Salle de Nuestra Señora in Barcelona's port area. There, from the age of six, he was brought up among the orphaned and abandoned in the school nicknamed the 'Port Asylum'.

'We're talking about the 1960s. Spain was under Franco's regime. Spain was underdeveloped. Many families couldn't support their children, there were many families, many children, who were orphans. So, the government created schools to take in boys and girls who faced difficult circumstances. Although, in my particular case, it was different.'

Educated alongside Canito at the school was Toni Frieros, who went on to become chief editor of the Barcelona-based sports daily *Sport* for over four decades.

'I have two brothers: one four years older than me, and another six years older. So, there were three of us. When my mother became a widow – my father died in 1966 – we all went to live at the boarding school. My mother was with us; she worked as a cook. It was a special case because none of the other children at that school – not a single one – had a mother or father there.

'It was a building that was divided into two parts. In one, for the youngest children, up to eight years old, there was a school run by nuns. From eight to 14, there was another part of the school that priests ran. So, the school was separated. For younger children, up to eight years old, it was mixed, but the school for ages eight to 14 was only for boys'.

'It was there we met Canito. I don't remember exactly how it started, but I suppose it was through football because Canito played football at La Salle, and my brothers also played, and that's where the bond and friendship began.

'Since Canito didn't have a father or mother, and no one came to visit him, my mother took a liking to him. As the cook, she always treated us a bit better; she'd give us sandwiches, and so on. She always had a very, very affectionate relationship with Canito. My brothers played football with him a lot, and when my older brother left the school, he went on to play for a local team called Iberia and played *juvenil* with Canito, they were team-mates.'

La Salle was strict, as Beltrán explains, 'The 1960s were years of an opening up in Spain ideologically, socially, and economically, but the boarding school remained very strict, led by harsh nuns, and there was little affection. He had no parents, siblings, or regular visits, only very occasional ones, such as for his First Communion. He had no emotional support, but what the nuns gave Canito was unique compared to other footballers of his time. He learned to express himself very well. He spoke articulately and wrote correctly. The strict, rigorous religious education he received gave him excellent verbal and written communication skills.'

That quality was also noted by Frieros, 'He wrote very well, with beautiful handwriting, and unlike a lot of footballers, he had culture – a street culture but a culture of life. Yes, he learned from the streets, from the *barrio*, from eating and spending time with normal people. Even so, he was well-spoken and wrote really well.

'I don't know why I didn't keep the letters he sent me from his time during military service in Cádiz. It's a shame, a real shame because he wrote so well. His handwriting was beautiful, and he knew how to express his feelings. When he wrote, he opened up. I really appreciated it when he wrote to me because I saw him as very human.'

Frieros's family eventually found an apartment and left the school about the same time Canito's years at La Salle came to an end. 'Around then, Canito kind of disappeared from our lives because once you turned 14, you had to leave the school.

'You could stay if you worked in the printing press run by the Barcelona City Council. You could study a course where you learned how to operate printing machines. So, some older boys stayed at another residence, separate from the younger kids, but Canito didn't; he left and went out to live on his own, and for a few years, we lost track of him.'

Left to his own devices, Canito made a living around Barcelona's port in any which way he could, as Beltrán details: 'He was figuring out how to survive as a young, street-smart boy. He earned a living in countless ways, including petty thefts, minor crimes, and doing jobs for the criminals of the time. He worked in loading and unloading trucks at Mercabarna, the central supply hub for Barcelona's markets.

'That's the most striking example of how hard it must have been. For a boy to do that job, but he worked at whatever he could because he was a kid who had to survive without a trade, money or a family.

'The Barcelona of those days is nothing like the Barcelona of today. Crime was high, and there were some very marginalised neighbourhoods. Many of these areas have been redeveloped, but the neighbourhood where his boarding school was, for example, was extremely poor and rife with crime and social issues. That area on the slopes of Montjuïc was near the city's largest cemetery, an industrial zone known as the Zona Franca and had three or four difficult districts.

'Specifically, the district he lived in from age 14 was called *Las Casas Baratas* (The Cheap Houses). These were social units built in the 1920s – low, single-storey homes resembling a village in the middle of the city. They were extremely modest and overcrowded. He continued having friends there; it was his natural environment. He always, always returned there.'

Football remained the one constant for Canito, offering a weekly change of scene as well as some pocket money. His name was soon being scribbled down in notebooks of scouts across the region as his athleticism and ability to play in a number of positions caught the eye and drew early comparisons with West Germany and Bayern Munich's all-conquering captain.

From Penya Barcelonista Anguera, then Iberia, Canito moved to Lloret, where attention from first division clubs intensified. Barcelona showed a prolonged interest but failed to come up with a contractual offer. Real Madrid scouts in the region also fed back promising reports. But it was one of their European Cup-winning dynasty that made the decisive move with José Santamaria signing Canito for Espanyol. Santamaria immediately sent him on loan to *Tercera* division Lleida to a manager he believed would instil some solid discipline in the 18-year-old.

It didn't quite work out that way. Exasperating his coach, arguing with local journalists and refusing to play unless the club bought him an all-white suit were highlights of an eventful season that nearly saw the loan ended on several occasions. On the pitch, though, he showed enough for Santamaria to incorporate him into the first-team squad in the 1976/77 season.

It was during his preparations for that term that Canito was reunited with the Frieros family, as Toni recollects, 'He came back from Lleida to Barcelona. Then I remember he got in touch with us – specifically my middle brother, Basilio, who was a goalkeeper, a very good one. It was June or July before the season started. Canito was training at the La Salle football field, which was a dirt pitch, and called my brother to help him practise his shooting.

'Then I don't know exactly how the conversation started, but it was something like, "Where are you going to live?" And he said, "Oh, I don't know, maybe I'll get an apartment somewhere." And we said, "*Hostia*, why don't you come live with us at our house?" We talked to my mother about it, and during his first two years at Espanyol, he came to live with us.

'That's when I started to have a closer, more personal relationship with him because I saw him every day. He would come home, sleep at the house, have breakfast, and then go train with Espanyol.

'My brothers were working and had their own lives, so I often went with him to training sessions at Espanyol's ground. I was 14 or 15 years old, and I would go to see him at Sarriá for the matches. At that time, I had more of a relationship with him than I did with my brothers.'

Frieros regularly experienced Canito's generosity first-hand, 'I remember he would come home from eating, go to bed, leave some loose money on the table, and say, "Take whatever you need, and tomorrow go get yourself a snack."'

There were gifts of sportswear and much larger gestures too. 'I remember that he paid for my schooling for two years. I went to a private academy, and he paid for it because he wanted me to be well off.'

Canito's first season at the top level was a promising one. Though Santamaria was reluctant to give him a starting role, Canito impressed in the opportunities he was given, including driving half the length of the field to score in a 4-1 demolition of Real Madrid at Sarriá.

Progress was abruptly interrupted by a call-up for military service. Canito was posted south to a base in Cerro Muriano in Córdoba, and predictably, those letters home to Frieros expressed frustration. 'He had a tough time during his military service because he was someone who struggled a lot with discipline. Not surprisingly, for him, being in the military was a waste of time, especially because it disrupted his football career.'

Fortunately, Canito was moved on to a base in Cádiz, where Espanyol struck a loan deal to allow him to continue his development in *Primera*. Cádiz finished bottom, but Canito enhanced his reputation. Memorably, he shut down Johan Cruyff during a man-marking assignment at Camp Nou. Cádiz ground out an unlikely 1-1 draw as a frustrated Cruyff drifted deeper and deeper in search of space, much to the disgruntlement of the home crowd – something Canito would come to be accustomed to himself in future seasons.

With *mili* out of the way, Canito returned to Espanyol, this time as an automatic starter under new manager José Antonio Irulegui.

'That season was his explosion,' says Beltrán. 'He was already expected to be a starter; the fans regarded him as a huge prospect. He lived up to all expectations. He was soon called up to the Spanish national team by László Kubala. His progress that year was remarkable.

'Despite his youth – he was just 21 or 22 – he had an authority in the starting eleven. He had charisma both on the field and with the people in the stands. He could score. He'd score four or five goals a season from sweeper or centre-back. He stood out a lot, and in Irulegui, he had a coach who liked to play good football.'

Frieros was also impressed, 'He was a creative defender who could carry the ball forward and make passes inside. He had great ball control, a strong shot and was a technical player. He had a mastery of the ball with both feet, which was rare then. Even today, it's difficult to find footballers who can play with both feet, but he could shoot equally well off either foot. He was very good.'

As always, along with the outrageous ability came glimpses of volatility. A three-game spell at the end of that 1978/79 season typified Canito. Superb and the scorer of the only goal as Espanyol beat Valencia live on national television, he was again on the scoresheet as they held leaders Real Madrid to a draw a fortnight later. In between was a bizarre 2-0 loss at Salamanca in which he was booked for arguing with his own captain, Rafael Marañón.

Beltrán takes up the story, 'Canito carried the ball from his own half, through one line, then another, then at the edge of the area, he took a shot that came close, but did not score. Marañón scolded Canito, seemingly for not passing the ball to him as he was in a good position, although Marañón later explained that he had been trying to tell Canito that he was drawing defenders away to create space for him. This misunderstanding led to a heated argument between the two, which involved a lot of gesticulating and shouting. The referee, hearing Canito yelling "*Vete a la mierda*" (Go to shit) at Marañón, showed him a yellow card for insulting his own team-mate.'

Match reports noted Canito rattling the crossbar with another long-range effort moments later before asking to be replaced despite Espanyol having already used both substitutes.

Those flashes of temper did little to dissuade suitors who were quietly manoeuvring into position for Canito's services. As so often is the case in Spanish football, it came down to a straight fight between Real Madrid and Barcelona.

For a long time, it seemed that Real Madrid's resolve to recruit a successor to their revered sweeper, Pirri, would prove decisive. It was a move endorsed by the incumbent himself, 'Pirri said that the player he most liked was Canito, and he recommended that Real Madrid sign him,' recalls Frieros.

Don Balon ran several front pages anointing Canito as a Real Madrid player. In February, one cover featured Canito perched on a ball at training alongside the headline: 'Canito: A leader for the future Madrid.' As far as the middle of May, an exclusive proclaimed that 'Canito is already a White,' reporting that the two presidents had struck a 50m peseta deal at a 'luxury Barcelona restaurant'.

The venerable magazine had got it wrong. Although both Beltrán and Frieros, to this day, wish it had been right.

'Undoubtedly,' argues Beltrán, 'for two reasons. First, from the very first day Canito arrived at Barcelona, things started off on the wrong foot. He had already clashed with Barça during previous matches, and even as a spectator in the stands at Camp Nou, he had got into altercations with fans. When he was presented, the fans received him poorly, insulting him. This bad reception created immediate tension, which would not have been the case had he joined Real Madrid, where the fans would have welcomed him.

'Second, it was well known that Canito was more inclined toward Real Madrid than Barça, and he likely would have been more comfortable there. Madrid had a history of managing difficult players better than Barça. At Barça, especially during Núñez's presidency, players with challenging personalities often faced stormy exits. In contrast, Real Madrid had a history of steering such players in the right direction – figures like Juanito being a prime example of how the club managed volatile characters effectively.'

Frieros agrees, 'I think so; Real Madrid would have been a better fit. Madrid is a club that protects its players more. He would have had more guidance compared to Barcelona. At that time, he didn't have any control over his life and just did whatever he wanted; he lived more at night than during the day.

'He suffered a lot because, although he was a physical prodigy, there weren't the same systems of control as there are today. People didn't take as much care of themselves. Today, players are much more disciplined, but back then, you might train a little, do the bare minimum, and that was it. It was very easy to lose your way if you didn't have an orderly life or a structured family. I think that he would have succeeded at Real Madrid. I have no doubt about that.'

Canito's love of the night was something Frieros had increasingly noticed when they lived together. On the surface, Canito epitomised 1970s glamour. His love of cars, fashion and the company of women inevitably invited references to *Saturday Night Fever*'s Tony Manero. Indeed, he spent many nights inside the velvet ropes of the city's nightclubs, such as the renowned Bocaccio on Carrer Muntaner, always impeccably dressed and hospitable company to be in.

Though just like Travolta's seminal character, it was a complex story. It wasn't simply a time-worn tale of a boy from humble beginnings giving in to hedonism and the bright lights.

'He didn't drink,' says Frieros. 'He didn't drink alcohol or smoke. The thing he liked was the atmosphere of the night. He enjoyed the nightlife. He liked the clubs. He liked... well, the girls and all that, but of course, he had no awareness that, damn, the next day at 10am, he had to train.'

CANITO: ONCE BARÇA, FOREVER ESPANYOL

On other nights, often on the eve of a home game, Canito would appear at a local bar in the Zona Franca. He would order a Coke and chat with friends before quietly settling their bills and heading home.

Beltrán's book features a beautiful black-and-white photo of a scene outside one such bar. Canito is hoisted high on the shoulders of beaming locals as news of his transfer to Barcelona became official. Young and old from all around the neighbourhood sharing the delight that one of their own was joining one of the biggest clubs in the world.

That the bar in question, as Beltrán observes, was the Peña Espanyolista Canito, an Espanyol supporters' club already dedicated to the man smiling in the centre of the photo, tells a story of its own.

* * *

For all the misgivings, life at Camp Nou started well. Indeed, lined up at centre-back on his home debut, Canito scored twice from open play as Barcelona thumped Real Betis 5-0. But Barça struggled, and Canito suffered as manager Rifé shuffled the pack in a vain attempt to find consistency. Mired in eighth and after a home defeat to Valencia in the first leg of a Cup Winners' Cup quarter-final, Rifé was sacked, and Helenio Herrera returned as manager almost 20 years after leaving the club.

Herrera surprisingly selected Canito at centre-forward as Barça attempted to retrieve matters against Valencia at Mestalla. The game finished in a chaotic 4-3 victory for the home side, but Canito scored twice, including a memorable goal hammered in off the underside of the crossbar.

Canito finished the season flitting between midfield and attack as Barça ground out a series of dull wins to climb into a UEFA Cup spot. One key victory came in that 1-0 win against Athletic, which would be remembered primarily for Canito hailing the news of Espanyol's goal at Hercules.

If his first season at Barça was a disappointment, the second was an outright disaster. The team floundered under the short-lived stewardship of László Kubala, who admired Canito but could not find him a set position. Worse was to come when Herrera was reinstated after just nine games.

Herrera soon became fed up with the player's antics, as Beltrán outlines, 'Canito had a deep attachment to his dog, a German Shepherd, and he wouldn't leave it at home. So he brought it to training and even tried to take him on the team bus on away trips, which created problems with Herrera.'

By December, Canito was reduced to early-round cup appearances and even then grabbed the headlines for the wrong reasons.

Ten minutes into a second-round tie against Lleida, an opponent's sardonic remark to Canito that he could see why he was only picked in the cups was met with violent retribution, and Canito was sent off. Jeered by his own supporters, Canito returned fire with sarcastic applause. At the end of its tether, the board instructed Canito to stay away from club facilities.

As the season drew to a close, he didn't wait around to find out his fate. While the club he was still registered with played out the final stages of the Copa del Rey, Canito boarded a flight with his former team and featured in all six games of Espanyol's May tour of South America. A midfield cameo against Boca Juniors that kept Diego Maradona in check in a goalless draw at La Bombonera was a reminder of Canito's quality.

The summer of 1981 saw Barcelona again raiding Espanyol, this time for goalkeeper Urruti. President Manuel Meler was able to smooth a deal with Nuñez to officially take Canito back to Sarría in return. Though almost inevitably, the tale of Espanyol's prodigal son would not turn out like the parable.

Just days after signing his contract, Canito exploded spectacularly during the final of a pre-season tournament in Badajoz against Atlético Madrid.

'Espanyol were on the end of some bad refereeing, which was not uncommon against Atlético,' recounts Beltrán. 'It was

1-1 near the end of normal time when tensions boiled over, and there were fights and arguments. Canito ended up being sent off along with three other Espanyol players. They were left with only seven players and ultimately lost 4-1.

'When the referee showed Canito the red card, he snapped. He angrily snatched the card, tore it up, and threw it away. Then, instead of heading to his team's dressing room, he went to the referee's room. He grabbed all of the officials' clothes, threw them into the shower, turned on the water, and soaked everything in revenge. Then he calmly went to his own changing room as if nothing had happened.'

The Extremadura Federation handed Canito a four-month ban for his actions, and the fallout from the 'Battle of Badajoz' lasted for days. Debates raged over whether such lengthy suspensions could be handed out for unofficial tournaments. In his column in *Mundo Deportivo*, Andrés Astruells opined that, 'The only one who can see the events in good humour is Barça president, Josep Lluís Núñez, who can breathe yet another deep sigh of relief for having got rid of Canito.' Some diplomatic manoeuvring by Meler, including committing to an exhibition game, eventually reduced the ban.

Despite strong performances on the field, the 1981/82 season proved to be tempestuous as Canito regularly clashed with his manager, José María Maguregui. The Basque's name is still employed today as a synonym for negative tactics – with Canito demanding licence to attack, the pair argued constantly.

'Canito wanted to play with freedom and joy,' says Beltrán. 'He preferred to be a libero who advanced with the ball. However, Maguregui didn't subscribe to that philosophy. He adhered to a more modern approach at the time, favouring four defenders and two conventional centre-backs. This was a shift in tactics that conflicted with Canito's natural style. For Maguregui, Canito had to conform and act as a traditional centre-back, but Canito resisted.'

The two managed to set aside their differences to memorably dismantle Barcelona at Camp Nou. Heckled by the crowd, Canito was commanding in an emphatic 3-1 win. 'I'm drunk with happiness,' he told reporters after the game, although he did summon up some magnanimous words for Barcelona on their title quest.

A month later, matters had soured badly. In the season's final game, Canito initially refused to travel to play Sevilla, only to be talked around. A 4-1 hammering did little to improve Canito's mood as he clashed with home fans, argued vehemently with Maguregui then set upon club masseuse Pepe Guijarro, who had attempted to separate the pair.

A few days later, newspapers were carrying declarations from Canito that he was quitting football, at least in Spain. The club briefed that they were open to rescinding his contract. Yet the soap opera rumbled on for months. *Mundo Deportivo* even designed a new stylised font and heading to introduce the stories. The 'Canito Show', the first instalment featuring a photo of the player gently cooing to a bird that had perched on his hand, would run and run.

The sad overarching storyline was that a talent once destined to star for Spain as they hosted the World Cup spent the summer of 1982 threatening to walk away from the game. 'The only thing that interests me about the World Cup is the Rolling Stones,' he told one interviewer who dared to engage him in football talk.

The drama continued to deliver its twists. Banished from the squad, at one point, he looked poised to join the New York Cosmos. Improbably, by August, he had found his way back into the fold, making conciliatory noises and even taking the captain's armband in a pre-season friendly. Yet, when the league resumed, Maguregui's refusal to name him in the first-team squad brought matters to a head. Canito delivered an ultimatum to the board that either Maguregui went or he would walk.

The board duly annulled the player's contract. 'Espanyol is the team of my life,' Canito declared. 'My departure is down to my incompatibility with the manager, who has made my life impossible. The club is more important than personal issues; I respect that because I love the club. One day I'll be back – even if it's to play for free.'

As fate had it, Canito was back just a fortnight later with his new club Real Betis.

'Canito had to make his debut for Betis in September at Sarrià,' explains Beltrán. 'It was another bizarre event. He'd left for free; he'd forced his departure. Other players that have done that to Espanyol have been booed, as would be expected at any club. When Canito returned, not only was he not booed, he was applauded.

'Espanyol lost the match, and the fans directed their anger at the manager. Sarrià wasn't like today's modern stadiums; players and coaches exited through the same gates as the fans. After the game, a protest broke out, with fans insulting Maguregui and demanding his resignation. When Canito emerged, the crowd lifted him onto their shoulders like a matador and paraded him around.

'I mean, he's left for free to the other team and just beaten us. But there was just an unconditional love between the fans and Canito.'

Canito was an automatic starter for Betis for two seasons. Life appeared to be good, from a distance at least. He again impressed in his duels with Maradona, now the world's most expensive player after signing for Barcelona. There was even a wedding at Seville's spectacular cathedral, but despite that tantalising glimpse of stability, the marriage didn't last, and there were worrying signs that his life was beginning to unravel.

As ever, there were fabled stories from his time in the south. From the times he handed out a 100 peseta note to each kid who asked for his autograph to the legend that he tore up his final cheque from Betis as he disagreed with the figure.

Unhappy spells at Zaragoza and in Portugal with Belenenses rounded off Canito's time at the highest level. At the age of 30, elite clubs were unwilling to take on the baggage that came with him. A career that had promised so much had failed to deliver on its glittering potential.

Canito returned to his native Barcelona, falling down the leagues and into bad company.

* * *

A lavish and generous spender during his playing days, it wasn't too long before money became an issue for Canito, and he fell into the seamier side of Barcelona nightlife. Drugs took hold – and eventually heroin. By the mid-1990s, Canito was almost unrecognisable, surviving day-to-day and spending nights in homeless shelters or bank lobbies. As someone who had always been benevolent to others, he was hurt to find himself abandoned.

'People have shunned me, and I don't think that I deserve that, but I need to hold on to the sense that, before anything else, I'm still a person,' he told *Interviu* magazine in 1996.

'Those who used to say "hello" now call me a pain and slam the door in my face. It's the poor people that have helped me more than the rich. That has been hard for me to take because when I had money, I would give a lot to anyone who asked for it.'

Desperation had reunited him with his sister, Fina, who had helped him battle his addictions. 'I owe her my life. My mother abandoned me totally, and the relationship with my wife broke down when my problems with drugs began. Right now, I'm not involved in drugs, but I can't guarantee that I won't fall again.'

Canito's addiction placed friends in almost impossible situations.

'I found out very late,' says Frieros. 'When he came to me asking for money, I had already started hearing rumours that he was using drugs. He had a strong connection with his neighbourhood, where he had friends in the *Las Casas Baratas*, where it was easy to get drugs.

'Of course, he wasn't asking for money to pay the electricity bill but to keep funding his habits, right? I remember one day he came to see me and asked for money, saying it was because he didn't have money to pay for something – I don't even know what.

'After that, he didn't come to me for money again. By then, he was already caught in a vicious cycle that was very difficult to escape.

'He already had circulation problems in his legs and didn't want me to know. He didn't want my brothers to know. He didn't want my mother to find out, because, I guess, he felt... ashamed, right? Of saying, "Damn, look at what I've become. After how you've known me, I don't want you to see me like this."'

Canito's collapse into dependency is something Frieros still wrestles with, 'I think that all of us could have done much more for him. All of us, really. When he started distancing himself from us, well... he did that because he had to live his life. He went to Seville and got married. I didn't even know. I didn't know he was married. He never told me. I found out through other people.

'Whether it was the people from Barça, Espanyol, Zaragoza, or Betis, we all could have done more for him. It's very difficult when someone doesn't want to be helped. He also deceived a lot of people, because when you say you need money to eat and then you spend it on drugs, well, that's not right, is it?

'Still, things could have been handled differently. It was a very different time, wasn't it? This was 25, 30 years ago. Society was different back then. Today, everything is much more visible, and there's more support. Things could have been managed differently.'

Four years on from the interview where he'd declared himself clean, Canito had fallen deep into addiction again and was taken in by his sister. His body was ravaged by drugs. The legs that once carried the ball so majestically from defence to attack were now barely able to support him as he crossed a room.

On 25 November 2000, Canito died in the arms of his sister. He was just 44 years old.

* * *

Three days later, he was laid to rest in the village of La Pobla de Montornés in Tarragona. His gravestone was simply carved with his name alongside the crest of Espanyol.

'I was at the funeral. I was in the church,' remembers Frieros. 'And it was a very hard moment. There were players from Barça, Espanyol, a couple of journalists, and those of us who were close to him. It shocked me. It really shocked me, because I knew he had circulation problems, but I didn't think it was that bad, you know? I hadn't received any news or information about how he really was. I think it surprised all of us.

'I consider him one of the people I've loved most in my life, because, to me, he was someone I idolised. Think about it – I met him when I was a child, just eight years old. By the time I was 12, he was already a professional footballer. And with me, he was always so kind.

'For example, the first tracksuit I ever had in my life was a gift from him – an orange Adidas tracksuit.'

The essence of an extraordinary life remains alive, with each matchday in its own way a tribute to Canito. Something Beltrán, whose work has helped bring the story to younger generations, explains.

'Canito remains a mythical figure, which is in some ways hard to explain considering he only played 100 matches in *Primera* for Espanyol. Lots of players have far more appearances for the club, yet Canito is one of the most charismatic figures in its history. The main Espanyol supporters' section is even named after him – you'll see flags bearing his face in the stands.

'He holds deep significance for the club and its fans, representing much more than his on-field contributions.

CANITO: ONCE BARÇA, FOREVER ESPANYOL

Espanyol is a small club living perpetually in the shadow of Barcelona, a giant that wins titles and signs the best players year after year. Espanyol, by contrast, is a club defined by resilience – remaining in La Liga despite limited resources and a lack of institutional support, often politically sidelined.

'This spirit of rebellion, resistance, and strength in the face of adversity, Canito represents that well. That makes him an enduring symbol for Espanyol supporters. If you ever visit the stadium, you'll find a huge photo of Canito playing in an Espanyol kit displayed in the supporters' section.

'It's beautiful.'

3.

Apocalypse in Aragón

UP OR down?

It was a hell of a choice, and there was only a split second to make it. He'd woken suddenly when his slumbering senses told him something wasn't right. An acrid haze had begun filling his room, seeping under the door and in through the air conditioning vents.

Bursting into the corridor, he'd searched in vain for the emergency stairs, instead arriving at the hotel's main staircase. The logical choice would be to go down, but thick plumes of smoke poured from below – the stairs' elegant carpets serving as tinder, powering the flames' ascent.

It would have to be up – maybe there would be an exit up there? But the second floor was arranged as confusingly as the first. The smoke grew denser, and the heat unbearably intense. Reluctant to go further, he found a room with a balcony and took refuge there. For a few brief seconds, he could just about breathe and feel the cool morning air on his scorched face. Then, an intake of oxygen and the cries from the street below brought him to the realisation that he had a very urgent decision to make. Although for Real Zaragoza's new signing, José Ramon Badiola, it wasn't really a decision at all. He simply had to jump.

* * *

The Hotel Corona de Aragón was, as the name suggests, the jewel in the crown of the city of Zaragoza. The region's only five-star hotel boasted 11 floors of luxury guest accommodation, lushly appointed meeting rooms, and a fine-dining restaurant. There was a gym equipped with a swimming pool and sauna alongside a hairdresser and beauty salon. There was even a crèche facility for pets. It was the natural port of call for anyone who was anyone doing business in the capital of Aragón.

Occupancy was regularly bolstered by events at the General Military Academy, situated on the city's northern outskirts. The academy is the main training centre for the Spanish Army and the national police force, *la Guardia Civil*, and has an illustrious history of instructing the Spanish elite. King Juan Carlos I graduated from there in 1957, with his son Felipe and granddaughter Leonor both following in his footsteps.

On the night of 11 July 1979, a passing out ceremony had brought a well-heeled crowd to town, and 190 of the hotel's 237 rooms were occupied.

Graduating as a second lieutenant was one of General Francisco Franco's grandsons, Cristóbal, which meant three generations of the dictator's family were guests at the hotel. Franco's widow, Carmen Polo, was joined by their only child, Carmen Franco, whose teenage children, Jaime and Aránzazu, had also come to Zaragoza to attend their brother's ceremony.

Another guest connected to the former regime was General Alfonso Armada, a staunch supporter of Franco who would go on to be one of the main protagonists of the failed military coup of 1981, for which he would be sentenced to 30 years in prison.

Other unmistakably military names such as Colonel Rodrigo Peñalosa Esteban-Infante, Captain Ángel Hernández-Perez and the former Olympic equestrian, Lieutenant Colonel Alfonso Queipo de Llano y Acuña also featured on the guest register that night, alongside the less elaborate but no less notable name of José Maria Zárraga.

As a player with Real Madrid, Zárraga had won six league titles and the first five editions of the European Cup. He'd captained the side in the latter two finals, including the famous 7-3 win over Eintracht Frankfurt at Hampden Park. Zárraga was in Zaragoza in his role as sporting director of Deportivo Alavés.

Languishing in *Segunda* and struggling financially, Alavés had sent a delegation to the city to complete the transfer of two of their brightest talents to Real Zaragoza for a combined fee of 35m pesetas. Over half of that sum had been secured early that evening as 23-year-old forward Badiola happily signed on the dotted line.

Fresh from a season where he'd scored 13 goals from the wing, Badiola was a player very much on an upward curve. Having joined Alavés from Athletic Club's youth set-up, he had sparkled in his two seasons in Vitoria, his new club amazed he'd been allow to leave Bilbao.

Quick and comfortable on either flank, Badiola had a trademark ability to deliver quick crosses with the outside of either foot and had attracted the attention of several *Primera* clubs, but it was Zaragoza he saw as the team that could match his ambitions. He delightedly sealed the transfer and was looking forward to moving to the city with Zárraga's daughter, his long-term partner.

The second part of the deal was proving slightly problematic. The Argentine forward and future World Cup winner, Jorge Valdano, was in disagreement with the Alavés board about the exact terms of his move. By way of making a point, he'd refused to travel, failing to check in to the hotel as arranged.

That Wednesday evening, the rest of the Alavés party dined in the bustling restaurant, toasting the deal that brought fresh funds to the club and progressed Badiola's career. After a nightcap at the bar, the group retired for the evening to their rooms on the first floor, unaware of the hellish scenes they would wake up to.

APOCALYPSE IN ARAGÓN

***

The churros fryer in the hotel's Cafetería Formigal had a history of flaring up, but as it was switched on for the breakfast service that Thursday morning, it quickly malfunctioned and ignited with more force than ever. Four staff members attempted to tackle the fire with extinguishers, but the strength of the flames proved impossible to quell, and staff abandoned the kitchen, raising the alarm to colleagues in neighbouring rooms and calling the fire brigade.

ABC reported that fire crews arrived within minutes, but the fire had already spread 'with extraordinary speed', roaring from the basement via a ventilation shaft to Piccadilly's Bar above. There, sofas, wooden furniture and carpeted floors fuelled the flames rapidly. 'The fire arrived quickly at the building's main staircase, which became a chimney which spread the fire and smoke to the floors above.' The main entrance provided a source of air that further fanned the flames.

The hotel proved disastrously ill-equipped to deal with the fire. The chief architect of the Zaragoza Fire Service later reported that the two emergency staircases were inaccessible to guests and could 'only have been known to staff'. One had to be accessed via a door with no exit sign. The other was hidden by rooms on each floor that functioned as storerooms with each door marked '*Privado*'.

Zaragoza police concluded that staff failed to fully initiate the hotel alarm before leaving. There was no protocol to shut down the air conditioning system, meaning deadly smoke was efficiently distributed into rooms as guests slept.

The blaze was soon evident on the first floor, where the group from Alavés occupied a block of rooms. The first to react was Zárraga, who provided the news agency *EFE* with a stunning account carried by several of the following day's newspapers.

'It was approximately 8.30am when, as I was about to have a wash, I realised there was a lot of smoke coming into the room, accompanied by an intense burning smell.'

Zárraga opened the door to his room and was met with thick smoke. 'There was a fire, a tremendous fire. I went back into the room, put on some trousers and shoes, and looked for an exit, the closest one, without thinking – I don't know why – to go to the staircase or the main door of the hotel.

'That's what saved me because it would have been impossible for me to get out through there. In my desperate attempt to escape, I found a staircase and bumped into one of the hotel waiters, who led me to another exit, which took us to the street.'

Safely on the footpath, Zárraga realised that in his panic he'd lost his shoes, 'But I ran desperately, I went to the part of the street below the first-floor rooms occupied by the club president, Hipólito Lastra, the secretary, Luis María Calvo, and the player José Ramón Badiola, and I began shouting to warn them about the fire.

'Both Hipólito and Luis María looked out. They had already realised there was a fire, but they were so worried that they did not react immediately. They went to Badiola's room, as I had done, and began banging on the door to warn him, but the door did not open. Then, I was shouting at the top of my lungs for them to jump into the street.'

Lastra and Calvo leapt to safety, but Badiola was unaccounted for.

The scenes surrounding the hotel were apocalyptic. US Air Force helicopters scrambled from the nearby base and rescued those that had made it to the hotel's roof terrace, depositing them safely in the nearby bull ring. Soldiers were mobilised to secure a nearby subterranean deposit of 150,000 litres of liquid fuel.

Fire crews attempted to rescue those trapped on balconies by ladder while others provided life nets on which to jump. Some felt they had no option but to leap, whether or not they had a net to aim for. The concierge of a nearby apartment block told reporters he'd witnessed four different people plummet to their deaths.

La Vanguardia recounted the unimaginably horrific scene of two young parents with no alternative but to drop their young daughter from the sixth floor towards a net. The girl did not survive the fall.

One image caught by photographers on the day was of a woman on a ninth-floor balcony, stretching out a hand towards a rescue platform. Aurora Merinero and her husband José Luis Serrano had been sleeping in after a late-night arrival when they were awoken by a telephone call. With flames having already reached the hallway, they fled to the balcony. While Serrano went back inside to retrieve some work documents, Merinero lost consciousness. She came round upon receiving a blast of water from a fire hose after cries from those on the roof alerted a crew who came to her aid. Her husband never made it back out of the room; his body was only identified after his wife described a recognisable scar to doctors.

Badiola's decision to go up a level had complicated his escape, but a fire crew had given him a net to aim for as he sized up his descent from the second-floor balcony. He found his target but rebounded, sustaining severe head trauma. He went into cardiac arrest and had to be given 45 minutes of cardiopulmonary resuscitation while being rushed to hospital.

Initial news broadcasts reported Badiola amongst the dead, a conclusion Zárraga also came to upon finding him.

'The confusion in those first moments was terrible, and I ran anxiously to the hospital where they told me many of the injured were. I found Badiola there. He was unconscious, scorched and blackened. They told me something about asphyxiation, and my first impression was that the boy had died.

'I was able to identify José Ramón by the bracelet he wears with his name, and I ran to inform Hipólito and Luis María. We returned to the hospital to receive the news that José Ramón had not died, although he had been found with burns and, above all, severe symptoms of asphyxiation. Now, despite the distress, we are calmer. José Ramón is being attended to, receiving an IV drip, and we hope he will recover.'

Valdano, for his part, had driven to Zaragoza that morning, unaware of the hell unfolding until he approached the old town. There, the circling of helicopters and the wail of sirens told him something was amiss. He rushed to the offices of Real Zaragoza, where he was stunned to hear what had happened.

Due to his reservation at the hotel, Valdano's name appeared on a list of those presumed missing at one stage. It took several frantic phone calls to reassure people in Vitoria and his family in Argentina that he was safe. His belligerence with the board had saved him.

Firefighters eventually brought the fire to a halt just before midday, but not before a death toll that would reach 83. The majority died from asphyxiation; others were killed in their attempts to jump to safety. More than 100 were injured. Badiola could only count his blessings that he was in the latter category – but he now faced the fight to save his career.

* * *

Badiola was discharged from hospital a month later. A plan was made to allow him to return to his hometown of Ondarroa for a month to make a gentle rehabilitation with training sessions entrusted to the player's brother-in-law, a Basque lower league coach.

Mundo Deportivo reported that the club's medical staff were keen to give the player space and advised him against giving any interviews, 'Confronting the experience suffered in the Corona de Aragón where he nearly met his death could badly set back his recovery.' In any case, the player was not given to discussing the incident. 'Badiola has refused to recall what happened that day as his subconscious attempts to forget it.'

While his team-mate recuperated slowly, Valdano quickly established himself as a mainstay after completing his transfer. He was an ever-present in his first season at Real Zaragoza and rarely missed a game in his five seasons at the club. When Badiola finally arrived in Zaragoza, he moved in with Valdano, hoping a familiar face would help him acclimatise to life in the city and football in *Primera*. Valdano, though, could see something was not right with his friend. Badiola failed to make an appearance in that first season and began behaving erratically.

The Badiola that Valdano knew from Vitoria was quiet and reserved. The Badiola that had – on the surface at least – recovered from the injuries suffered in the hotel fire displayed profound mood swings and bizarre behaviour. Scenes such as getting totally naked when feeling hot or smashing a bottle open at the neck to take a gulp of water were commonplace. On occasions, Badiola would finish training and hail a taxi, asking to be taken the 300km to Ondarroa.

His relationship with Zárraga's daughter soon broke off, and his parents moved to Zaragoza to support him, but over the course of three seasons, Badiola started just a handful of cup games for the club, alongside a sprinkling of substitute appearances in the league.

By the time Valdano had moved on to Real Madrid, rapidly accumulating silverware alongside the *Quinta del Buitre*, Badiola had already returned to Alavés in one last attempt to revive his career. The move failed to spark any semblance of his old self, and while his friend was tasting footballing nirvana with Argentina – playing in every game and scoring in the final of Mexico '86 – Badiola was back in his native Vizcaya, living in total obscurity with his physical and mental health continuing to decline.

* * *

Authorities swiftly declared that the fire was a tragic accident. By 10.15am the following day, the Zaragoza Civil Government issued a statement. 'Based on the collected data and witness testimonies, it can be concluded that the fire was an unfortunate accident, with no evidence suggesting deliberate arson. This conclusion has been corroborated by the insurance company's technical experts, following their own investigations on behalf of the property owners.'

The statement detailed that the blaze started in a container of the churros fryer that contained around 20 litres of oil and that the fire had spread rapidly due to the high flammability of materials and furniture in Piccadilly's Bar. The findings were endorsed by police after they had interviewed four staff members who had witnessed the start of the fire.

Franco's family escaped the fire relatively unscathed. His widow received brief treatment for smoke inhalation before the family were whisked back to Madrid. Still, the list of dead and injured was littered with military, police, and establishment names. The unique profile of the guest list, at a fragile time during Spain's transition to democracy, along with the astonishing speed at which the flames spread, led many to distrust the official verdict.

Soon after the blaze, the local newspaper, the *Heraldo de Aragón*, received a call purportedly from ETA claiming responsibility, though crank calls were common in the wake of major incidents. The same paper received another professing to be the inoperative left-wing organisation FRAP shortly after.

Suspicion naturally fell on the Basque separatist group, but ETA did not acknowledge responsibility at command level, as was its normal course of action.

Still, the verdict continued to be questioned. Families of the victims began a campaign to reclassify the incident as a terrorist act. The decades following the fire brought various judicial processes and reports. Claims of separate explosions or the apparent discovery of traces of substances planted as an accelerant among the cinders of the hotel regularly featured in articles, documentaries, and witness testimony.

While no action has ever been able to change the official classification, several rulings went some way towards assuaging, if not satisfying, those who believe it was a deliberate act.

In October 2000, José María Aznar's government concluded that the victims' families were eligible to receive compensation available to those who had suffered acts of terrorism, although without officially recognising that the fire was a terror attack.

Nine years later, the Supreme Court agreed with the theory put forward by an expert that the fire was the work of at least three individuals who had coordinated three almost simultaneous detonations before making their escape. However, the court's jurisdiction in that ruling only went as far as to posthumously award one of the deceased the Royal Cross of Civil Recognition given to victims of terrorism. Two years later, a Council of Ministers decreed that the same recognition be given to the rest of those who lost their lives in the fire.

The *Guardia Civil* went one step further, updating their records to classify the death of retired lieutenant Angel Cabello Iruela, who perished in the fire, as a victim of ETA.

For all its appalling record, ETA expressly denies culpability for what occurred that July morning. In 2018, the group's internal bulletin, *Zutabe*, recognised 758 killings and 2,606 'acts'. The report expressed a note of regret over the most shocking and bloody of its attacks – the 1987 bombing of a Hipercor supermarket in Barcelona – but categorically denied 'the authorship of false attacks such as the fire at the Hotel Corona de Aragón'.

A further attempt to reopen the files in 2022 was short-lived, with a court archiving the case after just four months, leaving the victims in a strange sort of limbo. Ramón J. Campo, an investigative journalist who has followed the case for the *Heraldo de Aragón* and co-directed the 2018 documentary *Los años del humo,* describes the situation as a 'triquiñuela' – a trick, or a ruse.

'It's a trick, so to speak. It's like saying, "You are victims of terrorism, but we don't know who committed it." That's the issue. The victims had been demanding recognition for so long… They are recognised, but only halfway.'

The fire at the Hotel Corona de Aragón remains Zaragoza's JFK case. Even good friends hold different opinions, their own theories. Some see a tragic accident, others a high-level cover-up. Some have even changed their mind. Ricardo Checa, the hotel's head of reception and acting manager on the day, believed strongly for decades that it was a deliberate attack but changed his mind after a conversation with an old maintenance engineer years later detailed the sorry state of the cafe's ventilation system.

***

The contrasting fates of Badiola and Valdano had always intrigued the radio journalist and writer Miguel Mena, and when he was asked to contribute to a 2007 book marking Real Zaragoza's 75th anniversary, he went on the trail of finding out what had happened to Badiola.

'I'd heard about it from my colleagues in sports radio. I'd come across the story before and asked what happened to Badiola afterwards, but no one could tell me. So, I started to investigate and found out that he had continued playing after the incident. He was even loaned to another team, and that sparked my curiosity; I wanted to know more about what had happened to him afterwards because I found it strange.

'I also started asking people why Valdano hadn't been there that night, and there were theories that it was just a stroke of luck, that he missed the train or something like that – but in the end, that wasn't the case. So, when they were working on this book and asked me to collaborate, I decided to investigate this real story instead of writing fiction.'

Mena's first port of call was Avelino Chaves, a revered figure in the club's history who, as sporting director, had constructed Zaragoza's most successful teams and was the brains behind the double signing of Badiola and Valdano. Chaves revealed that of the pair, it was Badiola whom they'd seen as the star and lamented failing to help revive his form after the fire.

Getting Valdano's number proved no problem. Finding a window to talk to one of Spanish football's intelligentsia, equally at home in a dressing room, boardroom or TV studio, was a little trickier. Mena was also mindful that Valdano may not want to speak at all, having recently recovered from another fortunate escape.

On a charity trip in Mexico in March 2006, Valdano was involved in a helicopter crash. Taking off from the roof of a 15-storey building, the overloaded machine immediately lost height in the thin Mexico City air, crashing to the ground on the residential street below.

Valdano had been the last to board, along with a young Mexican who politely offered up the choice of the two remaining seats. Valdano selected the seat in the middle and came around in a local hospital with several broken ribs and a collapsed lung, but remarkably no lasting damage. Juan Manuel Agudo Mille – the courteous fellow passenger who had taken the final window seat – felt the full impact of the crash and died of his injuries.

Eventually, Mena found Valdano with time to speak.

'He treated me very well. Very, very politely, and he told me – first, that he hadn't gone to sleep in Zaragoza due to disagreements with Alavés over money. He didn't agree with the terms of his contract, and that's why he didn't go there that night.

'Then, he told me about his relationship with Badiola, the connection they had, and Badiola's mental decline. Badiola could have been saved, but in the confusion, as the smoke was rising from below, he ran upstairs instead of trying to escape or jump from the window on his floor. So, he fell from a greater height and hit his head.

'When he returned to the team, Badiola was already behaving erratically – completely erratically. He started doing things that were... strange. He was never the same again.'

Valdano spoke of the night, in his time as manager of Real Madrid, when he heard a commotion in the corridor of the team hotel on the eve of a match in Bilbao. On opening the door, Valdano saw Badiola embroiled in an argument with security personnel. Badiola had popped in to see his old friend with no notion of phoning ahead nor explaining himself to the staff guarding the floor.

The pair embraced, but Valdano was upset to see his old team-mate so lost, consoling himself with the notion that at least he still followed football and could make a decision like coming to visit him when he was in town. Valdano remained convinced that the injuries and the experiences of the hotel fire had destroyed the career of a player he had always considered a special talent, one more talented than himself.

Mena then set about finding Badiola, working his way through the Ondarroa phone book until one day he found a relative who passed on the number of the player's mother, Manuela. Heartbreakingly, she described her son's decline, never the same after that tragic morning in 1979.

Badiola was a compulsive eater, drinker, and smoker – overweight and with soaringly high cholesterol levels. A world away from the lithe 23-year-old with the world at his feet that had toasted his future hours before waking up to a hellish inferno. When he wasn't hospitalised for treatment for his conditions, he passed his days at a day centre where he would rarely converse and seldom go out for fresh air.

His recently widowed mother had to pay for his upkeep, struggling to stretch her pension to cover the costs. The compensation promised by the government had been bogged down in red tape, and she had all but given up on receiving anything.

'She was a very kind woman, an elderly lady from a small town in the Basque Country,' Mena recalls. 'It was a deeply moving conversation because she was a woman carrying an immense, endless sadness.

'In fact, I remember that when I wrote the story, I decided to end it with her words because I felt that nothing else needed to be added. The last thing she said to me was, "I don't know if it was the smoke or the fall or what it was, but that day my son was lost forever."

'Even though I kept talking to her afterwards, I knew that was the ending. There was nothing more to say.

'She was a woman who... well, just imagine the situation. Losing someone is always hard – accepting a death is painful – but I think it's even worse when someone loses their mind because of an accident and falls into such a decline.

'For a mother, there is no comfort for that. No comfort at all.'

4.
Levante's Cruyff Turn

A SHRILL ring breaks the mid-morning silence in a chic Amsterdam apartment. Enjoying a restorative lie-in after a nasty bout of flu, a woman climbs out of bed, wearily ruffles her blonde, bobbed hair and pads through to the living room to pick up the telephone.

'Hello?'

'Sorry, he's not here right now. He's gone to a meeting at Ajax.'

'Yes, it is Danny, hi. Actually, wait a second. He mentioned you might call. I think he's left a statement for you. Let me see if I can find it.'

'Here it is. I shall read it for you.'

'The negotiations with Levante have not broken down, but we have still not come to an agreement. My father-in-law will arrive late tonight due to problems with his flights. We will then have all the information we need, and tomorrow, over dinner, we will discuss them. I will, therefore, give my definitive response tomorrow night or, at the very latest, by noon the following day.'

'Is that okay?'

'Great.'

'Well, look – personally, I love Spain and would love to go back, and everyone has told us what a beautiful city Valencia is.'

'Yes. Well, he's had a lot of offers, but unless there's a twist, he will go to Levante. Like the statement said, he will clarify it tomorrow one way or the other.'

'No problem. You're welcome. You too, bye.'

When the phone rang the following evening, it was Johan Cruyff himself, as promised, who answered and gave the most decisive of answers.

'We have studied the offer at length and read the reports from the club. We believe the deal can benefit everyone. So, it is decided, I will play 19 games for Levante with the objective of gaining promotion. After that, we will see.'

The following day's newspapers excitedly broke the news, even reporting a possible debut that Sunday against Sabadell. But soon that typically direct Cruyffian intention met the opaque and muddled world of *Segunda División* club finances. It would be another month, one involving the Spanish Federation, Leicester City and Helenio Herrera's underpants, before a 33-year-old Cruyff finally arrived as a most unlikely recruit in Levante's promotion push.

* * *

Exhausted by life in Barcelona, Cruyff bid farewell to Camp Nou in May 1978. He flirted with retirement but was besieged by mounting debts from a spectacularly bad pig-farming investment and a tax bill that incoming Barça president Josep Lluís Núñez refused to pay.

Cruyff was soon listening to overtures from the North American Soccer League. The Los Angeles Aztecs offered him the opportunity to reunite with his mentor, Rinus Michels, while also overtaking the Lakers' Kareem Abdul-Jabbar as California's highest-paid athlete. Despite six months of inactivity, Cruyff completed paperwork in Spain before boarding a flight and making his NASL bow at the Rose Bowl in Pasadena the same evening. Cruyff and Michels barely had time to get reacquainted before the player hurried out onto the pitch to score two goals in his first seven minutes of Stateside action.

Body and mind reinvigorated by the California sunshine and a spell with the Washington Diplomats, Cruyff returned to Europe at the end of 1980 feeling he had plenty more football ahead of him. He also eyed a return to the Dutch national team, who were midway through their 1982 World Cup qualification campaign.

Remarkably, the first to show interest on the club scene were Dumbarton, of Scotland's Second Division. Manager Sean Fallon flew to Amsterdam in an attempt to pull off an amazing coup but couldn't tempt Cruyff to the chilly banks of the Clyde.

Still, Cruyff wasn't entirely opposed to the notion of second-tier football. Indeed, despite interest from Arsenal, Chelsea and Espanyol, promotion-chasing Levante of Spain emerged as the club most likely to strike a deal.

It was a transfer that, on many levels, made little sense. A ten-year-old Emilio Nadal once had his hair playfully tousled by Cruyff when he went along to games with his uncle, a local radio journalist. Nowadays, Nadal heads up the club's historical heritage department but struggles to comprehend how the three-time Ballon d'Or winner arrived at Levante. 'The club's history has always been complicated, especially on the economic side. The financial situation has always been precarious and heavily reliant on the personal wealth of presidents and board members. In the 1970s, the problem was particularly bad because in the 1960s, Levante had spent a couple of seasons in the top flight, but they never took advantage of that.

'At that time, the club also moved from the old Estadio Vallejo to the current Ciutat de Valencia stadium. Today, it's in one of the new centres of Valencia, but back then, there was nothing around it; just farmland, and the access routes were awful. I remember going with my father by car; the roads were winding, old farm roads. There was no life around the stadium. The Orriols neighbourhood was nearby, but there were no bars or anything. That also diminished the club's fanbase.'

What Levante did have, though, was an audacious dealmaker in club president Francisco Aznar. 'He came from the world of *peñas* (supporters' clubs),' says Nadal. 'He had been the president of the *Delegación de Peñas*, but it wasn't common for someone in that position to go on to become the president of Levante. Usually, it was people from high society – typically businessmen. This man had been a *peñista*, a distinguished figure within the supporters' movement, and around 1979, he ended up becoming the president.

'He had grand, almost pharaonic plans for the club, and signing Cruyff was one of them. He dreamed of taking the team to *Primera*. Before Cruyff's arrival, the team was actually doing well in the league, and his arrival kind of disrupted everything. I don't think Francisco had a clear grasp of the club's actual financial situation or the reality they were living in.'

Where others saw the prohibitive wage demands of an ageing superstar, Aznar envisioned packed stadiums, a surge in club membership, high-profile friendlies, and a lucrative North American tour. Involved in a tight promotion tussle, Aznar believed Cruyff's arrival would provide a perfectly timed boost to separate themselves from the pack. Cruyff and his agent and father-in-law, Cor Coster, agreed, and Cruyff prepared to fly to Spain to make his debut on 1 February.

There was one problem. For all of Aznar's glimmering visions of the future, he hadn't been a particularly timely settler of debts in the past. Levante owed the current squad and former players close to 13m pesetas in unpaid wages. The Spanish federation felt more than a little uncomfortable with proceedings and refused to sanction the transfer.

Despite that and further issues with Cruyff's preference for wearing his own brand of sportswear, Aznar was adamant, 'He will play for Levante. I'm not some kid doing all this as a stunt.' Convinced that Cruyff's Spanish comeback game would draw a huge crowd, Aznar was keen for record gate receipts to remain in Levante's coffers. He assured fans and the press that Cruyff would arrive in time for the club's next home game against Getafe on 15 February.

Others were less convinced that the deal would be done. Unsurprisingly, the topic of Cruyff's future was a frequent subject at Barcelona press conferences, something that manager Helenio Herrera eventually found some humour in. Sceptical that Cruyff would end up in *Segunda*, he declared to reporters, 'I bet my underpants that Cruyff will not sign for Levante.'

As February wore on, it seemed increasingly certain that those undergarments would remain snugly around Herrera's waist. By Valentine's Day, Cruyff was still in the same Amsterdam apartment, answering calls from Spanish journalists with an increasingly exasperated tone, 'There's nothing happening. Levante's attitude doesn't seem serious, and I'm tired of waiting. I've seen no signs of life from them at all.'

Into the void rode Jock Wallace and Leicester City. Wallace had convinced the board that Cruyff could help lift his inexperienced team out of the relegation zone, packing out Filbert Street in the process. Reports put City's offer at £5,000 per game, doubling the eye-watering pay-per-play rate that George Best had earned at Hibernian. Wallace's grand vision of Cruyff orchestrating his young side never came to pass. The club's emerging striker, Gary Lineker, would have to wait a few more years before Cruyff was instructing him to play on the right wing.

Aznar had tested Cruyff's patience to the limit, but the Leicester link finally concentrated minds, and Levante dispatched lawyers to Amsterdam to close the deal. On Friday, 27 February 1981, Cruyff returned to Spanish soil. Touching down at Barcelona's El Prat airport, he was whisked through the arrivals lounge – a carrier bag with his customary two duty-free cartons of Camel in hand. He briefly stopped to speak to the journalists who had been running up their newspapers' phone bills with daily calls to Amsterdam.

'I'm finally here! The negotiations dragged on, but finally, everyone is happy. I've decided to play for Levante because life in Spain is good. The football is high quality, and the weather is amazing. It's true that playing in *Segunda* seems a little strange for a player of my quality, but not everything in life is about money or prestige. Levante offers a nice life, a good sum of money and a chance to get back into the business world. I can't really ask for more.'

As Aznar pinned the Levante club crest on Cruyff's lapel, Levante fans were adjusting to the notion that that transfer was actually happening. 'It all became real the moment Cruyff landed in Barcelona,' says Nadal, 'the day they pinned the diamond-studded badge on him. I've sometimes referred to it as *The Odd Couple*, like the Walter Matthau movies. It really felt like that – a bizarre pairing. Cruyff and Levante's inner circle just didn't seem to belong together.

'Looking at it now, it all feels surreal – Aznar presenting Cruyff with the badge, which might seem like a small detail, but at the same time, he's already laying out grand plans for a world tour and all these ambitious ideas when Cruyff hadn't even laced up his boots yet.

'Of course, everyone knew Cruyff would play, but only on his own terms when he felt like it. The whole thing felt like a fantasy, a world that didn't seem real at the time.'

Aznar was only too keen to proclaim victory over his doubters, 'With this deal, I've shown I'm not just some bluffer. The debts? Oh please! We owe nothing. The federation has received the necessary payments, and the squad has been paid. Right now, we have 5,000 members, but with promotion, we will have at the very least 21,000. I'm certain of that, and we already have the tours of Europe and America arranged.'

With that, Cruyff and Aznar went speeding down the Mediterranean coast to Valencia. While Cruyff met his new team-mates and settled into his beach villa at Platja del Saler, Aznar was still scrambling to get the transfer sanctioned by the federation. Finally, just after 10pm on Saturday night,

Cruyff was officially registered and able to make his debut in the following day's fixture at home to Palencia.

As Sunday morning broke, Helenio Herrera received a surprise visitor as he sipped his morning coffee. An enterprising photographer stopped by to ask for a snap of Herrera's underwear. The Barcelona boss took it all in good humour, 'I lost the bet! You have to recognise that Levante have pulled off a great signing. Congratulations to them.'

That afternoon, at the Estadio Ciutat de Valencia, the turnstiles clicked at an unprecedented rate as Levante took gate receipts of 5.5m pesetas, five times their usual matchday income. Cruyff took to the field in an uncannily familiar, *blaugrana* striped shirt and managed the full 90 minutes in a 1-0 win. Despite the result, he and his new colleagues seemed on different pages for most of the game, as Cruyff acknowledged: 'We certainly lacked some understanding, but that's natural as we only trained together for half an hour. But I'm convinced we can get promotion – as long as my team-mates understand my play and listen to my recommendations.'

The win took Levante third, a point behind the co-leaders, Rayo Vallecano and Castellón. It was a promising start for Aznar's masterplan but matters became more complicated as the media spotlight was drawn away by the dramatic kidnap of *Primera*'s leading goalscorer, Barcelona's Quini.

The following week, Granada welcomed Levante and Cruyff with open arms. The bumper crowd and the extra charge levied on club members were enough to clear that season's outstanding bonuses and debts. The home side cruised to a 1-0 win with Cruyff and the rest of the team again on different wavelengths.

It was Granada's best performance of the season, partly inspired by the buzzing atmosphere. A point picked up by Levante coach Pachín, whose observations did little to curry favour with Aznar and Cruyff. He was soon replaced by a former Barça team-mate of Cruyff, Joaquim Rifé.

Wins became scarce as Cruyff and his team-mates failed to click. 'The narrative in a lot of reports at the time made it sound like the rest of the team just didn't understand Cruyff,' says Nadal. 'Like Cruyff is a genius, and his team-mates couldn't keep up, but that squad had several players who had played in *Primera* and knew football. But the media pushed this idea that nobody could grasp what Cruyff was trying to do.

'That team had a strong, almost trade union-like camaraderie – it was a hard-working, battling squad without any one superstar. They were disciplined, clear in their ideas, and functioned as a unit. Then Cruyff arrived and completely disrupted that ecosystem. Until that point, the team had been performing well, competing at the top of the table, but after his arrival, they stopped winning games and eventually dropped to mid-table.'

Levante faded to tenth in the league, and there were some odd happenings at away fixtures.

While the exact details of Cruyff's financial arrangements with Aznar were never known, it was widely presumed that Cruyff took a healthy slice of the extra revenue his presence generated. Levante were welcome to make those arrangements for home matches, but it was rumoured that for away fixtures, Levante believed they deserved a cut of the bumper paydays their hosts were enjoying and negotiated to that effect.

Cruyff habitually travelled to away games with Aznar, arriving long after the rest of the squad. On the eve of Levante's fixture in Vitoria against Alavés, Cruyff returned urgently to Valencia, explaining that his wife, Danny, was unwell. *Marca*, though, relayed a story that Aznar had requested a payment of 1m pesetas from the Alavés board for Cruyff to appear. Eyebrows were raised, but Cruyff also withdrew from the Dutch squad that midweek – his first call-up in four years. Whatever had happened behind the scenes, the Alavés board was also in no position to negotiate with their gate receipts embargoed to resolve a dispute over Jorge Valdano's transfer to Zaragoza.

The fans in Vitoria were quietly disappointed, but the Andalusian public were far less forgiving a few weeks later. Cruyff was mysteriously scratched from the starting line-up at Linares at the very last minute, leaving the rest of his teammates to take the field to a cacophony of boos from a furious home crowd.

'All the players from that era will tell you that he didn't play that day because they couldn't reach a financial agreement with the president of Linares. I can't say whether that's true or just an urban legend, but it seems plausible. The club tried to profit off Cruyff in every possible way.'

The subsequent 3-1 defeat to the ten men of Linares effectively ended Levante's faint promotion hopes.

Aznar may have harboured dreams of being carried aloft by delirious supporters celebrating a famous promotion, but the reality was a far more ignominious experience. Levante's final home fixture of the season and Cruyff's last appearance for the club came in a passive 0-2 defeat to relegation-threatened Recreativo de Huelva. Sections of the home support were convinced that Levante had sold the match. As the game drew to a conclusion, Aznar and the board were surrounded by hordes of supporters screaming, *'Tongo, tongo'* ('Fix, fix').

Far from being venerated by home supporters, Aznar ended up fleeing through the neighbouring tennis club fearing for his own safety.

***

With Levante in disarray, Cruyff returned to Amsterdam. An international comeback had been rendered moot by the Netherlands' failure to qualify for the World Cup, but Cruyff felt there was still some top-level football in him – and he was right.

A glorious return to Ajax yielded back-to-back league titles and a Dutch Cup. It was a lucrative move as well. Cruyff and his father-in-law convinced Ajax to agree to a familiar-sounding deal. The club would split the additional gate receipts

Cruyff generated, paying half the amount directly into his pension fund.

By the end of the second season, Ajax were regularly drawing crowds of 50,000 to the city's Olympic Stadium. The club's board told Cruyff he was earning far too much money. 'But aren't you earning as much as I am? You've never had so many spectators,' came the typically blunt reply.

Feyenoord were only too willing to match the deal. 'That was very interesting, of course, because they had a stadium for 47,000 people,' recalled Cruyff of his move to Rotterdam. There, he delivered one of the biggest 'up yours' in football history – winning a league and cup double with Ajax's bitterest rivals in his final season as a player.

While Cruyff pursued silverware, chaos reigned at Levante. Aznar resigned just days after his escape via the tennis courts, leaving behind a financial mess. In early June, unpaid players and staff, true to their spirit of unity, barricaded themselves in the stadium for nine days and nights, demanding to be paid.

'There are photos of the dressing room where they had their mattresses,' says Nadal. 'They spent the whole day there. They didn't leave. The community showed solidarity with them, and restaurants and other places would bring them food. They told me they spent their days playing football and watching movies while the more veteran players were negotiating with the club. For the younger players, it was like being at camp; they woke up and played football – most of them still lived with their parents, but for the older guys with families who had to pay the rent, they really suffered. The situation was serious.'

Eventually, the players emerged, but the underlying problems were never seriously addressed. The following season was a disaster, with Levante losing 25 out of their 38 games. Failure on the field was compounded by a further administrative relegation as authorities finally ran out of patience with the club's financial incompetence.

By the time Cruyff and Jesper Olsen were playfully tapping home a two-man penalty routine in Amsterdam en route to another title, Levante were toiling to a 2-2 draw at UD Vall de Uxó as they attempted to tunnel their way out of Spain's labyrinthine fourth tier.

***

'After a brief spell in Spain with Levante…'

Cruyff's autobiography, *My Turn*, devotes exactly eight words to his time at Levante. In contrast, there are whole sections ruminating on the poor financial decisions that pushed him there, 'Believe it or not, I invested in a pig-breeding venture. How on earth did I get involved in that…'

From Levante's point of view, those bizarre few months leave the club and its supporters in a quandary. How exactly to remember the time they signed one of football's all-time greats? As the main custodian of the club's history, it's a question that Nadal has to grapple with, and, as he explains, it's not that simple.

'When you ask the players about their experience with Cruyff, it's interesting because there were two different perspectives. The more veteran players say things like, "Well, Cruyff didn't travel with us; he didn't do the same training as us. If he didn't feel like training, he wouldn't. When we went out, he wouldn't wear the official team gear. He wasn't really integrated into the squad's routine."

'The younger players would tell you the opposite – that Cruyff talked to them a lot, gave them advice, and had a very dynamic relationship with them. So, the younger they were, the more they spoke of him from a positive perspective. The older they were, the more critical they were.'

It's a legacy that occasionally lands Nadal some opprobrium. 'It still sparks a debate, even now. For example, at the stadium entrance, we have a photo of him next to Calpe, one of the club's great historical figures. Hardcore Levante fans get pissed off. They get really angry when I show it.

'Because Calpe is an emblematic figure, he comes from a second-, even third-generation football family. His father and brothers played in key moments of the club's history, and right next to him is Cruyff, who only played ten matches, scored two goals, and put in some pretty lax performances, but for people visiting from outside, the impact of seeing Cruyff is spectacular.'

Even the theory that Cruyff took the money and ran, leaving the club to fall apart, doesn't necessarily stand up to scrutiny. 'The club's economic situation was chaotic long before Cruyff arrived,' says Nadal. 'Could he have made it worse? Yes, but I don't think he ever actually got paid what he was supposed to.

'I believe he mainly lived off ticket sale percentages; I doubt the club paid him directly. Later, information started coming out that they wanted to pay him with shares of the tennis club, which is a clear sign that he wasn't receiving the money he was owed. If he had taken the shares, he could have become a multi-millionaire because later that land was re-zoned and is now a shopping centre.'

'*Una Leyenda Negra*' is a phrase that peppers Nadal's recollections – 'A Black Legend'. Three words that encapsulate one of the strangest chapters in Levante's history. A moment that Nadal still relates to tourists squinting disbelievingly at photos in the Valencia sunshine, while hard-bitten fans roll their eyes.

Hendrik Johannes Cruyff really did once play for Levante.

5.

The Spy That Wouldn't Break

Port of Spain, Trinidad, 21 June 1942

ACTING UPON instructions from MI5 in London, British authorities board the *Cabo de Buena Esperanza,* which has made its scheduled stop on its voyage from Barcelona in Spain to Puerto Cabello in Venezuela. Having removed and detained their suspect, they set about searching every inch of cabin 114, detailing each item in an inventory.

Among the mundane lies the incriminating. Unopened packets of German-made pharmaceuticals and notebooks with fictitious addresses that contain hidden formulae for invisible ink. The discoveries come as little surprise given the man in question 'was known to MI5 from most secret and reliable sources to be an enemy agent'.

His personal effects are boxed up, ready to be shipped to England, where he will spend the next three years as 'the most troublesome and difficult prisoner' British intelligence services have ever had to handle. Among those belongings is a clue to his old life, one element he is not yet ready to give up on – a pair of immaculately polished football boots.

Once a man renowned as the fastest winger in the land, one of a select group of history makers who lined up on the inaugural weekend of a national *Primera Division,* Juan Gómez de Lecube was now a Nazi spy.

* * *

THE SPY THAT WOULDN'T BREAK

There are many things a teenager might use their parents' credit card for on the internet while idling away the summer holidays. Procuring a trove of classified intelligence documents that uncover one of Spanish football's most intriguing stories is not usually one of them – but Oriol Jové wasn't like any other 17-year-old.

'I'm from Lleida, about 150km from Barcelona and Zaragoza. It's in Catalonia, but it's as close to Barcelona as it is to Zaragoza, kind of in the middle. It's not a very big city.

'I've always loved history, and since I was little, I've been interested in the history of Lleida's football team. One day, while researching the team's managers, I looked up the one from the 1951/52 season, and a file from the National Archives showed up on Google. I thought, "Wow, how is it possible that a coach from Lleida has a file in the National Archives of the United Kingdom?"

'I downloaded it, and that's when I discovered that he had been imprisoned in the UK for being a Nazi spy during World War II. From there, I started digging further and visiting archives to piece together his life. His story fascinated me from the very beginning.

'I didn't have a bank card until I was 18, so I had to ask my dad, "Hey, can you please help me with this? It's just three or four pounds, but I'm really curious." I'm 26 now, and I've spent all this time reconstructing his life.'

Jové's years of research culminated in an adventurously written book, *Lecube: El futbolista de Hitler*.

'When people ask about the genre, I always say it's a fictionalised biography but fictionalised in the sense that it has a structure similar to a novel. But everything in the book is backed by a document or testimony – there's nothing invented.

'In a novel, you can make things up to add more context or enrich the story, but here, for example, the fact that he read the *Daily Telegraph* in prison, there's evidence of that. I got so obsessed with the story, with knowing every little detail about his life, his espionage activities, that I achieved a level of detail that allowed me to write something that feels like a novel but is entirely based on real, documented information.'

Jové's enthusiasm is infectious, and there's an undeniable thrill in sitting in the hushed reading rooms of the National Archives in Kew, delicately turning the yellowed pages of the records, correspondence and interrogation notes kept on Lecube.

One batch of files that deals with his arrest in Trinidad and transfer to the UK arrives in a brown folder marked 'DEFENCE', with '1942' stamped on either side. The suspect's name is handwritten across the middle, and a note on square green paper has been stuck on top:

MOST SECRET

SPECIAL CARE SHOULD BE TAKEN TO MAINTAIN THE SECRECY OF THE DOCUMENTS ON THIS FILE. THEY SHOULD BE LOCKED IN A STEEL PRESS OVERNIGHT AND CIRCULATED BY HAND AT ALL STAGES.

WHEN ACTION HAS BEEN COMPLETED THE FILE SHOULD BE RETURNED TO MR. STEED

Pages of barely decipherable handwriting eventually give way to a series of telegrams 'Distributed as Most Secret'. Piece by piece the story emerges of a most peculiar life.

* * *

Born in the Galician coastal village of Ribadeo on 12 May 1902, Lecube's family soon moved to join relatives in Bilbao.

Tragedy struck before his fourth birthday when his mother died during childbirth at just 27 years of age. As the family attempted to rebuild their lives, Lecube and his three siblings moved in with a paternal aunt. One cousin of a similar age who lived with them was José Antonio Aguirre.

Aguirre won a Copa del Rey with Athletic Club in 1923 before moving into politics and becoming the first-ever president of the Basque Country. Sworn in at a ceremony in Guernica in October 1936, Aguirre was forced to flee the following summer when Bilbao fell to Nationalist forces. In exile, he coordinated the Basque nationalist effort and supported a progressive agenda until his death in 1960.

The family was reunited when their father remarried. They were brought up by their stern stepmother and were given a strict religious education. Jové's research found evidence of an early sojourn across the Atlantic, with Lecube spending some time in Argentina before returning to Spain, completing his education and coming more clearly onto the historian's radar through his abilities on the football field.

Lecube began his career with Gimnástica de Torrelavega, playing in the regional Cantabrian league but impressing enough in national tournaments to earn a call-up for the Cantabrian Select XI and consideration for the Spanish national side, who took on Switzerland in Santander in April 1927 shorn of players involved in the latter stages of the cup. Frustratingly, injuries prevented him from fulfilling either duty.

From Torrelavega, it was off to join a free-scoring Celta Vigo side. Lecube formed part of a prolific attack that hit an extraordinary 55 goals in 10 Copa del Rey games before being eliminated by eventual finalists Real Sociedad. That form earned interest from some of the ten teams the Spanish federation had anointed to form the first national league. Athletic de Madrid – yet to become 'Atlético' – and manager Fred Pentland secured Lecube's services, and he duly selected his new threat for that historic first round of *Primera* fixtures in February 1929.

He even made history of sorts, as Jové points out, 'Lecube gave the first assist in the history of the Spanish league. The first goal was scored by a player from Espanyol, Prat, but that was off a rebound. Then, the second goal was scored by Palacios from Athletic de Madrid, and it was from a pass by Lecube. So, he has the honour of providing the first assist in the entire history of La Liga.'

Researching footballers of the 1920s is not the simplest of tasks. Records are incomplete, newspaper reports are brief and rarely focus on the cult of the individual as today, but our protagonist had made some choices that make life a little easier for enterprising teenagers seeking information almost a century later.

Firstly, in tribute to the mother he'd lost at such a young age, he'd elected to be known by his maternal surname of Lecube. A poignant choice and one that stands out much better in the archives than his paternal name of Gómez.

Another was his unmistakable appearance, which made Lecube instantly recognisable in team photos, as Jové found. 'He stood out. Firstly, because of the white handkerchief he wore on his head. He wore it because he didn't have hair and was embarrassed about it. Imagine losing your hair in your early 20s, right? And then he also stood out for being very short.'

Yet it was another physical asset that meant that Lecube garnered more than his fair share of attention from newspapers and magazines. 'He was extremely fast – very, very fast. He was the fastest footballer in Spain at the time. I mean, nothing like it had been seen before. Later, of course, there were other players who were also very quick – like Gento with Real Madrid, but Lecube had done some athletics in his youth and was very, very quick. He could get from one goal to another in 11 seconds. That's 100 metres in little more than 10 or 11 seconds, so we're talking about speeds that even today could qualify for the Olympics.'

His startling pace and eccentric look in an era where photographers weren't routinely dispatched to football grounds meant Lecube became a favourite subject for illustrators. 'The fact that caricatures of him appeared in newspapers shows how important he was as a player. Not everyone gets drawn, right? They only draw important people – important and well-known footballers. In his case, I found five different caricatures of him.'

One cartoon features Lecube's handkerchiefed head perched on some handlebars, a testament to his nickname 'The Human Motorbike'.

Lecube and his new colleagues acquitted themselves well in that pioneering first season, but the summer saw Pentland return to Bilbao to lead Athletic Club to an unbeaten title win while his former charges slumped. A defiant 3-2 victory over champions Barcelona in which Lecube was sent off for fighting seemed to have given them a sufficient cushion, but three straight defeats sent Athletic de Madrid tumbling to an ignominious relegation.

Rather than seek a contract at another first division club, Lecube, at the age of just 27, decided to quit playing professionally. In part, the decision was made in order to follow another passion. One that involved the only thing that sped around the Estadio Metropolitano quicker than he did – the greyhounds.

Lecube's promotion of the sport took him all over Spain and even to the UK. Intelligence files detailed one trip in the mid-1930s to buy racing dogs. Eventually, Lecube realised he would need to add a more pedestrian pursuit to support his family, and he passed the exams necessary to become a government tax clerk and moved to Tarragona, where he'd been assigned.

The connection with football remained. There were fleeting attempts to tempt him out of retirement – a trial with Barcelona, a few friendlies for Valencia and some matches at a regional level, but football became an irrelevance with the onset of the Civil War when Lecube found himself in the wrong place at the wrong time.

'He was living in Tarragona with his family in 1936,' explains Jové. 'What happens in 1936? Franco's military coup takes place, and Spain is split in two. There's the Republican side, which was the established government, and then there's the Nationalist side, the part that Franco had taken over with the coup.

'On the day the coup happens, Lecube is in Zaragoza because he was building a greyhound track there. So, the coup traps him in Zaragoza. Which is one of the cities that falls to the Nationalists. Meanwhile, Tarragona, where his house and family are, is on the other side of the front.

'So, he's separated from his home and family by the war front. He can't cross the front line. He's able to move within Nationalist Spain, but he can't return home.

'He ends up going to the Canary Islands, where he had also organised greyhound races and other things, but he became involved with the Falange, which was the fascist party in Spain. By 1937 or 1938, he had become a centurion in the Falange in Las Palmas de Gran Canaria. This rank meant he was in charge of about 100 militiamen, commanding and leading them.

'His work with the Falange during the war involved monitoring ships passing through the Canary Islands. This was a strategic location, even more so with the Second World War approaching. The islands were crucial as a maritime checkpoint. That role he carried out for the Nationalist side during the Civil War became a key factor in his later recruitment by the Germans.'

When the war ended, Lecube returned to Catalonia but secured a transfer to the tax office in Barcelona. From Monday to Friday, he lived and worked in the city, catching a train along the coast to spend the weekend with his wife Elena and his six children in Tarragona.

The motivation behind this arrangement was a girl 20 years his junior whom he'd met in Las Palmas. Lecube set Amparito up in Barcelona, and the pair had a baby girl together in 1940. The double life he lived before his departure across the Atlantic would later form a key part of British attempts to break Lecube into confession and compliance.

When World War II began, Spain remained officially neutral despite Italy and Germany's support for Franco during the Civil War. While life went on relatively untouched by the horror raging all around, Spanish cities became intriguing theatres of espionage.

The *Abwehr* were able to operate within Spain and used that freedom to recruit agents to monitor and attack Allied naval assets. Their British counterparts, MI5 and MI6, quick to recognise the threat, ambitiously pursued Spanish-trained targets who they saw as valuable sources of information with the potential for being turned into double agents.

Lecube became known to British intelligence soon after his recruitment in May 1941. Run by the Naval Section of the German Secret Service, Lecube was designated to monitor the passage of ships through the Panama Canal and report back via a relay address in Buenos Aires in letters written in invisible ink. His duties also included acquiring a miniature Leica camera to photograph documents and supply sketches.

Frequent training trips to Madrid and his association with the known Mexican handler Luis Fernández de la Reguera were closely monitored. As was his young mistress, Amparito, who the services mistook to be his sister-in-law as she assisted Lecube in collecting the paperwork necessary to secure his passage to Panama.

The strongest intelligence came when intercepted communications revealed his codename to be *Espina* – 'Thorn'. Nearly 100 messages, decoded and transcribed by Bletchley Park, became the backbone of a dossier that convinced MI5's H.A.R. Philby that 'There are strong indications that Lecube knows a good deal about other German agents sent to South America' and 'should be a prolific source of information.'

The source of that information from Bletchley Park was deemed so sensitive that it was only alluded to in vague terms in official documents. Further information was strictly confined to face-to-face conversations.

British intelligence officers were understandably eager to arrest Lecube. They had to bide their time but knew where and when their opportunity would come.

'They were watching him,' says Jové. 'They couldn't arrest him in Spain, so they had to wait. One thing the British did very well during World War II was controlling ship movements between Europe and the Americas. Any neutral ships had to follow strict regulations.

'The *Cabo de Buena Esperanza* was a Spanish ship, and Spain, at least in theory, was neutral. The British had a system in place: all neutral ships travelling between Europe and the Americas were required to make a mandatory stop in Trinidad, a British colony at the time. This way, they could inspect them and stop them moving freely between continents.'

As the date of his sailing moved closer, Lecube continued preparing. Any good spy needs a good cover story, and naturally, Lecube's was a blockbuster.

The official purpose of his voyage was to reunite with his older brother, Luis Valentín, who had gone to seek his fortune in the Americas two decades before. The pair had last seen each other when Luis departed Bilbao as a fresh-faced teenager. In the intervening years, he had become one of the world's pre-eminent smugglers, known as '*El Cojo*' – 'The Lame One', due to the limp he carried from being shot in the knee by Colombian police.

El Cojo had mastered the jungles and waterways of the Chocó region of Colombia that bordered Panama, allowing him to go about his business several steps ahead of authorities. His legend was such that indigenous tribes believed he had magical powers that made him impenetrable to bullets.

While his younger brother prepared to cross the world to monitor the Panama Canal at the behest of the Axis powers, *El Cojo* had already monitored the area on behalf of the United States military. Their cousin, the Basque president-in-exile, had become a smart political operator in New York and had mobilised the Basque diaspora to aid Allied intelligence efforts. In return for his assistance, *El Cojo* had 13 pending charges against him dropped after his cousin bargained with the Panamanian and Colombian governments.

Jové believes there was an element of truth to Lecube's pretext, 'It's not incompatible. In fact, he was going to do both things at the same time. So, it served as an excuse to say, "No, no, I wasn't going to the Americas to be a spy. I was going to see my brother, to do business."'

Messages intercepted by MI5 revealed that Lecube's brother had helped arrange some of the required visas as his German handlers fast-tracked his training and started eyeing which sailing he should take. They settled on the *Cabo de Buena Esperanza*, which set sail from Barcelona on 1 June 1942.

* * *

British intelligence services were certain that the man in cabin 114 was the agent identified as *Espina*. One intercepted message sent three days before Lecube's departure confirmed that '*Espina*, like others, will investigate the strength, weapons, and equipment of the troops in the specified area.'

If further confirmation was required, it came in the last missive that mentioned Lecube's codename, communicating that he had been arrested in Trinidad.

In the eyes of MI5, the case against Lecube was overwhelming. They simply had to present the evidence and await the inevitable confession. After that, they would extract as much information as they could before deciding whether he would serve their purposes as a double agent.

Even his brother believed that Lecube would quickly be flipped. One MI5 telegram disclosed that 'Lecube's brother in Panama works for the FBI and has already denounced his brother as likely to be a German agent. He suggested, however, that might easily be got to double cross the Germans.'

Espina, though, would live up to his codename, proving to be a thorn in the side of Britain's usually unflappable intelligence operation.

Indeed, he began causing headaches before he set foot on British soil. When the boat transporting him and another two Spanish prisoners docked in New York for repairs, the trio set about petitioning to speak to the city's Spanish consul. When that request was denied, they began writing letters in batches, passing them to ordinary sailors in the hope that one might take pity and pass on their correspondence. Lecube also attempted to get word to his influential cousin, whom he knew was based at Manhattan's Columbia University during his exile.

One letter made it to the desk of the Spanish consul, who made a visit to the port. Hopes were briefly raised that the detainees might be taken ashore to plead their case in front of a sympathetic audience, but the consul was soon outranked and sent away, and the ship began crossing to England.

Lecube was immediately brought to London. First to the London Oratory School in Chelsea, which served as a processing hub for captured spies, then to the leafy environs of Richmond-upon-Thames. There, a Victorian mansion called Latchmere House had been converted into a detention and interrogation centre. Run on behalf of MI5 by Lieutenant-Colonel Robin 'Tin Eye' Stephens, Camp 020 had a prolific record of turning enemy agents.

However, from the very beginning, Lecube proved an obdurate opponent, as the camp's chief interrogator, Captain Edward Brereton Goodacre, laid out in a report in October 1942.

'At his first interrogation, LECUBE was told he had been arrested in Trinidad and brought to this prison here because the British Secret Services knew he was a German agent. His activities had been carefully watched for some months past, and we knew he was being sent to Panama on German instructions.

'If he wished to avoid the otherwise inevitable fate of hanging, his only course was to make a clean breast of things straight away. He would be given an opportunity to write a statement explaining his movements and associations in Barcelona and Madrid during the six or seven months prior to his sailing for Trinidad and if this were not satisfactory he need expect no further consideration.

'At his next interrogation he was told that if the statement he had produced were true he should swear that and sign and endorse it to that effect. This he did quite willingly. He was then told that his statement was so much worthless rubbish and general interrogation was begun.'

Lecube had an answer for everything. Associations with German handlers were either pure coincidence or people he'd been put in touch with to secure visas to reunite with his brother. His trips to Madrid were connected to a scheme to import cotton or buy a cafe. The pharmaceuticals found in his cabin were prescribed by the ship's doctor or given to him by a benevolent Dutchman.

Questioning evolved into an epic game of chess. Improbably given the weight of evidence against, Lecube appeared to have the upper hand. In his own mind, not only was he innocent, but it was also an outrage that he was even there. In a move that Lecube calculated would help prove his innocence, he revealed to his interrogators that the young lady they'd had under surveillance was not his sister-in-law but his mistress.

Officers seized on this information and attempted to use it to finally break Lecube. During one session, he was forced to write a letter to his wife, Elena, detailing his double life.

> My dear Elena,
> You will have heard that I was detained at Trinidad by the British authorities. I am now in prison. Even if the British do not hang me as a German spy, the best I can hope for is to remain in prison for the rest of my life. Consequently, it will obviously be impossible for me ever to see you or the children again. Please say 'goodbye' to them for me and look after them as best you can.

> It is my painful duty also to ask you to look after my former mistress, Senorita Amparito POWER and her infant daughter by me, now living at the Franciscan Convent de la Natividad de Nuestra Senora, at Viladomat 82, Barcelona.
>
> Although you are unaware of it, after meeting in the Canaries in 1937 we lived together for some years, latterly at Calle Manresa 4 and 6, 3° right, Barcelona. She is very young and knows little about the world, she will need your protection. I am sending you a photograph so that you may recognise her. Please bid her also a last affectionate farewell on my behalf.
>
> Your devoted husband,
> JUAN

Still, Lecube would not yield, and away from the interrogation room he was also causing problems.

'Normally, when spies are captured, they confess right away,' explains Jové. 'I mean, they put you in a concentration camp, they threaten you with death, and after ten minutes, almost everyone has already told the whole truth. Not him. He was inconvenient because he never, never, ever admitted that he was a German spy.

'Just for that, he was a pain in the arse for the British. On top of that, he's continuously protesting, writing loads of letters to the [Home Office] minister, to the king, to the ambassador. Then, he was involved in a plan to escape from the prison with other prisoners. He went on a hunger strike. He constantly complained.'

Lecube found no end of things to file grievances about – reading materials, lack of communication with other prisoners, and his health. One regular target was the food. In August 1943, he filed one complaint titled, 'Diet that is unbecoming of the Greatness of England.'

By August 1943, a frustrated MI5 officer, Helenus Milmo, opined that 'Lecube has proved quite the most obstinate and difficult prisoner whom we have ever had to interrogate and has steadfastly refused to make any admission of guilt. As stated, however, in previous correspondence, there is not the slightest doubt that this man is an important and dangerous German agent and, as such, must be detained at Camp 020 for the duration.'

A year later, still at a stalemate and with the value of any information Lecube held outdated, he was transferred to Dartmoor to wait out the remainder of the war. When the war ended, Franco's government requested the release of all Spanish prisoners held in Britain. Lecube was processed and sent home via Gibraltar, but even then, he spent weeks grumbling that $200 had gone missing from his belongings.

One of Jové's trips to an archive in Madrid was rewarded by the discovery of a letter from Lecube to Franco asking for assistance in claiming damages against the United Kingdom for his treatment there.

Back in Spain, Lecube was able to continue with his life, 'If you were a German spy and returned to Francoist Spain, nothing happened to you. Whereas, if you'd been a Soviet spy, you would not have been able to return to Spain because the Soviet Union defended communism, which was persecuted in Spain. In fact, the Spanish government even helped him request compensation from England – which he didn't get – but he was seeking damages and reparations for his detention and everything else.'

Lecube returned to the tax offices, living alone in Barcelona, ostracised by his family in Tarragona after the revelation of his relationship with Amparito. The lure of the football field called again and those boots that he'd lugged across the Atlantic and had sat for years in an MI5 storeroom were buffed and readied for action once more.

In 1951, Lecube took over as manager of second-tier side Lleida – then known as 'Lerida', with club names mandated to be in Castilian Spanish. True to form, Lecube didn't feel bound by the era's prevailing orthodoxies and proved himself an innovative coach in many ways ahead of his time.

'Ball on the ground, quick passes, one-touch passing, triangulation,' says Jové. 'The kinds of things that weren't common in Spain at the time where the style of play was more like in Italy. Like *catenaccio*, defend first and play not to lose with long balls.

'He brought this style of play, but it didn't work for him because he coached teams that had players who weren't very good. They weren't ready for it. This system only works when you have very good players who understand it well and have the qualities to execute it.

'So, even though, let's say, theoretically, this style of play made him famous – because newspapers interviewed him, "Lecube, that player from so many years ago at Atlético Madrid, turns out to have invented this new style of play." He was featured in newspapers, but in terms of sporting success, it didn't work out for him.'

As far as 1960, Lecube was still managing in *Segunda*. Manuel Sanchis, who went on to win a European Cup and four league titles with Real Madrid, marshalled the defence in his CD Condal side.

On 2 May 1966, after a battle with liver cancer, Lecube died in Barcelona at the age of 63.

A small obituary ran in the following day's *ABC*. 'Lecube was an extremely quick winger, one of the very fastest in races down the wing, a forerunner to Gento in those characteristics, although he never made it to international level. At Atlético, he played before the war and usually covered his head with a handkerchief, perhaps to hide his premature baldness. May this very noble and original player rest in peace.'

* * *

Lecube was laid to rest in Montjuïc cemetery, along with a lifetime of mysteries, contradictions and unresolved questions.

Was he a man of the hard right or just a pragmatist who swayed with the prevailing political winds?

'When it comes to ideology, it's such a personal matter that sometimes it's not reflected in the documentation,' says Jové. 'That's something only a person can say about themselves. My opinion is that he was a religious person, well, a very Catholic person, so he was likely right-wing. The thing is, he declared himself apolitical. He said he wasn't interested in politics at all.

'Whether you believe that or not is another matter because he said this while in prison at Camp 020. He told this to the British, and, of course, you're not going to tell the British that you're a fascist, that you support Franco's regime, because saying that would have worked against him.

'So from there, you might say, "Okay, but was he a Nazi spy or a spy for Nazi Germany?" Does it mean he had to like Nazism or admire Hitler? Not necessarily, because there were other spies who worked for Germany simply because the Germans paid them. These were years of extreme poverty. There was a fellow prisoner of Lecube who was a socialist and a Republican but became a German spy because the Germans paid for his trip to America.

'There are many cases of Nazi spies who weren't spies out of conviction or ideology but rather out of pragmatism. I believe his case is one of pragmatism as well.'

Lecube's eminent cousin, the first president of the Basque Country, offered his own view on the boy he played football with on the streets of Bilbao in one of his letters. 'My cousin became involved in that more because of his adventurous nature and his poor financial situation than because of his ideals.'

Debates like this have occupied Jové's mind for the last eight years. 'You're going to laugh, but sometimes I wake up in the morning thinking "*Ostras,* that thing I looked up could be related to this or that."'

Reconstructing a life, obsessively tracing documents and tracking down relatives has been an immersive experience. One that leaves Jové conflicted, 'I have some contradictions, because how can I *like* someone who was a spy for Nazi Germany? At the same time, after so many years of researching someone's life to the point where it almost feels like you know them, you do develop a certain affection for that person.

'Besides, yes, he was a Nazi spy, but, like we said, not out of ideology, but for pragmatic reasons. Independent of that, I have developed a fondness for him, and I like the fact that I spent eight years discovering things about his life, not in the sense of admiring what he did – not like, *"Wow, I like what he did!"* No, no, no.

'It's more that I find his life thrilling, fascinating. I mean, how does a football coach, a former player, end up as a spy? That's what I like – the story itself, for its sheer intrigue and value. Not *what* he did. How could I like that?

'But yes, I have developed a connection to the character. Because he has been with me for many years, and I do feel attached – not to *him*, but to the image I've reconstructed of him through my research over these eight years. It's a strange thing.

'And the truth is, I'm personally very happy because people who've read it tell me they like it. Honestly, I think if someone doesn't like the book, it's probably because it's poorly written – because the story itself is fascinating.'

Judging by the growing list of award nominations and rave reviews, that's not something Jové needs to spend too much time worrying about.

All in all, not bad work for a kid whiling away a summer.

6.

The Saviour of Mauthausen

'FROM NOW on, you are my son. Your name is Luis Navazo, you are Spanish and you were born in Madrid at Calle Don Quijote 43, Cuatro Caminos. And never say otherwise.'

The Americans had arrived and brought the liberation they had ached for day after infernal day, but amid the jubilation, panic gripped a blond boy just a day past his 11th birthday.

He'd arrived at Auschwitz with two parents but departed an orphan. Here at Mauthausen the guards had entrusted him to a tall, swarthy Spaniard named Saturnino Navazo, a charismatic man whose footballing prowess had earned him privilege, status and even a note of popularity from those tasked with grinding prisoners to dust.

From the day they met, the boy followed Navazo everywhere. He adored him, but now the end they'd so craved had arrived and the thought of a new beginning petrified the boy. He gave voice to the only thing that made sense to him.

'I want you to be my father.'

The answer came without hesitation and Siegfried Meir was no more. In his place stood Luis Navazo – a boy with a new name, a new nationality, and an address in a city he had never set foot in – and a destiny that depended upon him remembering it.

* * *

Born in Hinojar del Rey in the province of Burgos on 6 February 1914, Saturnino Navazo Tapia and his family moved to Madrid in the early 1920s to that address in Cuatro Caminos where his father ran a bakery.

Navazo came of age during a time of political upheaval in Spain, as the country convulsed from one form of government to another. After years of a faltering constitutional monarchy under King Alfonso XIII, a military coup in 1923 brought General Miguel Primo de Rivera to power. The weakened king backed the new regime, famously calling Primo de Rivera 'my Mussolini'. Like his Italian counterpart, Primo de Rivera attempted renewal through centralisation, sweeping infrastructure projects, and ruthless repression.

Initially Spain thrived, but an economic downturn, escalating debt and unchecked corruption saw Primo de Rivera's popularity plunge and he resigned in 1930. The king's attempts to restore an element of parliamentary democracy backfired disastrously as opposition to the monarchy surged. Emphatic victories for republican parties in elections the following year led to Alfonso XIII's exile and the establishment of the Second Spanish Republic – labelled '*la niña bonita*' (the pretty little girl) by those who felt the hope of change.

While politically the country was veering wildly, football was smoothly establishing itself as the country's main pastime. Initially enjoying popularity with high society and expats, the sport began rapidly expanding in major urban areas. Now attracting healthy crowds, a course to professionalism was set.

The game was thriving in Madrid, particularly in working-class neighbourhoods such as Cuatro Caminos. Tall, powerful and dynamic, Navazo carried all the traits of a traditional centre-forward but instead developed as a thrusting midfielder with an eye for goal. Those qualities saw him recruited by Club Deportivo Nacional de Madrid, who drifted between *Tercera* and *Segunda* and were a lively presence in the Copa de Castilla where they often went toe-to-toe with their more celebrated neighbours and won in 1934.

Navazo was reportedly on the verge of signing with top-flight Real Betis in the summer of 1936, but when the Civil

War erupted that July, his path changed. Instead of heading south with his boots, he was dispatched to the Republican front with a rifle in hand. During the merciless campaign, Navazo fought on the front line in Catalonia and Valencia.

When Nationalist forces prevailed in 1939, Navazo, like many Republicans, fled to France where he briefly settled in Toulouse. Then conflict stirred again with the outbreak of World War II as German forces swept through France and thousands of Spanish refugees were arrested. When Nazi officials asked the Franco regime if the prisoners should be returned to Spain, the answer was blunt. As far as Franco was concerned there were no Spanish living beyond Spanish borders.

Nazi authorities duly declared their Spanish prisoners as stateless – labelling their uniforms with an upside-down blue triangle – and began deporting them. In August 1940, a first train packed with nearly 1,000 Spanish exiles departed from the south-western city of Angoulême making the 1,000-mile (1,600km) journey to Mauthausen, in northern Austria. More trains followed as almost 10,000 Spanish prisoners were shipped to concentration camps, the vast majority ending up at Mauthausen which processed around 7,500 Spaniards during the war. There they served as slave labour, predominantly in its brutal granite quarry where prisoners were made to haul giant rocks up a 186-step 'staircase of death'. Fewer than half of the Spanish contingent survived.

Navazo arrived at Mauthausen in 1941 via an alternative route. Having fought alongside French forces as they attempted to resist the German tide, he was arrested and processed via Belfort in northern France to Fallingbostel in Saxony where upon discovering his nationality he was transferred to join his compatriots and assigned prisoner number 5656.

Strong and athletic, Navazo was better built to cope with the gruelling labour than others, many of whom died of illness, exhaustion or suspicious falls in the quarry. Though an accident while working in the quarry did cost him a finger.

Sundays came as a merciful day of rest, and those from the Spanish barracks who could muster some energy would pass an improvised football around between them to pass the time. Soon the Nazi guards became intrigued and organised Sunday matches were authorised by the camp's highest authority, the callous SS Captain Georg Bachmayer.

Navazo, as an ex-professional and the best player in the Spanish ranks, was given the task of organising the games. Sunday afternoons became filled with matches between different nationalities – Hungarians v Czechs, Poles v Spaniards – as fellow prisoners watched on enjoying a serene few hours' escape from the usual hellscape. On the balconies and rooftops above, Nazi soldiers also enjoyed the spectacle.

With Navazo providing the goals at one end and Juan Castañeda – a Barcelona youth player, whose son, Jean, would go on to play in goal for Saint-Étienne and France – keeping them out at the other, Spain were unbeatable. The Nazis came to value their Sunday entertainment so much that those involved began receiving preferential treatment – kitchen work instead of shifts at the quarry, extra servings of food and higher status in their respective barracks.

Football was providing an unlikely route to survival and soon Navazo would have a willing young assistant to help out on matchdays.

* * *

Siegfried Meir was born in Frankfurt on 4 May 1934 to Max Meir and Jenni Bacharach, a Jewish couple of Romanian heritage. His childhood was marked by the increasingly anti-Semitic policies of Hitler's newly-established Third Reich. Despite the increasingly hostile environment which drove hundreds of thousands of Jews to flee Germany, the family obstinately stayed put, a decision made by Meir's highly religious father.

'When someone has such intense faith in a religion – any religion – they are completely unhinged,' recalled Meir in the

2015 documentary film *Después de la niebla* (After the fog). 'They don't see reality. So, the education I was given was one aimed at preparing me for a future as, perhaps, a rabbi. My father was completely obsessed with religion, and his constant motto was, "Don't worry, nothing will happen to us. God will protect us."'

The family survived in Frankfurt until April 1943 when they were arrested and sent to Auschwitz. Upon arrival Meir was tattooed with his prisoner number 117943. He always recalled the woman who branded him seeing the fear in the eyes of an eight-year-old boy and promising him the 'prettiest tattoo of all'.

The new intake was sorted into two lines – one for women and children, one for men. Meir never saw his father again.

Soon after their arrival, Meir's mother fell ill with typhus and quickly deteriorated. With the situation hopeless, the Jewish women that supervised the barracks made the decision to end her life comfortably by an injection of air, sparing her the horror of being hauled to the extermination chambers. Meir watched his mother's final moments in the lodging they shared.

Meir soon contracted typhus himself, a fate that almost certainly meant a child would be executed, but remarkably, Meir was taken to the camp hospital and nursed back to health under the care of Josef Mengele – the doctor known as the 'Angel of Death' who performed genetic research on prisoners.

Meir often reflected on why he was spared at Auschwitz, despite the myriad opportunities to murder him. 'How could it be that, in a barrack where they killed children for experiments, I was saved?' He pondered in his 2016 autobiography *Mi Resiliencia* (My Resilience). 'That they cured me of typhus – an illness no one recovered from. If I look back and analyse it, it seems humiliating to have been in that situation, to have survived it; even though at the time I was glad to have been saved.'

'I was handsome, blond, had blue eyes, spoke exactly the same language as those who wanted to kill me, and I didn't understand that accusation of being Jewish. To me, it only meant the way my parents prayed, but I didn't understand why they were doing those things, and I still don't understand. That's why I was always furious – it was a kind of rage. I think that's what saved me – my anger, my rebellion. When you speak German and you speak it furiously, it sounds powerful. It's a language that hits hard when you shout it.'

That pugnacious streak would help change his destiny. Now orphaned and with the Soviet Red Army advancing through Poland, Nazi officials began evacuating prisoners away from Auschwitz and Meir was transferred to Mauthausen in January 1945.

* * *

Meir's arrival at Mauthausen caused a stir.

'I was afraid,' he recalled in his memoir. 'I didn't know what I was walking into. I was so full of rage that I couldn't control myself, and I caused a huge scene when they tried to cut my hair. I didn't realise how serious it was until Bachmayer appeared. When he told me he was going to take care of me, I didn't really know what that meant.'

A personal intervention by the camp's highest authority was usually an ominous sign. Again, somehow, Meir was spared.

'I thought the scene I had caused would end badly, and when Bachmayer said, "Nothing's going to happen to you. I'm assigning you to the Spanish barracks," I didn't really know what to make of it. I didn't know who the Spaniards were, because in Auschwitz there were no Spaniards.

'So, he took me to Navazo and said to him, "You're going to be responsible for him, make sure nothing happens to him. He will live here in this barrack, with you." He said it just like that, as an order.'

Left alone in Block Six of the sprawling concentration camp, a 10-year-old German boy and a 30-year-old Spanish refugee thrown together by circumstance, made an instant connection.

'I think we discovered something in each other at that moment, because he looked at me and I looked at him. I remember that moment vividly, because he smiled at me. I was nervous, but he smiled at me and he spoke to me, but I didn't understand a word he said because he was speaking Spanish, and I spoke German.

'I remember it very clearly, it's etched in my memory – that smile of his when he looked at me, almost laughing, as if to say, "Now what's going to happen?" But I didn't feel afraid. From that moment on, I was never afraid again.'

When the rest of the barracks returned from their day's labour, Meir – via some Polish prisoners – was able to tell his story. He took to life in Block Six, picking up Spanish quickly and was nearly always seen with Navazo. 'At first, I followed him around like a little puppy, always walking just behind him, until one day he put his hand on my shoulder – and from that moment on, we always walked together like that.'

Meir accompanied Navazo to work at the kitchen each day, despite grumbling from the guards that he was slowing down the peeling of potatoes. And then there were Sundays. 'I clearly remember the first time I saw him play football; he had a team with the Spaniards, and the first time I went to watch him play, I felt something very special. A very deep emotion.'

He had a front row seat and was soon making himself useful, helping organise shirts, boots and balls for the all-conquering Spanish team.

As winter turned to spring, American and Soviet forces were advancing through Germany as Axis resistance dissolved. Liberation was agonisingly close, but the prisoners of Mauthausen lived through the atrocious paradox that the closer that day was, the more hellish their ordeal became.

The camp grew critically overcrowded as the Nazis poured evacuated prisoners into Mauthausen and its sub-camps. Food supplies failed and typhus ran rampant. Sadistically, the camp kept its gas chambers operational even as American and Soviet troops met at the Elbe River, signalling that Germany had fallen. In the ten days leading up to the capture of the Reichstag on 30 April 1945, camp authorities slaughtered around 3,000 prisoners.

Finally on 3 May, Nazi forces fled and an international committee of prisoners managed the camp before the US Army arrived two days later. As the convoy rolled triumphantly in through the main gate, the influence of the Spanish Republican contingent was in evidence. A huge banner had been draped across the entrances: *'Los españoles antifascistas saludan a las fuerzas liberadoras'* – 'Anti-fascist Spaniards salute the liberating forces.'

After, Meir's plea received the answer he wanted more than anything else. All he had to do was convince them he was Spaniard too. That he was Luis Navazo of Calle Don Quijote 43, Cuatro Caminos, Madrid.

* * *

The Red Cross was charged with processing the camp's children and when Meir's turn came he told his story immaculately. Having entered Mauthausen as an orphan from Frankfurt called Siegfried Meir, he was leaving as Luis Navazo Tapia of Madrid, along with his father Saturnino and had the papers to prove it. A provisional identification card for civil internee of Mauthausen was issued with the exact details he'd memorised, his passport to a new life.

The pair were sent to Toulouse, then settled in the nearby town of Revel. Adapting was tough, with school a daily humiliation, as classmates several years younger than 'Luis' mocked his poor academic level. And he continued Siegfried's propensity for petty theft, a key survival instinct at Auschwitz and Mauthausen but distinctly problematic in polite French society. His new father patiently coached the habit out of him.

Navazo returned to the football field, enjoying success on the local amateur scene with Union Sportive Revenoise, and he became active with the exiled Spanish Socialist Workers' Party (PSOE), who had set up temporary headquarters in Toulouse.

He found work at a furniture restorers in Revel, specialising in painting and varnishing antique pieces. It was there he met his wife. The couple had four children together and Meir felt the dynamic between he and Navazo begin to shift.

'It can't be easy for a young woman to take on the responsibility of a teenager who isn't hers, whom she didn't choose,' he wrote. 'And even less so if the teenager is the baggage of the man she married. I wasn't happy. Navazo and I spoke a lot about it; we discussed it, he asked me to be patient, but in the end we decided the best thing was for me to move to Toulouse and return to the village on weekends.'

French law had frustrated Navazo's attempts to adopt Meir and after graduating from school under his Spanish name, Meir was forced to reclaim his former identity and become Siegfried Meir once more as he made his own way in the world. But he could never bring himself to speak his mother tongue again and forever felt a deep sense of ease whenever he heard it spoken.

From Toulouse, Meir soon felt the pull of Paris, where he found success as a singer under the stage name 'Jean Siegfried'. Then in the early 1960s he moved to Ibiza as the island began to boom. There, he found an element of fame as a fashion designer, restaurateur and nightclub owner, earning the nickname 'The King of Ibiza'.

By chance, business once took him to Madrid, where some associates were selling a pizzeria. The restaurant happened to be on Calle Don Quijote, in Cuatro Caminos – the very street he had so urgently memorised as a child. He knocked on the door of the old address, still etched in his mind after all those years, but nobody was home.

Navazo died in 1986 at the age of 72. Meir's memoir – written five years before his own death in 2020 – bears a simple dedication:

ONCE UPON A TIME IN LA LIGA

In memory of my parents
Saturnino Navazo, Max Meir and Jenni Bacharach

Some of the book's most moving passages describe the summers the two spent together in later life. An extraordinary relationship that began with so few words – decades later and despite all they'd survived – needed little more than that.

'We'd be at my house in Ibiza, just the two of us in the garden, enjoying the last rays of the sun. No words; just looking at each other, and every so often:

'"Do you realise?"

'"We're here."

'There was no need to speak. What more could we say? We both understood the whole universe was wrapped up in those two small phrases. There was no need to look back.'

7.

El Valladolid de los Colombianos

CARLOS VALDERRAMA had to look down to check what he felt was happening really was happening.

The corkscrew-haired Colombian had spent much of his afternoon at the Estadio Santiago Bernabéu in a running battle with his direct opponent, Real Madrid's Míchel. The pair had clashed on several occasions and the referee had once again intervened to restore peace as they awaited a corner in the Madrid penalty area.

Rather than risk taking another swipe in front of the officials, Míchel switched tactics, grabbing Valderrama by the testicles – at first almost tentatively, then again much more vigorously. Valderrama stood hands on hips, bewildered, glancing down to see the hand of Míchel before staring quizzically up at his marker.

Soon the corner arrived and the ball was cleared. The whole bizarre incident had lasted a matter of seconds but would occupy newspapers for days, a disciplinary committee for weeks and stand years later as one of the most indelibly odd images in Spanish football history.

It would also provide the one enduring highlight from one of La Liga's most curious recruitment experiments. When Colombian football's biggest names arrived at Real Valladolid in an ambitious attempt to power the club to new heights.

* * *

'A bit serious – Valladolid has always been that way,' says José Miguel Ortega, who followed Real Valladolid at close quarters for years as a reporter for *Marca* and Radio Nacional de España and the author of countless books on the club.

'Well, I'm not sure if we really are like that, but we do have the reputation of being serious, of not really liking the appearance of people like that. But back then, there was so much hope that with those three players, Valladolid was practically going to win the league, so people didn't mind. In fact, they loved them – they applauded all three of them like crazy.

'Of course, once things started going wrong, it turned into, "Hey, big hair, get out of here!" That's when problems began in the stands with all of them.'

Austere, orderly and conservative, Valladolid – an elegant city perched where central Spain begins stretching out to its northern coast – stands a world apart from the sprawling tropical mayhem of Medellín. But it was the direction the city's football club looked in the summer of 1990.

Real Valladolid largely epitomises the city itself. The club has spent exactly half of their history in Spain's *Primera División* and stand in a commendable 13th position in the all-time league table. Yet, for its admirable consistency, it's a club that, certainly up until 1990, largely coasted along serenely, rarely troubling the headline writers of the country's sports papers.

One man hoped to change all that. Gonzalo Gonzalo had already elevated the city's basketball team from mid-ranking plodders to European contenders. A pair of audacious signings from the Soviet Union had been the key. No sooner had Arvydas Sabonis and Valdemaras Chomicius stepped off the plane from Vilnius than they were averaging over 40 points per game together as the side rose up the rankings.

'He was a very open guy, very easy-going. He got along very well with journalists – especially me, because he had known me since I was a child,' recalls Ortega.

'His wife owned an electrical lighting shop. It was his wife who owned the business but he ran it too. He was very good at selling himself, great at self-promotion, and of course, with Fórum [the basketball team] he had a fantastic run.

'The president of Valladolid at that time was someone who wasn't well-liked by the public. His name was Miguel Ángel Pérez Serrano. People turned against him, and eventually, he was removed. In the end, Gonzalo Gonzalo was chosen as the new president. Gonzalo was a big fan of flashy, attention-grabbing signings – like Sabonis.'

Not given to idling, Gonzalo began eyeing up big-name arrivals even before his presidency was confirmed and had a particularly keen eye on a fashionable new head coach.

Francisco 'Pacho' Maturana was a manager whose stock was on the rise. A native of Medellín, Maturana had gone to secondary school with a certain Pablo Escobar but chose the more conventional career path of dentistry. As a player he had combined running a successful dental practice with a decade in central defence for Colombia's biggest club Atlético Nacional.

As he progressed into management, Maturana was creatively combining jobs again. After just one season in charge of Once Caldas, he was appointed as head coach of the Colombian national team in the summer of 1987. He was then courted by Nacional and ran the two roles alongside each other – basing the national side on the nucleus of his club squad.

It was seen as a controversial design, but one that soon paid handsome dividends. In May 1989, Nacional became the first Colombian side to win the Copa Libertadores. Five months later, seven of that side featured for Colombia in a World Cup qualification play-off win over Israel that returned Colombia to football's biggest stage after an absence of nearly three decades.

After his charismatic side progressed to the knockout stage of Italia '90, Maturana became a man in demand. Gonzalo moved quickly, so snappily in fact that Maturana's appointment had to be delayed while the president-elect hurriedly collected the 808 member signatures necessary to satisfy the club's statute book.

When Maturana finally landed in Spain on 1 August he was quick to pay tribute to the man who had brought him to Europe: 'I must express my appreciation to Gonzalo Gonzalo for the way he honoured me by choosing me to lead his team,' Maturana told reporters. 'I hope not to disappoint the expectations placed on me, and I will do my best in my role as manager of Real Valladolid.'

One name inevitably came up repeatedly at that first press conference. A man who'd shot to global fame that summer for all the wrong reasons after being robbed by Roger Milla far from his own goal as Colombia exited the World Cup in extra time against Cameroon. René Higuita was a fundamental part of Maturana's high-pressing style and Gonzalo's right-hand man, Javier Yepes, was certainly not ruling out a move. 'We would consider bringing Higuita in. He could even be signed as an investment by Real Valladolid. He's a goalkeeper who has introduced new ideas into the game and is a valuable asset for any team.'

Those remarks were revealing, not only for the eventual pursuit of Higuita but of Gonzalo's ultimately flawed concept that signings could pay for themselves. 'He believed football could bring in so much money that he could sign whoever he wanted,' sighs Ortega.

As he got to work Maturana had to largely make do with the existing squad, which wasn't without its talents. Despite Fernando Hierro's departure for Real Madrid, a young José Luis Caminero was attracting attention from bigger clubs while Gregorio Fonseca and Onésimo Sánchez formed a decent strike partnership.

While it would take some time for the superstars to arrive, there was one globally recognised name prowling around the Real Valladolid training facilities that summer. 'When Maturana arrived here, he was working during pre-season with the players, trying to instil a new style of play,' says Ortega.

'Arrigo Sacchi, the Milan coach, came incognito to observe him. He stayed for nearly a month. Nobody knew who he was, but he spent his time taking notes on Maturana's system.' The pair had struck up a close friendship after the 1989 Intercontinental Cup between Milan and Atlético Nacional revealed their shared tactical philosophy.

Less comprehending of Maturana's tactics were his new players, as Ortega recalls, 'For the Valladolid players at the time, Maturana's *zona* system was like a foreign language – it was hard for them to grasp, and it required a lot of effort. It was a high-pressing approach, extremely demanding. That was an issue, because the squad – both in general across Spanish football and especially at Valladolid – wasn't used to that level of physical work. The tactics required not only technical skill but also an enormous physical effort for the full 90 minutes. And that didn't sit well with some of the players; many simply didn't take to that style of play.'

It took until mid-October for Maturana's first victory to arrive and by Christmas, Valladolid were mired in the relegation zone with just two wins, but the new year, and the arrival of Maturana's compatriot – his trusted midfield lieutenant, Leonel Álvarez – saw the team finally click. An impressive second half of the season rallied the side to a top-half finish in a style that earned Maturana admirers.

Real Madrid had endured a torrid season where they had quickly tailed off the pace and cycled through managers. A pre-contract was agreed for Maturana to become the new Madrid head coach the following season. But Radomir Antić revived the side, rattling off eight wins from nine, including victories over Barcelona and Atlético Madrid. The late surge bought the Serb a further season in charge and Maturana's agreement was quietly filed away in an office drawer.

Unperturbed, Maturana looked ahead to the 1991/92 season, driving on his project at Valladolid and landing his two main summer transfer targets – René Higuita and Carlos Valderrama.

Prising Higuita away from Nacional became a convoluted process, but there were no such problems in tempting the other face of Colombia's World Cup campaign. So keen, in fact, was Valderrama to leave Montpellier and join up with Maturana, he left his national team's Copa America preparations to fly to Spain to complete the deal.

Valderrama was the picture of relaxed, Santa Marta beach cool as his beaded wrists jangled to join a three-way handshake with Maturana and Gonzalo for the benefit of the cameras. The smiles betrayed the storm that was blowing up back in Colombia. Valderrama's unauthorised departure from camp had infuriated the Colombian federation president, León Londono, who threatened to throw his captain out of the squad. It took a phone call from Maturana to defuse the situation – calmly talking his old boss down, 'I just explained to him that suspending Carlos made no sense, and the country wouldn't stand for it.'

Higuita finally set foot in Valladolid just as pre-season was ending. Although he'd been reluctant to move from Nacional and his home city of Medellín, his eventual transfer proved something of a relief, as Higuita had caused a scandal in Colombia by paying a visit to his new manager's old classmate, Escobar, in prison.

The image of the three superstar Colombians, with their moustachioed, wild-haired, buccaneering looks was striking. And a club more used to having their pre-season prospects passed over in a couple of nondescript sentences was suddenly having to get used to national and international attention.

'Their presentation in Valladolid was a massive spectacle,' says Ortega. 'It took place during a training session at the new Zorrilla stadium, and the place was nearly full with around 30,000 fans. Expectations were sky-high. People thought these new Colombian arrivals would dominate the league.'

'This was something new, not just in Valladolid, but throughout all of Spain. Higuita and Valderrama in particular were internationally well-known. Leonel was a bit less famous, but all three had played for the Colombian national team. They were key figures in that squad, which people had watched on TV during the World Cup. Colombia had been the tournament's surprise package, especially with their tactics and style of play. So bringing in three stars from that side made a huge impression.'

Higuita gave his new public an instant showreel of what to expect. In a friendly at Zorrilla against the Brazilian side Internacional, Higuita was at fault for two goals and escaped a blatant red card for dragging an opponent down in midfield. Though in typical fashion, in the resultant shoot-out he saved two penalties before converting the decisive kick himself.

Unsurprisingly, Ortega found Higuita an ebullient interviewee although Valderrama proved to be less so, 'Higuita was always joking around, always in a playful mood. Valderrama, on the other hand, was quieter, quite introverted. It was actually Leonel who adapted the best. He settled in well, and his performances were solid.'

For all the optimism, Valladolid made a disjointed start to the season at home to Sporting de Gijón. A good first half gave way to a nervous second, particularly after a Sporting free kick squirmed through the defensive wall, leaving Higuita scrambling in vain to keep the ball out. Fans left Zorrilla disgruntled as Maturana's men failed to react and lumbered to a 1-0 defeat.

Next was a trip to Real Madrid where Valladolid lost by the same scoreline – again to a goal where Higuita was unconvincing. But the performance was transformed, and Valladolid deserved more from a full-blooded contest where Valderrama imperiously pulled the strings. Madrid had to resort to hacking him down and some rather comical time-wasting from goalkeeper Paco Buyo.

The result would largely prove incidental as the fallout revolved around just one moment. 'Yes, the incident involving Valderrama and Míchel,' recalls Ortega. 'During a corner kick, Míchel touched Valderrama in his private parts, trying to provoke him. The idea was that Valderrama would react, maybe slap him, but Valderrama just stood there, looking at him as if to say, "What are you doing touching me like that?" It was a very amusing and strange moment.'

The clarity of the pictures caught by cameras, the high profile of the two players and the sheer oddity of it all were a perfect storm, and the incident became a sensation that was talked about for weeks on end.

In the following morning's *Mundo Deportivo,* the match report dedicated one paragraph to the rest of the game and instead focused almost entirely on those few seconds in the Real Madrid penalty area.

'Aldana scored – let that be noted for the record,' it began. 'But the most notable moment of the match starred Míchel.

'The Real Madrid midfielder quite literally put his hands to work – this time on Colombian Carlos Valderrama, a newcomer to Spanish football, and perhaps now considering writing a memoir after what happened.

'Valderrama and Míchel clashed just before Valladolid was about to take a corner kick in front of Paco Buyo's goal. The referee, Riera, intervened and for a moment it seemed everything had calmed down, but Míchel kept going, notoriously and blatantly pinching Valderrama's very masculinity.

'It was the "play" of the match – and of the entire matchday. Both players later got into something resembling a street fight, which is almost anecdotal in comparison. Míchel's "explorations" of Valderrama will not be forgotten in this league.'

Valladolid called for disciplinary action. President Gonzalo sent a letter to the federation stating, 'We find ourselves compelled to address you to express our indignation and rejection of the events that occurred at the Estadio Santiago Bernabéu, resulting from the unsportsmanlike and, in our opinion, indecent behaviour of the Real Madrid player, Sr. Miguel González, known as Míchel.'

Míchel himself sought to brush off the episode, 'It was just a joke. One of those things that happen in football that people don't understand.'

Unable to see the funny side was José Javier Forcén, of the Competition and Discipline Committee. He handed Míchel a 500,000 peseta (€3,000) fine for a 'lack of decorum', namely 'manipulating in public the gift that is exclusively given to males by nature'.

With the surreal chapter closed, Valladolid's improved showing at the Bernabéu proved to be something of an illusion and it took the side until October to register their first win. The mood was also growing sombre off the pitch, as an astonishing debt of 700m pesetas (€4.2m) owed to tax authorities became public knowledge.

Ortega explains, 'Valladolid was in a deep financial crisis. The players weren't getting paid, and it came to light that the club had accumulated a huge debt. Eventually, the mayor of Valladolid, a socialist named Tomás Rodríguez Bolaños, gathered local businessmen – mostly real estate developers – and urged them to put together money to save the club, not just from relegation but from total collapse.'

Gonzalo the dreamer who had brought in the four Colombians was forced off the board.

'The real issue at Valladolid wasn't just that the Colombians weren't performing as expected,' says Ortega. 'The club was failing to make the agreed payments for their transfers, and it was a financial mess.'

Tension transmitted itself to the stands, and Higuita's alternative take on the goalkeeping position was soon drawing opprobrium. Tired of basic errors, the Zorrilla crowd grew intolerant of Higuita's downfield sorties and attempts to flick the ball over oncoming forwards and began jeering their goalkeeper whenever he left his box.

'The fans didn't like him because he made some huge mistakes,' says Ortega. 'He was incredibly flashy when stopping balls that didn't require any theatrics. Instead of simply catching the ball, he'd spin around three times or do something dramatic.'

A broader debate on his style was taking place. *Don Balon* magazine ran a survey entitled: 'Is Higuita an acceptable goalkeeper for Spanish football?' canvassing opinions from fellow first division goalkeepers and greats such as Luis Arconada. Far from fuelling the debate, the answers were sympathetic, with the goalkeeping fraternity unwilling to criticise the Colombian.

Despite the support, it eventually became too much for Higuita. After another error-strewn display in the final game before the Christmas break against Tenerife, he made straight for the centre circle to wave goodbye to the home fans. In an impromptu press conference, conducted while he waited to provide a doping sample, he declared he was departing, 'I'm going to take a vacation and refocus my life away from Real Valladolid. It's decided. It's official.

'I'm not good. My head isn't in the right place, and under these conditions, I can't go on. The best thing is to look elsewhere. Of course, I wish this team the best. It's not the fans' fault or anyone else's. It's just that I'm not OK. My head isn't OK.'

With that, after just 15 games for the club, Higuita returned to Nacional – who, rather tellingly, had yet to receive a single dollar of his transfer fee from Valladolid.

With Higuita departed, the Colombian project limped on, until a few weeks later it imploded spectacularly in a game against Barcelona at Camp Nou. With 27 minutes gone, Valderrama fed a ball forward to Álvarez, who was clearly tripped. The Valladolid players stopped in anticipation of a free kick, but no whistle came. Instead, the ball was whisked downfield, where Michael Laudrup played in Julio Salinas for the opening goal.

Valderrama and Álvarez were incandescent and made their feelings plain to referee Andújar Oliver, but the official had a reputation for being particularly intolerant of dissent and haughtily produced red cards for both players.

'The team – especially the Colombians – were completely unhinged at that point. They knew that the club needed to get rid of them, and on top of that, they weren't getting paid. So they caused a whole mess during the match, and the referee ended up sending them off.'

The image of the pair sitting dejectedly on the floor in front of the Camp Nou dugout would be the last of them in Valladolid's violet and white colours. Days later, the duo departed, Valderrama to Independiente de Medellín, Álvarez to América de Cali.

Asked about the failure of the Colombian project, interim president Andrés Martín was frank in his assessment. 'Personally, I wouldn't have signed them. Though I'll tell you something, Cruyff, Maradona and Pelé all together would have failed here. You can't ask a player to do his job when he hasn't even been paid his salary from the previous season.'

Maturana limped on, but a year after being courted by Real Madrid, it became more of a question of when he would be sacked. That day came in April when the new board pulled the trigger with nine games remaining. The change did not have the desired effect and the club collapsed to relegation after an unbroken spell of 12 seasons in *Primera*.

***

Maturana wasted no time getting back into the swing of things, appointed as manager of América de Cali and immediately winning the title. Colombia called once more, and Maturana was re-appointed as head coach ahead of the 1994 World Cup qualifying campaign.

The qualifiers were played over an intense one-month period. It was a format that seemed to suit Colombia, who hit a strong vein of form and travelled to Buenos Aires for their final game assured of at least a play-off position and needing a draw to seal automatic qualification. After intense Argentine pressure throughout the first half, Freddy Rincón put Colombia ahead just before half-time.

Colombia then picked Argentina apart in a scintillating display of precise attacking football, running out 5-0 winners – a result that remains the most celebrated in Colombian football history.

While Maturana, Valderrama and Álvarez were receiving an ovation by the Argentine fans at the Estadio Monumental, fellow Valladolid defector Higuita watched on television from his cell at La Modelo prison in Bogotá. Higuita was being held without bail on charges of kidnapping. His involvement in negotiating the release of a teenage girl had broken Colombia's strict new anti-kidnapping laws. Higuita claimed he was being punished for the visit he had paid to Escobar and went on hunger strike to protest his incarceration.

After his eventual release, Higuita was in no shape to make the Colombian squad that travelled to USA '94 as what many people – including, famously Pelé – considered potential winners, but the weight of expectation and a horrifying backdrop of threats made against individual players saw the team eliminated after just two games. The subsequent murder of Andrés Escobar, the defender who had put through his own net in the decisive defeat to the USA, starkly illustrated the malevolent force that drug cartels had become in the country's football scene.

Back in Valladolid, a new president with genuine resources, Marcos Fernández, stabilised the situation and helped return the club to the top flight at the first time of asking where they remained for another long spell even qualifying for the UEFA Cup just a few years after the failure of their most exotic transfer plan.

Some three decades later, mention *el Valladolid de los Colombianos* to any Spanish football fan and only one memory will be conjured. The peculiar image of one of Real Madrid's greatest midfielders grabbing Colombia's most emblematic players by the balls.

Ingeniously, in 2017, the magazine *Libero* collaborated with Valderrama, using the incident to highlight the importance of testicular self-examination. Alongside slowed-down footage, Valderrama demonstrates the correct way to inspect for lumps.

'Throughout my career, I had many memorable moments, but there's one that really touched me,' Valderrama begins. 'I can still feel it.

'First touching my left testicle, from top to bottom. Then the right one, repeating the same movement, and a third one to see if both have the same shape, trying to find any lumps.

'So I want to thank you, my dear friend. For touching my balls in three simple steps. Like we all should do to prevent testicular cancer.

'Gracias, Míchel,' he concludes with that famous smile.

8.

Quini: Bound to Forgive

'IT WAS 1981.

'There were three major events. So, in terms of Spain's historical, political, and journalistic context, it was truly pivotal. It was a complicated, delicate, interesting, and exciting time.'

An economic crisis had sent unemployment and inflation soaring into double digits and contributed to the resignation of Prime Minister Adolfo Suárez in January, beginning a year that would contain enough drama and intrigue to keep scriptwriters and documentary makers busy for decades.

On 23 February, 200 *Guardia Civil* officers led by Lieutenant Colonel Antonio Tejero brazenly stormed parliament as it voted to swear in Suárez's successor, Leopoldo Calvo-Sotelo. With deputies held captive and tanks rolling ominously into Valencia, a nation teetered, but the coup collapsed after King Juan Carlos I's televised condemnation committed the country to following its constitution. The subsequent pro-democracy rallies reaffirmed Spain's modern path.

On a Saturday morning exactly three months later, gunmen swept into the Central Bank of Barcelona, taking around 300 people hostage. The assailants issued a demand for Tejero and three other authors of the coup to be released and flown to Argentina, but after a tense 37-hour standoff, police stormed the building, the siege ended, and investigators concluded that the political demands were merely a ruse designed to buy the gang time to tunnel their way out through the city's sewers.

Between those two shocks came the most bewildering and gripping saga of all – one that unfolded not in a parliamentary chamber or a bank vault but in a motorcycle repair workshop in Zaragoza. It was there that Enrique Castro González – better known as '*Quini*', the charismatic forward leading the league's scoring charts – was held for 25 days after vanishing from the streets of Barcelona on the night of a match.

* * *

'Bloody Sunday drivers.'

Juan, a waiter on the late shift at Can Fusté, looked out the front window to see a whiskey-coloured Ford Granada clumsily manoeuvring in the street outside. As he stepped out onto the pavement to take a closer look, he recognised from the number plate that the car belonged to Quini, who lived in a fifth-floor apartment above the restaurant. Before he could get close enough to speak to him, the vehicle sped off.

Inside the car was Quini, not behind the wheel but in the passenger seat. In a hint that this wasn't to be the smoothest of operations, he had to patiently coach his bemused captors on how to drive an automatic transmission, all while having the cold steel barrel of a pistol pressed to his neck.

Just hours earlier, he'd left the press room a few hundred yards down the Travessera de les Corts at Camp Nou in high spirits. He'd scored twice that afternoon as FC Barcelona thumped Hércules 6-0, and attention had turned to the following week's title showdown with Atlético Madrid.

Back at home, he'd made the flat look presentable for the return of his wife and two children, who had spent the week in the couple's native Asturias. He binned some tired-looking Valentine's Day flowers, set the video to record that night's goals show, and, at 8.30pm, called his in-laws to check his family's flight had left on time. Calculating the times in his head, he grabbed his keys and headed for the airport, taking the elevator to ground level, leaving the building and jumping into the car he'd parked by the bus stop.

As he put the key in the ignition, he became abruptly aware that he was not alone. Directed to the passenger side, he was made to stare straight ahead as his kidnappers made heavy weather of figuring how to move a car with no clutch pedal. Eventually, they screeched a few hundred yards up the road, where Quini was bound and hooded and transferred to a DKW van bearing stolen number plates. The player was padlocked into a wooden chest, and the van took off at full speed for Zaragoza.

At Barcelona's El Prat airport, 10km south of the city, Quini's wife, María Neves, had just landed. With no sign of her husband, she retrieved her bags from the carousel and attempted to soothe their restless 18-month-old son, Enrique, while their five-year-old daughter, Lorena, ran laps of the arrivals hall in search of her father.

After waiting around 20 minutes, María Neves, laden with bags and two uncooperative children, battled to the taxi rank and took a cab back to their home at Gran Via de Carles III, 52. After negotiating the front entrance and the lift, what she found when she opened the apartment door was deceptively reassuring. The lights were on, and the video whirred away, recording as it did every Sunday evening. On the couple's bed, the clothes that Quini had worn to and from that afternoon's game were laid out. Lorena came bounding in to exclaim that her father had brought home her favourite apple pie.

Puzzled but not alarmed, María Neves considered the possibilities – perhaps he'd gone out for dinner with someone from the club or been called into a late-night radio interview. She followed the usual evening routine, settling the children for the night. But as the clock crept past 1am, unease gave way to anxiety. She picked up the phone and called Quini's closest team-mate, Alexanco, to explain the situation.

Alexanco had been out with colleagues that evening but hadn't seen Quini since saying goodbye to him at Camp Nou. Concerned, he and his wife, Margarita, headed to Quini's apartment, where more calls were made. Soon, the club's public relations officer, Óscar Segura, arrived. Together, he and Alexanco began scouring the city, starting with the airport, then the hospitals. They even checked the few bars still open to stragglers in the early hours of a Monday morning. Finding nothing, they returned to the apartment, where Barcelona vice president Joan Gaspart had joined the gathering. After further discussion and a series of fretful phone calls, it was agreed that Alexanco and Segura would go to Santa police station and formally report Quini as missing.

As kiosks rolled up their shutters that morning of 2 March, the freshly printed newspapers they laid out for sale were already old news. Within hours, a scrum of reporters and concerned fans gathered outside Quini's apartment building. The mid-morning discovery of his Ford Granada – parked near a local marketplace, unlocked, with the keys still inside – escalated matters to a distressing new level.

***

His captors could scarcely have chosen a more widely admired figure. Quini had broken into Sporting Gijón's first team as a teenager and spent the next decade scoring over 200 goals for the club, becoming a regular for the Spanish national team. Barcelona had courted him for years but only landed their man when he turned 30. Even then, he had begun life in Catalonia as prolific as ever.

Yet it was his off-field character that truly endeared him to fans – even those of rival clubs. Antonio Rubio, an investigative journalist who co-wrote a book with Quini and liaised adeptly with the police, the club, and the family during the ordeal, explains:

'Quini was as great a person as he was a player. He was a simple, down-to-earth guy. At no point did he let fame or the status of being a star player go to his head. That made him very relatable – very close to the people, and that's one of the reasons why the whole Quini episode was felt so deeply by Barcelona fans – maybe even more so than with other players.'

As the news spread, visitors began arriving at the apartment to show solidarity. The presidents of both Barcelona and Espanyol, Josep Lluís Núñez and Manuel Meler, were among the first, followed by a steady stream of players from both squads. Barcelona's club doctor, Carles Bestit, prescribed sedatives for María Neves to help her rest.

Newspapers and radio stations in the city received dozens of bogus calls, but on the Monday evening, the phone rang in the living room of Quini's flat. Gaspart answered. A voice on the other end of the line said there was a letter hidden in a hole in the ceiling of the bathroom of Bar Lidia on Carrer de la Riera Blanca, just 1km away.

Police were dispatched to retrieve the note, but the proprietor was unable to shed any light on who may have left it. Back at the apartment, María Neves instantly recognised her husband's handwriting, but the letter contained little helpful information. A further call came that evening to confirm the message had been retrieved and to arrange to speak directly with María Neves the following day.

As promised, the call came at exactly midday on Tuesday. Officers quickly set up a recording device before María Neves picked up the phone. The voice on the line assured her that Quini was alive and well and made one thing clear, that there was no political element, all they wanted was money – 100m pesetas, to be paid by the club, not the family.

The call was brief and mostly calm, aside from one chilling remark, 'Quini is fine, but if you want proof, we can send you a finger, an ear – or send him in *trocicos* (little pieces).'

Police played the call back, zeroing in on that moment of menace. The investigation was being led by an elite unit, says Rubio, 'The team handling the case specialised in bank robberies and similar crimes. The chief inspector was Francisco Álvarez – known as *El Técnico* (The Technician) – a meticulous and highly skilled officer. He was the one who first mapped out how the kidnapping might have unfolded, and he was lucky to have a streetwise, experienced team around him.'

One word in the call captured the officers' attention and that was *'trocicos'*. The diminutive *-ico* form was commonly used in the neighbouring region of Aragón – a small linguistic slip but the first real clue.

* * *

Around 250km away, in a makeshift hideout beneath a motorcycle repair shop on Calle Jerónimo Vicens, near Zaragoza's Old Town, Quini was being held. Two of the kidnappers – Fernando Martín Pellejero and José Eduardo Sandino Téjela – ran the garage and had devised the plan alongside Víctor Manuel Díaz Esteban, a spare parts dealer they knew from Barcelona.

They were far from slick, seasoned criminals. Often flustered when locals dropped by with bikes, they also seemed ill-prepared for the dietary needs of a professional athlete, at one point complaining about how much they were spending on sandwiches.

The instructions they gave to Quini's wife were often confused and erratic. They demanded 100m pesetas, five million of which was to be in used notes, but they procrastinated over the method of collection.

By the end of the first week of Quini's captivity, the focus had shifted to football. The president of the Spanish Football Federation, Pablo Porta, insisted the league go on as planned, with Barcelona travelling to Madrid for a pivotal fixture against Atlético. Initially, Bernd Schuster refused to play, but the midfielder had a late change of heart and travelled with the squad.

The team took to the field without anyone in the number nine shirt. Quini's replacement, Andrés Ramírez, instead wore 14, and Barça desperately missed Quini's cutting edge as they went behind after 20 minutes but failed to capitalise on the pressure they piled on their hosts.

Cruelly, Quini's captors told him the game had finished goalless, the next day justifying the lie so he got a good night's rest. The result was a shuddering blow for Barcelona's title hopes, now four points behind leaders Atlético, and with a gaggle of teams bunched behind them.

The days stretched on, and the atmosphere at Quini's apartment was one of fraught exhaustion. 'The issue was having to be on alert 24 hours a day for phone calls,' says Rubio. 'And making sure the calls weren't cut off and there weren't any technical problems. All of that, plus going to the places the kidnappers indicated to prove that Quini was still alive, because even though they weren't professionals, they weren't totally stupid – and they were calling the shots on how everything had to be done.'

There was an aborted handover at the Park Hotel next to the city's Parc de la Ciutadella, the kidnappers claiming Alexanco had arrived too late. There was an elaborate plan for the same player to deliver the money to a hotel in Perpignan over the French border, which was again abandoned.

Barça lost again, this time at Salamanca. Then, they dropped points at home the following week after failing to score against Zaragoza. By this time, Quini had been given a 19-inch television set and was following the highlights on a Sunday evening, able to see for himself how the team were struggling without him.

The impasse moved into its fourth week when the gang struck upon a new idea. On Monday, 23 March, they phoned Quini's apartment, and Alexanco took the call. He was given the details of a bank account in Geneva and instructed to make a transfer from Andorra.

Within hours, police capitalised on the mistake. 'The key error was that they opened a bank account in Switzerland under their real name,' Rubio explains. 'Legally, it was an international crime, so the Swiss authorities allowed the account holder's identity to be revealed.

'They had made a deposit into that account in order to allow a withdrawal, and with the matter in the hands of the Spanish justice system, the Swiss cooperated. Once they had the name of the person who had opened the Swiss account, they traced it directly to Zaragoza.'

On Wednesday afternoon, Pellejero entered a branch of Credit Suisse in Geneva, checked the balance of his account and withdrew a modest amount. He bought a ticket to Paris from a travel agent before flagging a cab to the airport. As the taxi pulled up, Spanish police officers swooped.

Pellejero immediately confessed his involvement and provided the address where Quini was held. Police from Barcelona raced to Zaragoza, where local and national police silently surrounded the garage. Inside, Quini was watching Spain take on England at Wembley. The second half had just begun, with Spain leading 2-1, when armed officers burst through the door. They encountered no resistance from Díaz, who was preparing Quini's evening meal.

On hearing the commotion, a petrified Quini hid in a corner behind his foam mattress. It took a few moments for a policeman to convince him he was safe, and it was real. He showed him his badge. 'I'm not trying to trick you,' he said. Quini burst into tears.

***

TV and radio broadcasts of Spain's Wembley win were interrupted to break the news that Quini was free, and it was news of the latter that dominated the following day's papers – the national team's historic first victory on English soil a footnote.

The player was taken to the central police station in Zaragoza, where he made a brief witness statement to police and gave a short press conference. He was then whisked along the motorway, with a cavalcade of police vehicles sounding their horns in celebration. The convoy arrived in Barcelona at 2am, where he was checked over by medics and finally reunited with María Neves.

In the Barcelona trophy room the following day, Quini gave a lengthy account of his ordeal to reporters, including his relationship with his abductors, 'They flattered me, saying I was a great athlete and that they respected me, that I shouldn't be afraid. They told me they had asked for 100m pesetas, which seemed ridiculous. I wrote letters and recorded some words because they asked me to, but I had no idea how things were going outside. I told them things only my family could know so they would realise I was alive.

'If I saw them right now, I wouldn't know what to say. They treated me well, and I don't blame them for anything in that regard. The only thing that hurt me was being in that "cave", without space and eating only sandwiches.'

Despite everything he'd been through, Quini declared himself ready to play in Barcelona's trip to Real Madrid just four days after his release, but manager Helenio Herrera petitioned that the best course of action was to recuperate physically and spend a quiet weekend with his family. Quini reluctantly agreed, thanked Real Madrid for inviting him and María Neves to watch the game as special guests, and disappeared to the countryside for a few days.

Before kick off in the Estadio Santiago Bernabéu, a statement was read out, 'Real Madrid delightedly celebrates the happy outcome of the kidnapping of the player Enrique Castro "Quini" and congratulates the state security forces for their brilliant intervention in the case.' The announcement was generously applauded by the entire stadium.

The camaraderie was short-lived, though, as Madrid raced into a 3-0 lead after just half an hour and saw the game out comfortably. Title contenders at the time of Quini's disappearance, Barça had slipped to fifth in his absence. In the four matches he'd missed, they'd picked up just one point and scored a solitary goal.

Quini scored and played for over an hour in a midweek friendly against third-tier side Vilafranca, then made his league return – still with a decisive lead in the goalscorer standings, despite a five-week absence – to a huge ovation at Camp Nou against Real Valladolid.

Barcelona salvaged their season with a 3-1 win in the final of the Copa del Rey. Quini scored twice against his beloved Sporting Gijón, the club he would return to after adding another Spanish Cup, a UEFA Cup Winners' Cup and another *Pichichi* during his four seasons at Camp Nou.

***

With the help of Antonio Rubio and another journalist, Enrique García Corredera, Quini quickly documented the episode in the book *Quini: Del secuestro a libertad (Quini: From kidnap to freedom)*.

'I don't remember exactly whose idea it was,' says Rubio. 'We spoke with Óscar Segura – who was the most involved and the person we were closest to – and we proposed the idea of the book to him. Once Quini was released and had had a few days to recover and rest, Óscar presented the proposal to him. We spoke with him and a publisher in Spain – the most important one at the time – Manuel Lara from Editorial Planeta.

'That allowed me to convince Quini to tell us how he had experienced it – because he was the only one who truly knew first-hand. We reached an agreement, and he came to my house two or three times. We had in depth conversations there.

'We did it in a week, but we already had the experience and background of everything we'd reported. We had an advantage in that my neighbour, Montserrat Roig, was an excellent writer, so we locked ourselves in and wrote all day long. Then Montserrat would go over the text in the evening and at night, editing it.

'Then we had the opportunity to get Manuel Vázquez Montalbán – who was a very well-known author and big Barcelona supporter – to write the foreword, so we managed, in a short period, to bring many people together to get the book published as quickly as possible.'

A theme emerged from those long chats with Quini – he felt no malice for what had happened to him. For him it was the desperate act of three men suffering from Spain's economic slump. When the case went to trial in January 1983, the three accused were each handed prison terms of ten years and a day. Quini was awarded 5m pesetas in damages – which he waived.

Quini's attitude throughout the trial was conciliatory. He took the wives of his captors for breakfast – one of them confessed she'd helped make the wooden box he'd been transported to Zaragoza in, thinking it was for a motorbike. His testimony enabled his kidnappers to spend their sentences in a lower category of prison and eventually to rebuild their lives. Quini once recalled a chance meeting with one of the men years later. They shook hands and the abductor gave Quini his phone number, should he ever need anything.

Quini himself had to overcome what life threw at him in later years. In 1993, he lost his brother, Jesús, who died after saving two children from drowning on the coast of Cantabria. He fought off cancer a decade and a half later. When he died in 2018, the public outpouring of emotion and the tributes centred not on the goals he'd scored and the medals he'd won but on the lives he had touched and the way he'd made people feel – even those who had wronged him.

'I like to remember him at his peak,' remembers Rubio, 'when he was scoring goals and was close to the people. He was especially good with kids. He had passion and never said no to an autograph, a photo, or anything like that. He was a footballer of the people, a man of the people.

'Not all footballers return to where they came from, but he returned to Gijón because he still felt he was from there. And despite having earned money and so on, his people, his home, and his family were there.'

9.

Once Upon a Time in the Desert

IN A saloon bar on the edge of the desert, a man strides in, tosses his dusty Stetson on the counter and orders a beer to slake his high noon thirst. As he lowers his formidable frame onto a bar stool, the usual thing is on his mind – Native Americans. It was his job to find them, but lately, they'd become particularly elusive.

Thirst quenched, he signals for a refill – one to sip rather than gulp. His brow cools, his body uncoils, and he begins to take in his surroundings, casting a glance around the scattering of fellow patrons. His gaze falls on an athletic figure on the far side of the room. As he drains his glass, he considers the man, his build and features, figuring that maybe he's just what they are looking for. In any case, there wasn't time to be picky. They needed someone, and he looked as close to it as he'd seen for a while.

Ordering two more beers, he draws himself off his stool and strides across the room. Placing one glass down in front of the man, he takes the seat opposite and comes straight out with it.

'Hey buddy, how would you like to be in a movie?'

Twenty-four hours later, the pair are at work in the Tabernas Desert. For Antonio Tarruella, a budding actor-come-director, it's just another daily grind in the sweltering heat. For his new recruit, Florencio Amarilla, it is a thrilling breath of fresh air. Yesterday, he was a retired footballer contemplating his future – today, he's an indigenous Yaqui, enlisted by Raquel Welch and Burt Reynolds to a militia hell-bent on settling an old vendetta.

The film's other megastar – the obligatory irascible sheriff – was also an elite sportsman. Jim Brown had carried a ball further than anyone in the history of the NFL; now, here he was in the south of Spain, reinventing himself as an actor.

Amarilla could see the parallels and could sense the opportunity. Almería had become the global headquarters of Western film-making, with film companies sweeping into the region to rattle through productions. This unlikely boom meant extras, stand-ins, and bit-part actors were in demand. Even more so if they had what, by the loose standards of the time, passed as a Native American appearance.

Of indigenous heritage and brawny build, Amarilla was a casting director's dream, and *100 Rifles* became the first of over 100 film credits. A winger who once fired his country to a World Cup finals was now on the way to becoming the first Paraguayan to win an Oscar.

***

With cactus-pocked deserts, canyons and ravines, Almería, tucked away in the south-east corner of Spain, offers a more than passable impression of an Arizona, a Texas or a Montana. Over 3,000 hours of annual sunshine and scarce rain provide stunning natural light and a reliable shooting schedule. Crucially, in the 1960s, it was a far cheaper place to make a film than the country it was imitating, which made it the ideal location for a growing sub-genre.

An enterprising group of Italian film directors had begun reimagining the classic American Western, a genre that had faded from its glorious past. Given a grittier spin with sparse dialogues and intense close-ups and driven by dramatic scores, the 'Spaghetti Western' exploded with the extraordinary success of Sergio Leone's *A Fistful of Dollars*.

Made on a miserly budget in the province of Almería in 1964, a copyright snag stalled its US release until three years after the final cut. Even then, the producers' wariness of the American public's reaction to this interpretation of the cherished Western meant that European names were substituted for American-sounding alternatives. Leone was credited as 'Bob Robertson' and the legendary composer Ennio Morricone was listed as 'Dan Savio'.

Those fears were misplaced as the film became a hit. The delay had the unintended benefit of allowing the sequels *For a Few Dollars More* and *The Good, the Bad and the Ugly* to be released in quick succession, capitalising on the success of the original and catapulting the film's main star, Clint Eastwood, to superstardom.

The triumph of the Dollars Trilogy saw the production of Spaghetti Westerns multiply rapidly, with an impoverished corner of a country emerging from international isolation at the forefront. Accustomed to seeing its sons and daughters departing in search of prosperity, Almería began welcoming international film crews and the world's biggest movie stars.

Franco's pervasive, ultra-conservative regime proved surprisingly amenable to the unexpected gold rush. Indeed, the expansion aligned with the dictatorship's latest objectives. Economically, it attracted much-needed foreign investment, while politically, it allowed the regime to present itself to America as a staunch anti-communist ally. The sighting of Hollywood's biggest stars on Spanish soil was also a boon to the country as it sought to boost its image internationally.

So obliging was Franco that he often made the military available to assist with production. The climactic three-way duel in *The Good, the Bad, and the Ugly* takes place in a vast cemetery made up of 5,000 graves just south of Burgos. To speed up construction, hundreds of soldiers from the nearby San Marcial barracks were enlisted to help. Some even supplemented their income as extras in battle scenes.

Down in Almería, tarmac was hurriedly laid down for trailers to roll and planes to land upon. Gran Hotel Almería sprang up on the city's seafront to provide luxury accommodation and poolside cocktails for the likes of Yul Brynner, Charles Bronson and Alain Delon.

Locals adapted quickly, with many picking up second jobs on location that paid in one day what they usually earned in a week. Farm hands with horse skills were prized, and carpenters could suddenly name their price. An entire generation of Andalusian 'cowboys' was born – skilled stunt actors able to be thrown into a bar fight or flung from a horse at a moment's notice.

Also in demand was anyone who could perform the role of a Native American. With production at full tilt and cultural sensitivities an afterthought, the bar for what qualified as an Indigenous American was set particularly low. A swarthy complexion was enough for a local to be dispatched to the costume trailer, emerging in an implausible confusion of Sioux and Apache dress.

A face that comprised native features could go a long way, and that was what caught the eye of Tarruella when he happened upon Amarilla in a bar in Almería. Like many Paraguayans, he was of Guaraní heritage and a Guaraní speaker. Though unrelated to any of the Native American languages, it was mysterious enough for directors to use for the few lines of dialogue the script demanded.

Amarilla's encounter with Tarruella came at a perfect time. At 32, his career was winding down a decade after his starring role at the 1958 World Cup. His performances in Sweden had earned him an opportunity for a new life in Europe, which he seized with both hands. Here was another life-changing moment. He would not let this one go, either.

**

Amarilla was born in 1935 in Coronel Bogado, a small town in southern Paraguay. Little is known about his childhood, but it is believed he never met his mother and spent much of his early life in Argentina before returning across the border as a gifted teenage footballer. His talent took him to the capital, where he signed for Club Nacional, and his explosive left foot and performances on the wing soon led to an international call-up.

Amarilla was given his opportunity as the Paraguayan team was rebuilt after failing to qualify for the 1954 World Cup. In the preliminaries for the following edition, Paraguay earned a hard-fought win over Colombia in Bogotá, which they followed up a fortnight later with a 3-0 win in the reverse fixture. Those victories set up a decisive clash with Uruguay, who were in their first-ever qualifying phase, having won the World Cup twice.

Uruguay were demolished. After just five minutes, Amarilla opened the scoring with a trademark long-range effort and completed his hat-trick on the hour mark. There was still time for two late goals to crown a 5-0 win. It was a victory celebrated in the streets throughout the country and still revered in Paraguayan football history.

At the finals in Sweden the following summer, Amarilla impressed again. In their opening game, Paraguay went toe-to-toe with a potent France side including Just Fontaine and Raymond Kopa. Amarilla thundered a free kick through the wall for the opener, then levelled the game from the spot at the end of a breathless first half. Paraguay had the temerity to take a 3-2 lead before a flurry of French goals saw the game end in a 7-3 scoreline, which didn't truly reflect Paraguay's efforts.

A victory over Scotland raised hopes of progress to the quarter-finals, but Paraguay ran out of time as they chased a win against Yugoslavia. The draw saw them eliminated, but their enterprising efforts, along with the entrepreneurial instincts of an Armenian agent, saw many of the squad earn moves to Spain.

Included in Arturo Bogosian's stable of young South Americans was Amarilla, who was signed by first division Real Oviedo along with compatriot Jorge Romero, who legend has it believed he was signing for Real Madrid. Oviedo provided Amarilla with an early test of his acting skills. With overseas squad places at a premium, their new winger was required to invent a Spanish mother to accommodate Oviedo's growing South American cohort.

After three respectable seasons on the north coast, an Achilles injury saw Amarilla end his contract and head east to Barcelona for treatment. After recovery, he won a contract with Elche, where fellow Paraguayans Juan Ángel Romero and Cayetano Ré had established themselves.

He found life on the Mediterranean to his liking, playing for several clubs along the coast as he descended the divisions. He finished his professional career with Club Deportivo Almería. The financially troubled club disappeared in 1968, but Amarilla stayed, making the city his home.

With film production ramping up rapidly in the region, the timing worked out perfectly. The same year his club went bust, Amarilla had his chance encounter with Tarruella and instantly transitioned to his unlikely new career. His physical gifts, charisma and some equestrian skills picked up in his youth meant he was rarely out of work and soon racking up credits on increasingly high-profile projects.

A diversion from the constant stream of Westerns came with the 1970 war drama *Patton*, a three-hour-long biopic of the American Second World War General George S. Patton. The film swept the following year's Academy Awards, taking seven prizes, including Best Picture, and gave Amarilla the claim to be the first Paraguayan Oscar winner.

The same year, Amarilla reunited with Jim Brown and was joined on the main cast by Lee Van Cleef in *El Condor*. Supporting roles alongside Brynner, Bronson and Leonard Nimoy followed. Eventually, Amarilla worked under Leone when the director returned to the region in 1971 to film *A Fistful of Dynamite*.

Amarilla was well-liked, striking up lasting friendships with an array of household names who found his backstory intriguing. In down times on set, it was not unusual to see Amarilla juggling a football in full war dress or explaining the finer details of the game to curious transatlantic colleagues. The midweek schedule also allowed him to keep playing, turning out for several regional league sides in the latter years of his thirties and then moving into coaching.

***

Inevitably, the dilution of quality and a change in cinemagoers' tastes saw the revival of the Western ebb away. Though Amarilla remained adaptable to a new generation of film-making, featuring in Arnold Schwarzenegger's breakthrough *Conan the Barbarian* in 1982.

While Almería remained a viable location, the stampede had well and truly subsided by the 1980s, leaving the province and Amarilla to reinvent themselves once more. In the city, photos of Leone, Bronson, Eastwood and Brynner still hang on the walls of the Gran Hotel Almería. The hotel exudes a faded grandeur, the rooms more functional than fabulous these days.

Out in the desert, some of the abandoned cowboy towns have been converted into tourist attractions by shrewd locals who snapped up the disused sets before eventually selling them on to hotel groups. For a fistful of euros, film buffs can watch pistols being drawn at noon at *Oasys MiniHollywood*. For a few euros more, they can head further up the road and explore Fort Bravo on horseback.

The Almería Western Film Festival held each October draws thousands of visitors, packing out the city and both resorts and proving this corner of Andalusia is still a draw for A-listers. At the 2024 edition, Viggo Mortensen picked up the Best Feature Award for *The Dead Don't Hurt*. 'The Western genre isn't dead. It's got endless stories waiting to be told,' he declared in his acceptance speech.

Amarilla was not among the lucky few who capitalised on the legacy of the Spaghetti Western; instead, as his acting career faded, he returned to football coaching at amateur level while selling shoes and books to make ends meet. Into his 70s, he worked as a kitman for *Tercera* side CD Comarca de Níjar. Unusually, he had made the stadium, nestled at the foot of the Sierra Alhamilla, his home, despite offers of alternative accommodation by the club.

'I like to live free. I get up early, walk, run, drink a *mate*. I'm happy like that. Then, for the rest of the day, I'm sorting out the equipment, completely at the team's disposal.' Amarilla was a popular figure, the club president remarking that he'd never seen anyone receive so many Christmas gifts. There were regular trips to Oviedo, where directors still invited Amarilla to matches.

In August 2012, some 44 years after that meeting in a bar, Amarilla died in the village of Vélez Rubio at the age of 77. His final scenes played out in the province he'd made his home, from its football fields to its deserts and canyons.

La Sala de Prensa

The Media

10.

The Prince of the Night

tiki-taka, *n.*

Etymology: < Spanish *tiki-taka* (2006 or earlier).

Association Football.

A style of play characterised by highly accurate short passing and an emphasis on retaining possession of the ball.

***

IT STARTED as a bit of fun. A light-hearted way of capturing the mesmeric, all-conquering style of FC Barcelona and the Spanish national team that set the world abuzz towards the end of the 2000s. Almost inevitably, the phrase came to be disliked, derided even – a byword for possession for possession's sake.

Loved or loathed, the term would become etched into the football lexicon. It even made the unlikely leap from the cacophonous commentary booths of Spain to the cloistered calm of Oxford University when the word was codified into the English language in 2022 by the *Oxford English Dictionary*. Which perhaps made for a fitting posthumous tribute to the man who bounded onto Spanish television screens 'dressed like an English lord', blazing the phrase into public consciousness.

Andrés Montes's commentary style was as distinctive and idiosyncratic as the man himself. Rhythmically delivered in his trademark attire – complete with Windsor glasses and bow tie – and peppered with nicknames, catchphrases and wordplay.

Montes's unique talent saw him rise from local radio to the witching hours of NBA coverage before fronting Spain's free-to-air football as both Barcelona and Spain emerged from the doldrum years with a new, distinctive brand of football that he managed to encapsulate in just one word.

For all the on-screen exuberance, Montes cut a much more circumspect character away from the microphone. An introverted extrovert, marked by an extraordinary childhood – a black kid raised in 1950s Madrid by a woman who answered a newspaper advert – and plagued by insecurity and a permanent preoccupation with his own health.

***

'His life was like a movie; from the day he was born. His success was like a movie too,' smiles Antoni Daimiel, and no one would be better placed to write the script.

Paired on commentary together in 1995 when *Canal+* bought the rights to show live NBA in Spain for the first time, Daimiel and Montes immediately struck up an enduring friendship. 'It was interesting because there was an age gap between us, but we got along really well. There was great chemistry, a strong connection – not just professionally, but personally as well. For different reasons, he saw in me something that he valued. He used to tell me that he was surprised that at 25 or 26 years old, how composed and thoughtful I was. So, he would consult me about many aspects of his life and career, and he liked to hear my opinion.

'For me, I appreciated his friendship because he was unpredictable. He was someone you could never quite anticipate – what he would think, what his take would be on any given topic. He always had a unique perspective on everything. And I like people like that – people who challenge my thinking, who make me reflect on things from a different angle.'

Another cool head brought in to soften Montes's ebullience was the journalist Santi Segurola, who had long suggested bringing the NBA to the channel. When that day finally arrived, it came with a special assignment. The station's director, Alfredo Relaño, proudly announced to Segurola that he had secured the rights and already knew who the lead commentator would be – Andrés Montes. 'I think he'll be perfect for the time and the type of programme, but I think I need someone to calm him to control him a bit, and I'd like that person to be you.'

Segurola was initially reluctant. 'I don't like doing television – not at all. I'm not good on it, I don't feel comfortable on it, but somehow, I saw it as a mission, almost like a duty. *Canal+* was part of the media group I worked for, and I had been following the NBA for many years, so I agreed. That's how my partnership with Andrés started.'

Montes had caught Relaño's eye from a segment on the station's cult show *El Dia Después*. The programme, hosted by Michael Robinson, sought out the lighter side of a weekend's football matches. In one game at a resurgent Atlético Madrid's Estadio Vicente Calderón, the cameras were drawn to a local radio commentator whose quirky appearance, frenetic energy and thundered mantras such as 'Something is happening in the south of the city!' made for a wildly entertaining montage.

Thrust together in a stuffy office in the Madrid night, the trio set about making a product of the pictures beamed to them from across the Atlantic. Daimiel and Segurola alternated playing the foil to Montes, who, as Segurola recalls, was determined to make the most of his break. 'The truth is, he knew that this was a huge opportunity for him – that the NBA represented his dream chance to make a leap, as long as he could achieve two or three things.

'The first was captivating an audience, which at the time was uncertain. At first, it was very small. Even though there was excitement, no one really knew how viewers would respond, especially considering the games aired between 2am and 4.30am.

'The second was figuring out what kind of commentary could be done. This was an era without the internet – statistics weren't instantly available. You had to read them in *USA Today* from the previous day by actually buying the newspaper. Now, broadcasts have access to all kinds of data, but back then, it was a primitive world.

'I think he quickly understood that at those late-night hours, the best approach was to be dynamic and entertaining – to make the broadcast feel spectacular and fun while, of course, not losing sight of the game itself.

'He also realised early on that he had the chance to become a recognisable character. Until then, people had only heard him on the radio, but on TV, he was even better – his image was striking, and his style fitted perfectly. He knew that the way he appeared on-screen would play a major role in the success of the show. And the truth is, he became an almost instant success.

'He was expansive, entertaining, and had a blistering ability to come up with nicknames. More than anything, he had a talent for making sure that a two-and-a-half-hour game didn't feel tedious. Instead of just focusing on UCLA cuts or pick-and-rolls, the key was making sure people didn't fall asleep, that they stayed engaged with the game – and he achieved that from day one.'

Daimiel similarly describes Montes's style, 'It very bold, very different, very imaginative. There's a tradition, especially in Latin America, of giving players nicknames, calling them something specific based on their characteristics. He had that instinct, I think it was in his DNA – he enjoyed it and had a natural talent for it, an incredible imagination – and it served him well as a commentator.'

Montes opened each night's broadcast with a chirpy, 'How's it going? Welcome to the club,' and he treated his growing membership to a rechristening of the era's biggest stars. Michael Jordan became the wordy but self-explanatory '*Bienvenidos al Vuelo numero 23: Aerolineas Jordan*,' Shaquille O'Neal was tagged '*Articulo 34*' - an imagined part of the

US constitution that entitled Shaq to do whatever he liked, whenever he liked to opponents, while Dennis Rodman's fashions and ever-changing hairstyle earned him the moniker '*Cruella de Vil.*'

Three-pointers were greeted with cries of '*Ra-ta-ta-ta-ta!*' or '*Triiiiiiiple!*', big plays with '*Jugón! Jugón!*' a clever assist '*una declaración de amor*' (a declaration of love). While a clumsy pass invited a whimsical reference to *The Flintstones* with a '*Wilmaaaaa!*'

As counterweights, Segurola and Daimiel worked perfectly. Daimiel, young, considered and knowledgeable, became the long-term sidekick to Montes. To this day, the two are almost always mentioned in tandem.

Segurola, for his part, feels he delivered on his two-year mission. 'I was the counterbalance. I tried, in some way, to keep Montes's expansiveness under control, to make sure it didn't go too far, but honestly, I think he controlled *me* more than I controlled *him*. I was the serious one, the boring one, the one who told NBA stories, but he was 80 per cent of the broadcast. He was an animal of communication. I wasn't that, but I was good at having a solid dialogue with him.

'Half the time, we'd end up talking about anything. We talked about jazz – he loved music and since I also love music, our conversations often drifted into musical discussions that I imagine hardcore basketball fans must have found frustrating. But I think he and I understood that part of the job was to create a viewing experience around the NBA that made the audience feel comfortable – and in Andrés Montes they found a personality that truly fascinated them.'

Montes had essentially gone viral in a pre-social media age, and it wasn't just his voice he used to garner an audience.

Segurola often refers to Montes as 'The Prince of the Night'. 'At midnight, he would arrive dressed like a dandy, always.'

The famous look comprised an immaculately shaved head, round Windsor glasses, a high-quality blazer over a colourful shirt, topped off with a bow tie. Below the waist were tailored trousers and the finest English leather shoes.

It wasn't an ensemble that was particularly practical in the sweltering *Canal+* offices, as Segurola remembers, 'We worked in a tiny, sweltering studio where our makeup would literally melt. It was overwhelming. At times, I think we were on the verge of passing out from the heat. The lights were blazing right in front of us, we were working under really precarious conditions, but we managed to pull it off however we could.'

Somehow, after hours of full-throttle commentary, Montes would emerge blinking into Madrid's morning light as immaculate as he had arrived.

Though Montes was naturally inclined to dress well, Daimiel points out there was an element of foresight behind the finery. 'Before he started at *Canal+* on the NBA, he had gone through a tough time professionally. He had been out of work for a while and had started working at a radio station, covering football and other sports, but for very little money.

'So, when the opportunity in television arrived, he thought that his style of dress was something that could also draw attention and promote him as a personality in the media world. That's why he always wore the bow tie.

'He liked luxury. He had grown up in a difficult, impoverished environment in Madrid, so when he finally started making money, he wasn't the type to save or put it aside – he spent it as soon as he earned it.'

Daimiel chuckles about one trip they took to the United States, 'I remember one time in New York; someone had told him about a shop in Manhattan that only sold bow ties, so he bought something like 35 or 40.'

Sometimes, the image came at a physical, rather than financial cost. 'He used to shave his head every morning. One morning we were in a hotel in Chicago, and he must have done it in a rush or something, but he cut quite a chunk on his head: not just a bit of skin but flesh too. So he knocks on the door of my room bleeding, having used up all the toilet paper in his room.' Daimiel duly handed over his supply.

When the two met later in the lobby, Montes arrived clutching two carrier bags full of bloodied loo roll. When Daimiel enquired why he hadn't just left them in his room for the cleaners, Montes shot back, 'This is Chicago. They'll think we've killed someone,' before finding a side street to surreptitiously dump them.

It was on the very first of their many trips to America that Montes revealed a more anxious side of his personality to Daimiel. 'It was two or three months after we'd started working together. I remember we were sitting together on the plane. I think we were flying from Madrid to Atlanta. As soon as we sat down before take-off, he took out this case to prick his finger to check his blood sugar levels. I asked him what it was because I'd never seen it before, and he promptly told me that of the three illnesses that cause the most deaths in Spain, he had all three.'

Montes obsessed about his health. Though, as a diabetic with underlying heart issues who'd lost a kidney to cancer treatment, he was fully justified in doing so. 'He had a fear of illness,' says Daimiel, 'so he was always on alert to whatever illness, he'd always be going to the doctor, and I always knew him like that, from the day I met him until the day he died.'

Spain's crumbling football stadiums, Daimiel notes, did Montes few favours. 'He always complained because there were stadiums like the old Atlético stadium, the Vicente Calderón, where the commentary booths were all the way at the top, and there were no lifts, no assistance. He had to walk all the way up, and his health wasn't great for that.'

Those health concerns formed part of a multifaceted character. For all the on-screen geniality, it could often be a different story away from the studio lights, as Segurola explains, 'He was an extrovert in front of the camera, but away from the camera, he was a man that, at times, conveyed a certain angst.' Segurola also detected a melancholy, 'There was something of a certain sadness about him.'

Daimiel adds another layer, 'He was strange. He was a unique person. In personal interactions, you couldn't always predict how he'd respond. If someone was introduced to him, he'd greet them, but from that moment he'd either like you or dislike you.

'If he didn't like you, he could be a bit hostile, quite blunt. Not particularly friendly. Though if he *did* like you, even if he knew nothing about you, he would immediately establish a deep level of trust. Right away, he'd ask about your family, "How much do you make at your job?" or "Are you having any problems?" These kinds of questions in your very first conversation.'

It's perhaps unsurprising that such a composite personality had emerged from what was a remarkable upbringing.

Montes was born in Madrid in 1955 to Antonio Montes and Zenaida Manfugás, a Galician merchant and a Cuban pianist who had met on a train journey in Venezuela. The couple had moved to the Spanish capital when Manfugás was accepted into the Madrid Royal Conservatory to continue her classical training, but the success of Fidel Castro's revolution drew her back to her home country.

Daimiel takes up the story, 'When the revolution triumphed, his mother felt she had to return to Cuba. She put an advert in a newspaper, *ABC*, to find a woman who could care for her son for a while. They found a single woman to look after him, and she left. Then time passed, years passed, and she never came back. So, he, from the age of four, grew up thinking that his mother was the lady looking after him.

'He told me once that his mother had written him some letters, but the lady who looked after him hid them. It's like a story from a film.'

When his father died, Montes was left alone at the age of 11 with the woman he considered his 'true mother', Lorenza, and no connection to any extended family. Occasionally, his birth mother returned to Madrid, usually as part of a concert tour. There were meetings but little connection. 'She expected Frederic Chopin but met an outcast,' Montes once told friends of one unfeeling reunion.

Montes also had to navigate the experience of growing up as a black child in Madrid. 'He was a black kid in Madrid at a time when there weren't any black people in Madrid,' says Daimiel. 'There wasn't really immigration back then. There was nothing. So I imagine he suffered some marginalisation. At school, kids shouting, "You're black", the usual stuff. He told me once that on the bus, some people would actually get up and move to another seat so they wouldn't have to sit next to him. He went through all of that.'

He may not have grown up to be the next Chopin, but by the turn of the millennium, there was a generation of Spaniards for whom Montes's melodic refrains were more evocative of the night than any nocturne. In 2001, Pau Gasol – dubbed 'E.T.' by Montes for his 'extraterrestrial' level of play – became the first of a talented generation of Spanish players to be drafted by the NBA, driving interest in the sport and the league's popularity even further, with Montes at the forefront.

Rival channels began wondering if Montes could boost their ratings. When the nascent *La Sexta* audaciously acquired the rights to the 2006 football and basketball World Cups, they poached Montes to lead the channel's coverage. The move ended their decade-long alliance, but Daimiel could understand why they'd chosen his partner, 'They signed him because they considered him a media personality. He went beyond being a pure, play-by-play football or basketball commentator. They believed he was someone who could attract viewers, build an audience – not just because of his commentary, but because he was a unique figure.'

Montes faced a whirlwind start. 'He left *Canal+* on 1 May 2006, and the first thing he had to do at *La Sexta* was the World Cup, and then the basketball World Cup in Japan.' Despite the challenge, Montes acquitted himself well.

'It's true that I was his friend, but I tend to be quite objective in my professional judgments. I've been a journalist for over 30 years, and I don't base my opinions on what is supposedly considered successful. There are commentators I personally like who might not be widely popular, and vice versa.

'Setting aside my friendship with him and looking at it from a purely analytical perspective, I believe that during the 2006 World Cup in Germany, he was spectacular. For me, he was a 10 out of 10. He was fantastic throughout the tournament; his work was outstanding.

'Then he also covered the Basketball World Cup, and he did well there too. He felt very comfortable, and of course, Spain ended up winning the title, which made everything even more special. His arrival at *La Sexta* was a huge success – very positive.'

It was in Germany that Montes employed the term '*tiki-taka*' for the first time as Spain came from behind to overcome Tunisia in Stuttgart, and it was rolled out with increasing frequency, often rattled out three or four times in a row as Montes spearheaded the channel's domestic football coverage. *La Sexta* won the right to broadcast the one weekly free-to-air La Liga fixture, generally the highest-profile game of the week. Montes gelled immediately with co-commentators Julio Salinas and Kiko Narvaez and transferred his style from the early hours of the morning to the peak hours of Spanish television while losing none of his rambunctiousness.

As ever, the nicknames flowed. A Spain attack could begin with '*El Tiburón*' (Carles Puyol 'The Shark'), move through midfield with 'Humphrey Bogart' (Xavi, who played it again and again...) and 'Sweet' Iniesta before being finished off by 'MaraVilla' (David Villa 'The Marvel').

Alongside *tiki-taka*, countless new catchphrases were reeled off. From the catchy but nonsensical '*Fútbol con fatatas*' to the bellowed '*¿Dónde están las llaves, Salinas?*' ('Where are the keys, Salinas?') directed at his co-commentator when neither side were able to string two passes together.

Montes was in full, irrepressible flow, but there were some early signs that his offbeat approach may not have been to everyone's liking. Cesc Fabregas's half-time introduction against Tunisia sparked Spain's fightback and the inaugural use of Montes's most famous phrase, but *Mundo Deportivo* lamented that the commentary had 'called Cesc everything other than his name.'

It seemed that those who'd signed Montes based on his ability to draw an audience were beginning to fear that the opposite could be possible, as Daimiel explains, 'His style in football, let's say that it drew attention. It clashed with the people that were more orthodox, more conservative, that didn't like that someone came from doing NBA to doing football. Clearly, his style was very invasive. He pulled you out of the routine experience that most football fans were used to.'

Daimiel believes that input from above was not something that Montes welcomed, 'What happened with his *La Sexta* broadcasts, where he covered one La Liga match per week, was that he wanted to keep his style, but he was very dependent on his mood, you know? On feeling comfortable.

'With me, covering the NBA, he was at ease. The bosses didn't even watch us. We were working at 5am or 6am with just a small crew, and he felt free, comfortable.

'*La Sexta* was a big television network, an open, mainstream channel with a big structure – lots of executives, advertisers, people telling him, "Hey, maybe don't say this," or "It would be better if you did that."

'That made him uncomfortable and when he wasn't comfortable, his talent didn't flow as naturally.'

By Montes's third season at the station, a muting of tone was clearly detectable. In October 2008, he was on duty for the breakout performance of Pep Guardiola's early tenure at Barcelona, a 6-1 demolition of Atlético Madrid at Camp Nou, which saw Barça 3-0 ahead after just eight minutes. The hallmarks were still there – the nicknames, the taglines – but used much more sparingly. Despite the chaotic nature of the opening half an hour, Montes's usual intense cadence had noticeably slowed.

Towards the end of that season, Montes was informed that his contract at *La Sexta* would not be renewed. 'He took that badly,' remembers Daimiel. 'Not so much because he was losing a well-paid job – of course, that mattered – but more because he felt it wasn't fair. He believed he had done a good job and that his departure wasn't about performance or the audience getting tired of him.

'He thought other factors were at play. He felt he had enemies in television, people who didn't want him there, and he believed that was the real reason why they didn't keep him on.'

Montes's last contractual obligation was an enjoyable one at least. He travelled to Poland to front the channel's 2009 EuroBasket coverage. After a stuttering start, Spain found their feet during the knockout phase, crushing Serbia in a one-sided final to add a European crown to their World Championship win. As the arena emptied and the confetti was swept up, Montes thanked colleagues and crew in the gantry and said goodbye with his signature bittersweet sign-off – '*la vida puede ser maravillosa*'.

'I say farewell to all of you in my last broadcast with *La Sexta*, and I'm going to say the same thing I've said in the three-and-a-bit years since I arrived here at *La Sexta*: Life can be wonderful. Goodbye friends.'

Tragically, those would be the final words ever spoken on air by Andrés Montes.

* * *

Less than four weeks later, on a Friday evening, Daimiel received a phone call.

'That Tuesday, Andrés and I had dinner together with another friend, and that Wednesday, I remember perfectly, I was driving home from work, and he called me. We talked like always, just a normal conversation, like any other day. The Thursday, he didn't call me, which was rare but not that strange. I wasn't worried or anything like that. Then Friday evening around 6pm, I was having a shower at home when a friend called me.'

The friend explained that someone at the *EFE* news agency, whose head office was directly opposite Montes's apartment building, had seen an ambulance and paramedics outside. Rumours that something had happened to Montes or his wife were circulating, and calls to his phone were going unanswered. Worried, Daimiel asked to be kept informed.

Five minutes later, the friend rang again with terrible news, 'They've told me Andrés has died.'

Daimiel dressed quickly and raced to Montes's building. 'When I arrived, the police were already there, along with an ambulance. They weren't letting anyone in. After about half an hour of waiting there, I saw the stretcher come out, with his body already covered by a sheet, being loaded into the ambulance.'

Montes was just 53 years old. The cause of death was given as a cardiac arrest.

The public reaction to his death was huge. As Segurola – who penned a tribute for *Marca* entitled, 'The Prince of the Night' – recalls, 'The impact of Andrés Montes's death – among all the sports journalists I've ever known – was the most profound, the most incredible. The feedback I noticed, especially from young people, was overwhelming. He had an extraordinary connection with the youth, those who grew up in the 1990s and the 2000s.

'It was a huge shock, and honestly, as I think back, I can't recall the death of any sports journalist, maybe even any journalist in general, that generated so much sadness, so much grief, and had such a massive impact on people.'

Daimiel can see why, 'First of all, he'd been on television almost every day for 13 years, so he felt like someone close to the people. Also, his way of communicating brought him even closer. People would meet him on the street and speak to him like he was a friend or family, but he didn't know them at all.

It was his style that provoked that familiarity and trust, and then, well, he was a young person, so there was a tremendous impact.'

One of the most heartfelt tributes came from Gasol, part of that generation that stayed up all night hanging on Montes's every word, by then en route to becoming a first-ballot NBA Hall of Famer. On the way, Gasol and Montes had formed a close friendship.

'The news of the death of Andrés Montes has left me frozen. A person who contributed to making basketball in Spain more followed and loved. A media reference of our generation and a basketball lover. We are going to miss him a lot. Our thoughts are with him and his family. Farewell Andrés, E.T. will miss you.'

Montes's colleague Salinas led the respects from the football world. 'Andrés will go down in history for bringing a different approach to football commentary. His career was long, but he became super famous in recent years. He has given us many lessons with his phrases, and we must remember one that he repeated many times – life can be wonderful.'

In 2021, Montes was inducted into the Spanish Basketball Hall of Fame. The honour was accepted by his sons Orson and Nelson, who took to the stage in their father's signature jacket and bow tie. Nelson delivered a poignant speech, 'My father used to say that fame is fleeting and that when you die people won't remember you. This is quite the opposite. Twelve years have passed and here we are. If he were alive today, he wouldn't understand it.'

Nor you suspect, would he fathom having one of his most famous utterances eternally preserved by lexicographers of a foreign language.

11.

They All Have Their Idols

ANDRÉS PALOP'S giddy explanation wasn't necessary. Michel Platini had recognised it straight away. Twenty-four years had passed, but he recognised the shirt. He hadn't forgotten its former wearer either – the man that Palop was paying tribute to. 'He's here somewhere, I invited him,' Platini beamed as he draped a winners' medal on the goalkeeper's shoulders.

Seated a few blocks away and talking emotionally on the phone, Luis Arconada looked up at the giant screen in Vienna's Ernst Happel Stadium and saw it. It was unmistakable with its navy blue shoulders and cuffs, dark green body and bright red Spanish federation badge. It was the very jersey he'd worn on the most excruciating night of his otherwise brilliant career.

Now that famous number 1 shirt was being worn by Spain's number 13 as Spain concluded Euro 2008 with a narrow yet irrefutable victory over Germany. It was a win that ended years of frustration to herald an era of ascendancy. Palop had chosen the occasion to remember the goalkeeper he and a whole generation had idolised and make a gesture that he hoped would help turn a page in history.

As an homage, it couldn't have been more perfect; it was a beautiful culmination of planning, coincidence, and sheer luck. One only made possible by the man on the other end of the line with Arconada.

Aitor Aguirre and Sergio Manzanera, (bottom row, armbands attached) line up with team-mates before Racing Santander's fixture with Elche, 28 September 1975. Fundación Real Racing Club

Aitor Aguirre (armband visible) heads Racing ahead in the 29th minute from a cross from Sergio Manzanera. The two were met by armed police at half-time. Fundación Real Racing Club

Aitor Aguirre
Fundación Real Racing Club

Sergio Manzanera
Fundación Real Racing Club

Fire crews attempt to rescue guests trapped on balconies during a fire at the Hotel Corona de Aragón on the morning of 12 July 1979

Many guests including Real Zaragoza's new signing José Ramón Badiola attempted to jump to safety as the blaze engulfed the hotel

José Cano López — better known as 'Canito'
Fundación Del RCD Espanyol

Johan Cruyff's registration card from his spell with Levante
Levante UD SAD

Cruyff (bottom row, second from right) lines up for Levante ahead of his debut against Palencia on 1 March 1981
Levante UD SAD

Juan Gómez de Lecube, arrested by British forces in Trinidad in June 1942 and held until the end of WWII. National Archives Files KV2/1456 & KV2/1457.

Real Madrid's Míchel pays controversially close attention to Carlos Valderrama of Real Valladolid during a match at the Estadio Santiago Bernabéu, 8 September 1991

Andrés Montes (left) and Antoni Daimiel on NBA commentary duty in Chicago, June 1996.
Antoni Daimiel

Luis Arconada is unable to stop Michel Platini's weakly struck free kick in the Euro 1984 Final between Spain and France in Paris, 27 June 1984.

Andrés Palop (first from left) celebrates Spain's Euro 2008 win by paying homage to Luis Arconada wearing his shirt from the Euro 1984 Final

Michael Robinson shares a joke with long-term commentary partner Carlos Martínez, January 1993

Carmen Avendaño, the founder of Érguete, the organisation born out of the struggle against drugs in Vigo in 1984

Raimundo Saporta, president of the 1982 World Cup Organising Committee received by King Juan Carlos I in December 1979

Ronaldinho drifts past opponents during Barcelona's 1-1 draw with Sevilla in September 2003. A game that kicked off at 12.05am after a dispute between the two boards.

Real Sociedad captain Inaxio Kortabarria and his Athletic Club counterpart José Ángel Iribar carry the banned Ikurriña on to the field before the Basque derby at Atotxa on 5 December 1976. The flag was legalised the following month.
Argia eus licensed under CC BY-SA 4.0

Carnival icon Manolo Santander as 'capo' of La Familia Pepperoni, the act behind Me han dicho que el amarillo, *now Cádiz CF's matchday anthem.*
Kiki Fotógrafo

Legendary Cádiz fan 'Macarty' embraces club president Manuel Irigoyen after the team secured Primera survival in the 1987 relegation play-offs.
Kiki Fotógrafo

Two of of the La Viña barrio's most beloved characters, 'Macarty' and 'La Uchi', share a moment during the city's carnival
Kiki Fotógrafo

THEY ALL HAVE THEIR IDOLS

* * *

'I believe that Andrés Palop and the Spanish national team gave Luis Arconada back the recognition he deserved for the trophy he should have lifted at the Parc des Princes.' Journalist José Miguel Muñoz was the architect of the tribute and the man sharing that celebratory phone call as Arconada watched on in delight as Spain celebrated their first trophy in over four decades.

Spain had become wearily accustomed to disappointment. Sharp Italian elbows, implausible Egyptian officiating and a blur of penalty shoot-outs littered pre-tournament montages, but one moment stood out for its cruelty. The Parisian heartbeat in which a tame free kick squirmed under the body of Spain's captain and agonisingly over the goal line, gifting away the one final they had made in all those years.

It was a mistake that broke a million teenage Spanish hearts. One more than most. 'We're talking about 1984. I was born in 1969. I was 15 years old; I watched it at my parents' house and I cried. I don't think I've ever cried more while watching a football match,' remembers Muñoz.

Muñoz grew up in Jerez but had long since sworn an allegiance that set him apart from his peers.

'I was the black sheep. Everyone, if they weren't supporting Sevilla or Betis, then it was Barcelona or Madrid. All the kids supported one of those teams. But me? I was a fan of Real Sociedad. I would walk down the street wearing a Real Sociedad or Arconada jersey.

'People would say to me, "You're weird, aren't you? How can you support Real Sociedad?" And I'd always reply – "Because of Arconada." Always, it was because of Arconada. I've been a Real Sociedad fan because of him. My love for the club has always been tied to Arconada.

'Since I was a kid, I've always been clear in my ideas. I used to play as a goalkeeper, and the first time I saw Luis play, it was love at first sight. He had qualities as a goalkeeper that captivated me. I wasn't tall, and he wasn't particularly big either, but he had such powerful legs that he could fly in an incredible way. That's where my admiration for him began. I started following him, however I could in those days, mainly through the radio and the occasional match on television. Back then, they only aired one match, and you had to be lucky for it to be the game of the week. It wasn't like today, where we have on-demand TV.'

Living as far away from San Sebastián as it was possible to be in mainland Spain meant Muñoz had to be intrepid if he was to meet his hero.

'Every time he played in Andalusia, I would sneak out of school. I'd grab my bag, but inside, I had photos, flags, pennants – 70,000 things of Arconada. I'd head straight to the hotel and find out where they were staying. When I think about it now, it's crazy. I mean, my son is 16 years old now, and I think, if my son at eight years old had done something like that, I'd say, "This kid is nuts."

'Back then, you had to call a hotel, and this was a child calling, not an adult. If Real Sociedad were staying at that hotel, I'd go there, ask around, and wait. If they didn't let me in, I'd pretend I was going to have something at the bar or that I was looking for my dad. Then I'd search for Luis around the hotel.'

'That's how it started. In Cádiz, Málaga, Seville – when they played Betis and Sevilla – in Córdoba, Almería, Huelva, all over Andalusia. I'd take a bus or a train, just with my milk and eggs, and go. Looking back on it now, I realise how crazy it was, but I'd wait for Luis to appear, and when he did, I'd go up to him to get him to sign the photos I had of him.

'He'd sign four photos, leave, and then I'd come back to find him again. He'd say, "But I've already signed for you." And I'd reply, "Yes, but I have six more photos." He'd sign those six as well, and so it went, year after year, and kept building from there.'

Muñoz was on to something. By the early 1980s, Arconada's popularity was such that the best-selling Christmas gift for several years was a replica of his goalkeeping jersey. 'In sky blue (the best seller), orange or green but always with the famous navy shoulders,' wrote Alfredo Relaño in *El Pais*. 'In those years, every boy in Spain wanted to be Luis Arconada.'

Arconada had led Real Sociedad to the pinnacle of the Spanish game, captaining them to their first-ever league titles. He was the undisputed number one for Spain, for whom he also led the side on the field. Known for his agility and reflexes, Arconada often made important saves with his feet – a trait that has passed down Spanish goalkeeping lineage.

Not by coincidence. Similar in style, Iker Casillas often tells the story of when his mother encouraged him to eat sardines by pretending to have a phone conversation with Arconada about the importance of fish in a young goalkeeper's diet: 'At seven years old, I looked at her and thought, "If she's spoken to Luis Arconada and he told her that I need to eat fish, I'm going to start eating fish,"' Casillas recounted when the pair got together to officially open Gipuzkoa's cider season.

It was perhaps a blessing for Casillas that he was a little too young to remember when Arconada led the Spanish team on the short journey to France for the 1984 European Championship.

* * *

Expectations were low after a disappointing performance as hosts of the 1982 World Cup. Indeed, it had taken the most bizarre result in Spanish football history to scrape through qualification.

A loss in the penultimate game in Rotterdam left Spain with the improbable task of needing to beat Malta by 11 clear goals to qualify. The improbable looked impossible after 24 minutes when a Maltese goal drew the teams level, but 60 barmy minutes later, Spain had a 12-1 lead. There was even time for a 13th to be disallowed before the final whistle blew and fans poured onto the pitch at the Estadio Benito Villamarín.

At the finals, Spain were drawn with Romania, West Germany and Portugal – thus avoiding the hosts and favourites, France. They were pooled with Yugoslavia and the talented Belgium and Denmark sides.

After two draws, Spain's final group game became decisive.

Their opponents, West Germany, knew a point would qualify them for the semi-finals. Spain depended on the result in the other match. Topping the group carried the additional incentive of avoiding France, who had powered to the last four with three wins and nine goals – including seven from Platini.

Arconada was unusually hesitant in a first half where Spain had to contend with an injury in defence and some pinpoint German set pieces which left their crossbar shaking. As newspaper *ABC* noted, using a Spanish idiom, a more recognisable Arconada emerged in the second half, 'He removed the thorn of the first half with several magnificent saves.'

Shots from Rudi Völler and Klaus Allofs – twice – were beaten away before a superb reflex stop denied Karl-Heinz Rummenigge, who had freed himself brilliantly to shoot high and hard from close range.

On 80 minutes, news filtered through that Portugal had taken the lead in Nantes. Mere survival for Spain would not be enough, although there was some confusion. *Mundo Deportivo* reported that the team were initially instructed to hold the ball and settle for a draw. It took a frantic relay of information from the Spanish press corps to get word to the bench that, as things stood, Spain would be eliminated.

Antonio Maceda was sent forward, and the German defence fatally failed to account for the centre-back as he headed a 90th-minute winner completely unmarked from Juan Señor's perfect cross.

The unlikely group win set up a semi-final against Denmark in Lyon.

The Danes would not afford Spain the luxury of another nervous start. After just seven minutes, Arconada acrobatically tipped a looping header onto the crossbar, only for Søren Lerby to crash the rebound over him for the opening goal.

Spain attempted to react but found themselves outmatched in both skill and physique. 'It was not a battle, more an attempt to bring down a colossal statue with kicks to the shin,' reported *ABC*. Arconada kept Spain alive with a double save before, once again, the unlikely figure of Maceda rifled home a loose ball to level the game. Even then, Spain only survived to extra time after Arconada dived full length to keep out Michael Laudrup's low drive.

In the very last action of extra time itself, Denmark won a free kick, which Preben Elkjær struck viciously, forcing another astonishing save from Arconada, who scrambled to his feet to block the follow-up opportunity.

It was on to penalties. Arconada thought he had made the breakthrough, saving Laudrup's attempt, but referee George Courtney instructed a retake and booked Arconada for his protests. Laudrup gladly took advantage of the reprieve.

As the shoot-out effectively reached sudden death, Elkjær blazed over, allowing Manu Sarabia to send an unconvincing Spain to the Parc des Princes for the final.

In the other semi-final, France had beaten Portugal in an all-time classic. With home advantage and featuring the midfield *Carré Magique* (Magic Square) of Platini, Luis Fernández, Alain Giresse and Jean Tigana, France were firm favourites, but as so often is the case, the occasion was nervy with few chances.

Little of note had happened until the moment that would go down in history. Just before the hour, France were awarded a generous free kick for what little contact Salva had made with Bernard Lacombe barely a yard outside the Spanish penalty area. So close to goal, Platini opted not to flight the ball over the wall but to drive it to Arconada's side. Anticipating the former, Arconada motioned to his right, but the shot was weak enough that he had no problem readjusting to make a comfortable dive to his left to meet the ball.

Disastrously, the ball dipped slightly and squeezed under the body of that famous jersey, sending it trickling towards the goal line. Arconada made one last desperate stretch, but to no avail. Platini sunk to his knees as his team-mates engulfed him in celebration. Arconada sprung to his feet, booting the ball downfield in bewildered self-reproach.

Spain desperately sought an equaliser but Bruno Bellone clipped a late goal on the break to confirm a first major tournament trophy for the hosts – the crowning achievement of a classic French vintage.

Arconada's error eclipsed the heroics he had performed to drag his team to the final and cast a shadow over the remainder of his international career.

In a World Cup qualifier against Wales the following April, a mix-up involving the two heroes of Euro '84, Arconada and Maceda, gifted Ian Rush the simplest of goals. Unbeknown to Arconada, the last of his then-record number of Spanish appearances came in a grisly 3-0 loss at the Racecourse Ground in Wrexham.

The spectre of the Paris mistake had been raised, and the gloves were passed to Athletic Club's Andoni Zubizarreta. Although it was denied that Arconada's omission from the squad was permanent, the situation became clearer when he suffered a severe knee injury in September 1985.

Arconada was out of the reckoning for the 1986 World Cup squad, and the issue was no longer brought up at press conferences.

Despite regaining a high level after his recovery and his relative youth, Arconada was never again selected for Spain. An imperfect ending to one of the most enduring international careers.

* * *

Spain may have cruelly given up on Arconada, but his number one fan certainly hadn't. What's more, the relationship between the two was evolving.

'I started buying every football newspaper and magazine I could find – Spanish, English, German – anything related to football that arrived at the *kiosko*. I was lucky because my mother used to buy magazines from that same newsstand, so the owner let me browse through all of them. Whenever I saw Arconada featured, I bought the magazine, cut out his pictures and started creating a scrapbook.

'I was about 14 years old, maybe 15, when I created that scrapbook, and it felt like it created a bond between Luis and me. When I showed him the book to have him sign it, he was amazed. He asked, "Who made this?" I said, "I did." He replied, "Do you realise the amount of work and documentation you've done here?" I explained to him how I'd compiled it.

'Luis signed it and then asked me, "Can I take this with me?" I told him, "No, it's mine. It took me a lot of effort to make it." He then proposed a deal, "Let me take it so I can show it to my wife. I'll bring it back the next time we meet."

'I had made a photocopy of the book in black and white, not like today, where you can have high-quality reproductions. Luis said, "Please, let me take it. I really want my wife to see it." From then on, his wife, Carmen, also spoke to me. She told me it was incredible and said, "I've seen many children and adults who are passionate about Luis and love him, but never to the level I've just seen or that Luis has told me."'

Muñoz was coming of age. He'd long since abandoned his dreams of becoming the Andalusian Arconada, but he was able to leverage the relationship he'd built to prise his way into the world of journalism.

'Yes, thanks to Luis and some friendships I had with players. I don't know if you remember, but in Spain, there was a very important magazine, even on a European level, called *Don Balón*.

'Back then, I used to call *Don Balón* and say, "I have some news. This player is signing for Real Madrid." They'd ask, "How do you know that?" And I'd reply, "Because I'm friends with the player." At first, they didn't take me seriously, but when the transfer happened, they called me back, "Hey, how did you know?" I said, "I already told you that I have friendships with players, and through those connections, I hear things."

'From there, we started building a relationship, and I kept calling them with news. When Luis retired, I was also the one to break that story. At one point, they said to me, "Look, we want you to work with us." And I became the director of *Don Balón* in Andalusia.'

From *Don Balón*, Muñoz moved to work for *Marca* in Madrid. '*Marca* was the best university because the level there was incredibly high. It was like a 15-year university degree. It was impressive, truly impressive. At least the *Marca* I experienced was the pinnacle. For any journalist, working at *Marca* was like playing for Real Madrid or Barcelona.'

When *Marca* bought out the Seville-based sports daily, *Estadio Deportivo,* Muñoz returned south, 'They wanted me to implement *Marca*'s editorial style there and teach the team how we worked at *Marca*. So that's how I ended up in Seville, continuing with both *Marca* and *Estadio Deportivo* during those last two years.'

Muñoz's devotion to journalism hit the rocks after a run-in with Real Betis's bombastic president, Manuel Ruiz de Lopera.

'Lopera wanted to control everything. He wanted to control the media, know everything you publish, how you publish it, and who your sources were, and as you know, for a journalist, sources are sacred.

'I had very good relationships with players from that era at Betis – Denilson, Joaquín, Alfonso, Toni Prats, Finidi and many others. Naturally, you'd find out about many things happening in the dressing room, and Lopera didn't like that.

'So, he sent me a warning and told me to stop publishing certain things. The next day, I wrote him a letter – an editorial in the newspaper. In it, I sarcastically apologised for reporting stuff he didn't want me to report, for not saying he was blond, handsome, and had blue eyes. I challenged him, and it cost me my job.

'He demanded my head, and *Marca* gave it to him.

'I felt a lot of frustration, and for the first time, I stopped believing in truth and journalism. I thought, "This is all a lie. It doesn't matter if you report something that's true. If your boss doesn't want it published because someone asked them not to, you have a great story, but in the end, you lose."

'I felt powerless. I didn't want anything to do with it for almost a year. I didn't read; I didn't engage. I sued *Marca*, won the case, and got compensation. It was a moral victory, but it didn't satisfy me. It wasn't enough.

'You know how it is when you work in journalism or writing. My time at *Marca* – I lived for it. I'd be on vacation, and they'd call me, "You need to go to New York." And I'd leave my vacation. I'd leave my wife on the beach and go.

'That's when I learned that work is important, but family is more important.'

Muñoz was stung but soon found out that in a deeply divided football city, whatever annoyed Ruíz de Lopera delighted his arch-enemy, the Sevilla president José María del Nido.

'Del Nido heard about how I stood up to Lopera. He called me and said, "I want journalists like you on my team. I want brave people, people who don't back down, even if it costs them their job. You need to come work with me."'

Muñoz joined Sevilla's media department and couldn't have picked a better time to do so.

* * *

Through the highs and lows of journalism, Muñoz had kept in touch with Arconada and started to accumulate an enviable collection of memorabilia.

'During a trip to San Sebastián with Betis while I was working at *Marca*, I went to Luis's house in the afternoon to see him. That day, he took out a collection of shirts and said to me, "Take the two you like the most."

'It was a tough decision because he had the jersey from the first league title, the jersey from the season when Real Sociedad went 32 matches unbeaten. There were so many, so many memories to choose from.

'The first shirt I picked was from the European Championship final. I chose it because of its sentimental value, for what it represented, and for how I experienced that final as a child watching it on TV. I don't think I've cried more in my life than during that match, especially after that goal.

'For the second, I was torn between several. Luis's jerseys were unique. Most keepers wear the kit provided by their club, but for Luis, it didn't matter what Real Sociedad wore; he always wore Adidas, which he bought himself. He got them from Adidas in Germany. They were his – they didn't belong to the club, and he always kept his kit in his own bag. No one else touched them.

'If he lost a match, he'd switch jerseys, but if he won, drew, or played well, he'd keep wearing the same jersey until they lost.

'The other one I picked was from the "Match of the Stars". In that game, the goalkeepers for the European team were Peter Shilton and Arconada. It's a shirt from Johan Cruyff's brand.'

In his new job, Muñoz encountered another charismatic goalkeeper. Andrés Palop was 31 when he arrived at Sevilla in 2005, having spent a decade as an understudy to Zubizarreta and then Santiago Cañizares. Finally given an opportunity, Palop soon made up for lost time.

In his first season, Sevilla won the UEFA Cup, thrashing Middlesbrough in the final of a competition they would come to dominate. As holders, they were moments from an underwhelming elimination in Donetsk when Palop's headed goal rescued them. They won the tie in extra time and eventually progressed to an all-Spanish final in Glasgow.

At a soggy Hampden Park, Palop kept Espanyol at bay with a string of saves before stopping three of four penalties in the shoot-out. Sevilla retained their title while Palop picked up a deserved Man of the Match award and a place in Sevilla folklore.

Palop went from getting splinters on the bench to starring in adverts, 'A few weeks before the famous header goal, his contract with Nike ended, and he signed with Adidas,' recalls Muñoz.

'The Adidas representative told him, "Andrés, remember, you've joined Adidas, where Nothing is Impossible." Not long after, that crucial match happened, where Sevilla had everything on the line. Andrés went up for the corner and scored. Adidas later made an advert featuring that play, with that tagline: "Nothing is Impossible."'

Soon after Palop's arrival, he and Muñoz struck up a rapport over one mutual fascination. 'Palop said, "I've been looking forward to meeting you because I've heard you're very close to Luis." So I explained the connection. Then, he came to my house and saw Arconada's jerseys. He was so excited, like a little kid.'

As Euro 2008 approached, Palop's form put him in contention for a place in the squad.

'Through contacts, I learned that Luis Aragonés was seriously considering including Palop,' remembers Muñoz. 'Not as the starting goalkeeper, but to be part of the squad. I mentioned it to Andrés, who confirmed, "Yes, the federation called me, and it's possible." We talked and talked until the big day eventually arrived, and the rumour turned into reality.

'Then Andrés said to me, "I've been thinking. We need to do something to honour Arconada. Any ideas?" We chatted, and we naturally thought of that famous Euro '84 final in France. Andrés said, "If Spain reach the final, would you lend me Luis's jersey?" I said, "Andrés, are you crazy? Spain never gets past the quarter-finals." He replied, "If I'm going, it's to win the Euros."

'So, we agreed that if it happened, I would get the shirt to him so he could go out on the field in it.'

Palop's ebullience trumped Muñoz's pessimism as Spain waltzed to Vienna, winning all three group games, but it was only after a quarter-final penalties win over their historic bête noire Italy that a nation began to feel something akin to authentic excitement.

Russia were summarily dispatched in a one-sided semifinal, leaving Spain to face Germany and Muñoz to figure out how to transport a shirt from Seville to Vienna.

'Andrés got in touch, and we made it happen, but I wasn't the one who brought the shirt because I'd had an accident at home and ended up with 89 stitches on my face. But through a friend of his who was heading to Vienna, we sent him the jersey.'

The plan was falling perfectly into place before something they hadn't even considered added another beautiful twist.

It hadn't occurred to them that handing over the trophy in his role as president of UEFA was the man who'd struck that fateful free kick, Michel Platini, but it immediately struck Platini that the first person he should invite to the final was Arconada.

'Luis called me,' recalls Muñoz, saying, "Hey, Platini has contacted me. They want me to attend the final; what should I do?" Luis had distanced himself from the media over the years. He was worried about going and having people talking about "Arconada" all over again.

'I told him I thought it was a wonderful opportunity, especially considering that Platini was UEFA president and their relationship. It felt like the planets had aligned for him to attend, and, above all, it was a testament to Platini's class because not every president or high-ranking official has the sensitivity to recognise that this man has been treated unfairly because of one goal.'

With the shirt safely packed in Palop's bag, all that was needed was for Spain to oblige and claim their first title since 1964. After a jittery start, Spain took control, and after Fernando Torres put them ahead with a first-half goal, they never looked likely to surrender their advantage.

As the final whistle blew, the Spanish bench rushed onto the field. Palop hoisted Carles Puyol, bear-hugged Xavi and helped throw Aragonés in the air before taking advantage of a lull to dash down the tunnel. He emerged wearing the shirt. It looked magnificent – indeed better than the shirt he had worn on the bench all tournament. The manufacturer's logo had been tactfully covered over to avoid any dispute.

Team-mates quickly clocked it, as Muñoz explains, 'David Villa saw Andrés with the jersey and said, "Hey, Andrés, what's that?" And Palop replied, "It's the shirt Arconada wore at Euro '84. Today, I'm going to honour him." Villa then said, "Damn, I should've brought my Quini one from Sporting de Gijón. Wow, what a beautiful gesture to pay tribute like that."'

As Palop climbed the steps, waiting to meet Platini, Muñoz was on the phone to Arconada.

'There's an image on TV where he's talking on the phone. A UEFA employee points with their hand and says to him, "There, there, look there," pointing at Andrés wearing his jersey. At that moment, Luis was on the phone with me, and I said, "Hey, Luis, look for Palop, look for Palop." He asked, "Why? Why?" And I just said, "Just look." Then, at one point, he looked, saw him, and said, "What a bastard! What have you done? What have you done?"

'Luis comes across as a reserved man – which he really isn't, as he's very warm. It's rare to see him like that, especially in public, but that was about the most emotional I've ever seen him.'

A few handshakes and backslaps later arrived that other Arconada disciple, Casillas. He hoisted the trophy that had painfully eluded his idol all those years ago. Palop and that enterprising boy from Jerez had helped set the record straight, and it couldn't have been more perfect.

***

In another quirk of Spanish goalkeeping injustice, Palop never saw the field for his country. He was destined to be the man who won a European Championship yet never won a cap, but his and Muñoz's stamp was still visible when Spain won the biggest one of them all.

For the 2010 World Cup in South Africa, Adidas modelled the Spanish goalkeeping shirt on that 1984 version. Casillas clambered onto the presentation stage in Johannesburg with a familiar green-bodied, navy-shouldered top, an ensemble which also included a nod to Arconada's famous white socks.

'We gave the idea to Adidas, and we didn't charge them anything for it,' laughs Muñoz, who nowadays knows a thing or two about selling shirts. Muñoz has long been in charge of Arconada's social media accounts, and he proudly shows off some of the replica jerseys and T-shirts they've recently launched.

Muñoz has become the custodian of all things Arconada. 'He gave his jerseys to me, not to his kids. Even his trophies, he gave them to me. When I asked him, "Luis, why me? I don't want your children to be upset," he said, "I've talked to them, and we all agree that you're the best person to have these, and you'll take the best care of them."'

Part of Muñoz's role involves fielding the many requests from people asking to meet with Arconada. 'Every week, I get messages from people in their 40s and 50s and even from kids who want to fulfil a dream for their father. Their father says, "I can't die without meeting Arconada," and they reach out to me through Luis's social media. Just last weekend, a young woman surprised her boyfriend, a firefighter from Madrid, by arranging for them to travel from Madrid to take a photo with Luis. We keep making those dreams come true.'

Life has come full circle with Muñoz now the gatekeeper, but he's as aware now as he was when flitting furtively around hotels as a young boy of the superpower footballers possess to make people incredibly happy with simple gestures.

THEY ALL HAVE THEIR IDOLS

'My dream was to become a footballer, and I used to go see Arconada. I know what it took for me to get to him. If I had been a footballer, I would have made it easier for any kid who came to see me'.

'And I think that's true for all footballers – they all have their idols.'

12.

Tell Me a Story

THEY CALL it *la sobremesa*.

While much of the world hurries to pay the bill and rush some goodbyes, in Spain, they tend to linger. With the rituals and routines of a meal behind them, it's time to sit back and take another glass of wine, a *digestif*, or a gin and tonic served in a glass so large it could house a school of goldfish. It's when hours drift away in conversation, storytelling, and laughter.

There's no equivalent word in English. Nothing as satisfying as the Spanish term, at least, and yet, it was a lad from Blackpool who became its most prodigious practitioner – holding court as lunches that began in the searing heat of a Madrid afternoon stretched into the cool of the evening or as dinners drifted into the early hours of the morning.

'Michael saw more waiters with their coats on than anyone in history. They'd have all the chairs up on the table, and he'd still be sat there ordering another gin and tonic.'

Perhaps it was only right. After all, Michael Robinson's life had become a kind of glorious *sobremesa* of its own – freed from the structures and strictures of professional football into a world of intrepid tales and generous humour.

'We met for lunch, and it just went on. Michael was one of these people where you would find yourself trying to leave for about three hours because you've got things to do, but he wouldn't shut up, and, well, you're actually quite enjoying it.

You keep trying to go, but somehow you never manage to – he would tell such great stories.'

Robinson convinced himself and then his adopted country that there was another, more human side to sport, and he tempted people to stay a little longer at the table, long after the final whistle had blown – to listen, to laugh, and to see the game, and life, in an entirely different way.

* * *

It's difficult to convey just how much of a cultural phenomenon Michael Robinson became in Spain to those who hold memories of him leading the line for Manchester City, Brighton & Hove Albion or Queens Park Rangers or partnering Ian Rush and Kenny Dalglish at Liverpool. When Robinson and his creaking knees departed for an end-of-career jaunt in La Liga from which he basically never returned, he largely faded from the British footballing public's memory. Yet all the while in his new home, he was enchanting television audiences and becoming a fundamental part of a sporting media that he was helping to reshape.

Luckily, *The Guardian*'s Spanish football writer Sid Lowe has the perfect point of comparison to help explain just how significant Robinson's impact was.

'There's a great English measure of fame,' says Lowe, 'if you've been a puppet on *Spitting Image*, you've made it. Well, in Spain, Michael Robinson's puppet *presented Spitting Image*.'

'Their version was called *Las noticias del guiñol* and was done as a news bulletin in which Michael Robinson was the presenter. So, for me, that's a nice way of expressing how big he was here. If being on *Spitting Image* is a measure that you've made it, then, bloody hell, how big do you have to be to be *presenting Spitting Image?*'

When Lowe arrived in Madrid to begin his own Spanish adventure in 2001, Robinson was already firmly established as a huge media presence and became a profound influence on Lowe – even if the beginning of their relationship was a little fraught.

Unsurprisingly, it all started with not one, but two, extended lunches.

'I contacted him to do a piece with him. He phoned me, and he was really warm, and I remember it really striking me that Spanglish thing he used to say, "I really want to attend you, but I don't know when, blah blah…" In the end, he said, "Look, come to this restaurant and have lunch with me." It was De María, which is at the top of the Castellana, the Argentinian one where a lot of players go.

'So I went for lunch with him, and his dad was there. We were there for hours, and the gin and tonic came out because the gin and tonic always came out. At one point, Michael said, "Look, my dad's here. I'm really sorry. I've got to take him home. Otherwise, we'd stay out all night," and we'd been there for five hours or something anyway.

'The next time I saw him, we met for lunch, and then it really did go on. There's a context here that I'm of an age and I'm a Liverpool fan. I remembered Michael, and he was a big deal to me. So I'm sitting there and Michael starts telling me stories about Liverpool from the 1980s, which is my Liverpool. I'm sitting there like, "This is amazing." I've got someone telling me a story about Kenny Dalglish, and I'm all over it. He was just great, great company.

'The thing about that meeting, in that interview, was that he said something which could be perceived as slagging off Raúl. He said something like, "I wouldn't cross the road on a rainy night to watch him play." Now, the point he was making was that Raúl wasn't as talented as the other *Galácticos*, but he had something. I think he referred to him as a "dark, mysterious animal", which was his way of saying, you know, he's not flashy, but he's amazing.

'As you can imagine, the Catalan papers picked that up and span it. So Michael rings me quite late – like 1am or something on a Friday or Saturday night. I didn't hear it, but the answerphone message was basically him, a bit flustered about it.

'I actually suspect that one of the reasons we got on was because I rang him the following morning and basically said, "That is what you said, and it's written in context, and you're Michael Robinson – you can say whatever you like, and what you said isn't even bad." We had a long conversation then – as tended to happen with Michael – the conversation drifted off somewhere else, and by the end, he'd forgotten what he'd been worried about. He probably liked that I didn't just say, "Oh, I'm really sorry." I think that conversation ended with him saying, "Alright, let's go for lunch."'

That a benign comment made to a UK-based newspaper could start a minor media storm was a testament to how big a deal Robinson had become in the decade-and-a-half since he slipped into the country in the depths of winter.

***

Robinson's playing career began at Preston North End, where his potential tempted Malcolm Allison's Manchester City to pay £750,000 to sign him in the summer of 1979. Labouring under a price tag only eclipsed by Trevor Francis's seven-figure move to Nottingham Forest the same year, Robinson was offloaded to Brighton a season later.

There he found form and his best friend in football in the headbanded centre-back and captain Steve Foster, 'We arrived about nine months apart, we both signed ten-year contracts,' remembers Foster.

The pair thrived and drove Brighton to the 1983 FA Cup Final, where they faced Manchester United. Foster was suspended, but Robinson demonstrated his strength deep in extra time when he bulldozed Kevin Moran then Gordon McQueen and rolled the ball perfectly to Gordon Smith. But Smith fired his shot at goalkeeper Gary Bailey's legs, inspiring Peter Jones's unforgettable radio commentary, 'And Smith must score,' a line etched into Brighton folklore.

Foster returned for the resulting replay, but United ruthlessly ran out 4-0 winners. With Brighton also suffering relegation, the club began selling its assets. Robinson's muscular performances had caught the eye of Liverpool, the team he'd grown up supporting further up the west coast in Blackpool.

At Anfield, Robinson won a league title, a League Cup and, most famously, a European Cup when Liverpool overcame Roma at the Stadio Olimpico on penalties. But despite demonstrable contributions to the side's success, Robinson forever suffered with a strain of impostor syndrome about representing his boyhood club.

'Every time I spoke to Michael about Liverpool,' says Lowe, 'there was a kind of wonder, a kind of joy and a sort of disbelief that he was *allowed* to play for Liverpool. You know, this sort of gratitude for having been given the chance to play for them. I think Michael always felt that he wasn't really good enough.

'I don't know if Michael expressed it when he played for Liverpool, but certainly later on there is a real sense from him of seeing Liverpool as a cause, as the nearest thing to a Spanish club. Obviously, Michael's whole media career was built on this idea of expressing what it is that links us to our football teams. So the idea of "You'll Never Walk Alone", the Kop, Anfield – all those things really suit Michael because Michael is this guy that is all about the people. And there was a massive warmth, he had become very close to a lot of people at Liverpool.'

After an intense two-year love affair with Liverpool, Robinson moved on to QPR, where his knees clashed disagreeably with Loftus Road's unforgiving plastic pitch. Though he did find riverside life in west London to his liking and struck up another close friendship, this time with someone who had nothing at all to do with football.

Mark Lister ended up following Robinson to Spain and became godfather to his children Liam and Aimee. It all started from a chance meeting in a deserted pub. 'I was in a bar down by the river, and the only customers were me and Michael. The barman introduced us; we shook hands and exchanged a couple of beers.

'I was obsessed with football as a kid but then completely lost it – I went down a bit of a hippy route, so I didn't have a clue who Michael was, which I think was the basis of our friendship, that I wasn't a fan. There was a sort of instant chemistry. Two hours later, I was round his house playing backgammon.'

Robinson and Lister grew close as the opportunity to move to Spain arose as Osasuna sought to reinforce their front line midway through the season. 'They desperately needed a centre-forward. Michael had no intention whatsoever of going to Spain, but they checked on his availability. He invited me up to Chelsea on New Year's Eve, and the board of Osasuna came over to see him play. He didn't have a particularly good game, but they decided to sign him. Two or three weeks later, I drove him to Heathrow to get on a plane to Bilbao.'

Lister can also lay claim to involvement in one of the most-told fables of Robinson's move, that of trying to locate Osasuna on a map – gloriously unaware the club was from the city of Pamplona. 'I was actually with him, me and him with an atlas looking for it. We were in his house down by the Thames. About 40 people claim that story, but it was me and him.'

Knowing where Osasuna was based was one thing – actually getting there became an adventure in itself. When Robinson landed at the airport in Bilbao in the January of 1987, the club sent Danish striker Michael Pedersen to pick him up and provide an English-speaking welcome. But a freak snowstorm had hit northern Spain, and when the pair reached Vitoria, they found the road to Pamplona was closed. They lucked out though, when Osasuna arranged for them each to have a suite in the finest hotel in town, where they stayed for three nights, and, as Robinson said in his 1996 autobiography, *Las Cosas de Robin*, 'There was nothing we could do apart from gorge ourselves on good steak and wine.'

When Robinson finally arrived in Pamplona he was dropped at his hotel late in the evening and greeted warmly by the hotel manager, who offered him something to eat and just about managed to convey to Robinson that he would be picked up for training the following morning at 9am. To Robinson's bewilderment, when he emerged on to the training pitch he saw the hotel manager again and thought to himself that he must just be a huge fan. It took him until well into the first session to realise his new boss, Pedro Mari Zabalza, managed both Osasuna and the Hotel Ciudad de Pamplona.

Robinson's adaptation to life in Spain provided many an anecdote for future retelling. From being sent to the bar to order *'cinco hijos de puta'* (five sons of bitches) by giggling team-mates to slapstick acts of blasphemy on the club's official church visits.

With few English speakers in the squad or the city, Robinson had no option but to adapt. 'It was a huge advantage that he went to Pamplona as he had to learn Spanish very quickly,' says Lister.

On the field, Robinson had a mixed start. His debut came in a 4-1 loss to Athletic Club at San Mamés, where he lost his marking assignment at corners for two of the goals. His second game saw him open the scoring in the first minute against Real Madrid in the Santiago Bernabéu, although Osasuna eventually slipped to a defeat. A week later he scored the only goal at El Sadar and was also sent off for an altercation with an Espanyol defender which seemed to instantly endear him to home supporters.

Though Robinson was never a prolific goalscorer for the club, that popularity endured as Osasuna escaped relegation via a rather odd three-way play-off series. In his second season, Robinson tempted his former Liverpool colleague Sammy Lee to defect from QPR and Osasuna were transformed, finishing in their joint-highest-ever league position of fifth.

Robinson and his wife, Christine, were falling deeply in love with life in Spain but by his third season Robinson's right knee was flaring up again. One of the few highlights of that final campaign came when Lister was paying his friend a visit – a night he still sheepishly remembers.

'We had dinner on the Saturday night, and Michael said, "I'd love to stay, but I'm playing tomorrow, so I'm going to bed. Here's the keys, let yourself in." I stayed out with some of his friends, went to a disco, and had lots and lots of gin and tonics. I got back to his flat at about five in the morning, put the post box key in the main door and broke the lock.

'I had to ring him. He came downstairs, and I've never seen him so angry. He said, "If this happens again, just go straight to the airport." He was quite right.

'The next day, I went to the game against Athletic, not feeling too well. It was 0-0, and I was thinking it was all my fault. Then late on, Michael scored the winner. He wasn't one to bear a grudge anyway but after the game he came out and gave me a big hug.

'He dropped me at the airport in Bilbao the next day, and we saw Howard Kendall, who was manager of Athletic at the time. Michael said, "Hello, Mr Kendall," and he said, "Oh bloody hell, I've seen enough of you this weekend."'

Robinson was decisive again at El Sadar against Malaga a few weeks later as Osasuna strung a decent run of results together. But during a home win against Betis in January 1989, Robinson rose to challenge for a header and landed jarringly on that right knee. Hobbling off the field, he knew it was time to call it a day and spent that Sunday night sleeplessly churning his decision over in his mind as his leg throbbed with pain.

The following morning he went straight to the training ground and told his manager and his team-mates of his decision. He then sought out his wife who he hadn't had the heart to tell and called by a restaurant he knew. The door was locked as it was still setting up for lunch, but the owner recognised Robinson's distress, invited him in and poured him a glass of Rioja as he wept at the realisation that at just 30 years of age his career was over.

Robinson met with Osasuna's president, Fermín Ezcurra, who suggested he see out his deal, prioritising playing home games, but Robinson couldn't countenance the idea and asked that his contract be torn up, not wanting to earn while he was unable to physically perform.

That Wednesday, his retirement was announced publicly. 'Club Atlético Osasuna has lost one of its most charismatic and beloved players,' began the report in *Mundo Deportivo*. 'In a gesture of honesty towards the club and its fans, Michael Robinson decided to hang up his boots. His knee problems have proved tougher than his own pride.'

'After 15 years of playing football, it is very hard,' Robinson told reporters. 'But I have my pride and dignity – I can't crawl around the pitches as it wouldn't be good for the club or the fans. I have been very lucky to play for this club and to have a crowd like the one in Pamplona. It's been a pleasure to live and play in the city.'

***

Suddenly cast into retirement, Robinson initially bounced between Spain and England working for *Eurosport* selling television rights for boxing and other events, but it was Italia '90 that changed everything. Spain's national broadcaster, *Televisión Española*, offered Robinson work as a pundit covering Group F which contained England, the Republic of Ireland – who Robinson had represented 24 times thanks to his Irish heritage – as well as the Netherlands and Egypt.

As well as giving Robinson his break in television, it was an event that fundamentally changed his perspective on the sport.

'The way he told it, it was almost a eureka moment,' Lowe explains.

'Michael always said to me that when he went to the World Cup in 1990, he saw things that he never saw as a player. He sees the fans, he sees the party, he sees all this stuff. As a player, all he saw were the fans in the stadium itself, because you get taken to a ground, you get taken to a hotel, you don't see it all.'

'I remember him saying to me, "I never knew as a player what this meant to so many people and how big it was. It was a good job I didn't because I would have gone to pieces." He used to talk a lot about the pressure of playing in front of the Kop and the pressure of not wanting to let anyone down.'

Shortly after that World Cup, Robinson found the perfect platform for his fresh outlook when Alfredo Relaño, the director of the new subscription television channel *Canal+*, offered him the opportunity to work on their flagship programme *El Dìa Después* (The Day After).

The show was broadcast each Monday and ostensibly looked back over the weekend's games. There was some tactical analysis and discussion of key incidents, but what set the show apart was its eye for the quirkier side of the game and its focus on fans – a theme that became stronger as Robinson's influence grew. The programme became a sensation and one of the few broadcasts that *Canal+* made available for free.

'*El Dìa Después* was a social and cultural phenomenon beyond football,' Lowe explains. 'It didn't matter if you weren't really into football; you watched it, and people loved it. Michael absolutely loved it. I think what he did was create a space that everyone shared.

'*Canal+* was codified, and basically, the screen would be fuzzy black and white – I remember watching football matches through the fuzz because I didn't have the subscription, trying to work out if I could see what was happening, but they put *El Dìa Después* out for free. There was a conscious attempt to say – and obviously, Michael massively bought into it – "This is for everyone."

'This was the collective cultural experience for a massive chunk of Spain. From a newspaper point of view, it managed to be like a national newspaper that had loads of local news, because, of course, what you did by having a video from Cádiz or Osasuna or Valladolid was you had people in Cádiz or Osasuna or Valladolid watching it thinking, "We might be on."

'I remember Michael saying to me he had a golden rule, which was, "You never do a video of a fan who is trying to get on the telly. You're not there to put him on a telly because someone is going, Look at me. No, you're there to document them."'

After moving from pundit to presenter, Robinson also took over the production of the show. 'Michael's directorial approach, I think, is really, really significant and there's a real depth to it,' Lowe remembers.

'I went with Michael one Monday to watch it being made. Essentially, he would send his kids – and he always called them "his kids" – away for the weekend. Obviously, they send people away with certain ideas in mind, but generally it was, "Go and tell me a story." He would get them in on a Monday in a big office and say, "Right, tell me what you've got." They'd all sit around the room and they would watch each other's videos and they would laugh. He'd be like, "That is brilliant, we're doing it." Then they would discuss whether it was a two-minute video or a four-minute video, how much they would edit it and all this sort of stuff.

'I think he wanted it to have a purity, so if one of his team came back empty-handed, he'd accept that, because he didn't want anyone to force a story, to go looking so hard that it didn't feel natural. There was a real kind of "go and show me the world" about it. It was genuinely inspiring.'

As part of his *Canal+* contract, Robinson also provided co-commentary on the highest-profile game of the week. That, combined with the astonishing success of *El Día Después*, meant that Robinson's profile soared, and soon he was everywhere from the front cover of *PC Fútbol* – Spain's answer to the *Championship Manager* computer game – to providing the voice of Doris the Ugly Stepsister in the Spanish versions of *Shrek*.

He soon had illustrious company for those long lunches and dinners. His old Liverpool colleague Graeme Souness once recalled receiving a call from Robinson as he left a restaurant alongside Seve Ballesteros. Robinson was bemused as fans bounded up to him for autographs while neglecting Ballesteros.

Lister, who had also moved to Madrid by then, remembers one night when he and Robinson arranged to have dinner. 'We agreed to meet at this restaurant where the footballers tended to go. Then he rang me about an hour and a half later and said, "Mark, I've got a problem. We've arranged to meet, and we will meet, but I've got a couple of friends who want to come. Do you mind?" I said, "Who are they?" And he said, "Luis Figo and Mick Hucknall." I said, "Yeah, okay. They can come."'

It was a mania that Foster witnessed after he'd retired and started taking monthly trips to Madrid. 'It was incredible. Everyone wanted to be with him or to be seen with him.' Robinson, though gregarious when approached, was never entirely at ease with the attention, often favouring bars or restaurants where he knew he could relax in peace.

When Foster was in town, Robinson made sure he got the full experience. 'He used to take me into the commentary box when he was working. I remember going to Valencia against Man United once.' Foster also had his own seat in the *Canal+* studio to watch *El Día Después* go out live each Monday. And, of course, he was always one of the most enthusiastic participants in those legendary long lunches. 'I think we set a record for the number of times we had lunch, carried on talking, and ended up having dinner at the same table. The restaurant would close around five or six and reopen at eight or nine – but they'd just leave us there with the keys.'

For all of the celebrity company and fondness for the finer things in life, beneath it all, as Lister points out, there was a professionalism and determination that underpinned Robinson's media career.

'He was a brilliant communicator and a great raconteur; he just had a way of saying things – and he was very, very, very driven. I mean, just unbelievably. It wasn't that he had this gift – well, he did – but really, it was 90 per cent hard work. He really, really worked. He took it incredibly seriously.

'He had a funny timetable but was never late for anything. He might get home at 2am or 3am, but he's on that plane at eight the next morning. He had that incredible discipline.'

Something else that wasn't as it appeared on the surface, particularly in his breakthrough years on screen, was Robinson's command of Spanish. An undoubted part of Robinson's charm was the particularly Anglo-Saxon manner in which he spoke his second language.

'His Spanish was fantastic,' says Lister. 'But he was famous for speaking bad Spanish. He used that well; it was almost like wearing a costume. There was a story that he used to spend a month in the UK every year under contract so as not to lose his accent. Not true – absolutely not true.'

The myth served as a measure of how fascinated the Spanish public had become with Robinson, but in 2005, after 15 years of unequivocal success, a brainwave in the boardroom of *Canal+* saw *El Día Después* unnecessarily reinvented, leaving Robinson furious and disillusioned.

'Michael really disliked what they did with *El Día Después*. That genuinely hurt him,' says Lowe. 'Basically, they ditched it for a programme called *Maracaná*. They tried to put it in a studio with an audience wearing football shirts. They wanted it to be a bit of a circus. It was all very forced and lacked the finesse of the video segments in *El Día Después*.

'Now, on one level, you could say, well, that suits Michael, doesn't it? Because he was about people. He was about the madness, but Michael thought they made it tacky and cheap, because, for all that Michael was about the people, he was also about quality and was very conscious of not dumbing things down.'

Lister's analysis of the *Maracaná* debacle is even less forgiving. 'It was probably the lowest point of his life when they tried to make it into a comedy show – and it was a *complete* disaster. I think Michael did two shows and resigned. He just couldn't do it. He got huge, huge respect for doing that. It was crap, it was just so wrong.'

El Día Después eventually returned in something approaching its original form in 2009 and is still produced to this day, but Robinson never went back after the *Maracaná* fiasco. Instead, when he found his verve again, he began making documentaries, producing *Informe Robinson*, a show similar in style to the human-focused ESPN *30 for 30* series, although pre-dating its American equivalent by a couple of years.

With its high production values, the output, figuratively and literally, had Robinson's name all over it. Something the man himself was keenly aware of, says Lowe.

'A lot of the people who worked with him at *El Dia Después* went to work with him at *Informe Robinson*. People like José Larraza and Nico Abad. These were people he trusted and was really fond of. And Michael had this very clear sense that this is his team, these are his people – and he always tried to talk about them and acknowledge them. He never wanted it to be about him.'

On one occasion, that trust to produce the goods even extended to Lister. 'He gave me a camera crew and unlimited budget to do one about the Grand National,' says Lister. 'Horse racing is my passion, and there's worldwide interest in the Grand National, so he gave me, not an open chequebook, but not far off, and we did that. It was the year Comply or Die won the race.'

Sure enough, the archives feature an *Informe Robinson* on the 2008 Grand National, as exquisitely produced as all the rest.

The series would shine a light on unknown stories and unfamiliar sports but also featured some of the world's biggest stars, who eventually didn't even need to be approached.

'I was told by someone who worked with Michael,' says Lowe, 'that it got to the point where they had too many things to do, because they would have footballers phoning them up and saying, "You've got to do one on me. Why haven't I got an *Informe Robinson*?" There was this real thing of, why does [Rafael] Nadal want to do this? Because it's Michael Robinson. People were coming to him because he was such an expression of the way sportspeople felt they should be treated. I think

Michael understood a fundamental truth of sport, which was this is about people who are committed and have a passion and give everything for it, because however shit a sportsman you are, you've still got to work really bloody hard at it. But Michael also understood that it could be fun if it was done right.'

Dovetailing with *Informe Robinson* was a radio programme titled *Acento Robinson* – a playful nod to Robinson's Blackpudlian lilt – which went out each Sunday on Cadena Ser. It was on that station, on the drive-time show *La Ventana*, in December 2018, that presenter Carles Francino broke the bleakest of news.

'I've been thinking a lot about how to start the show today because it's not easy at all. I've spent the whole morning going over it, but I think the best thing is to get straight to the point because everything gets mixed up – friendship, bad news, and how to face it. So here goes, my friend – our friend – Michael Robinson has cancer.'

'That's it, I've said it. From now on, we'll let him speak since he's the one who gave me permission to say it. Michael, good afternoon.'

Robinson explained that he had incurable melanoma, the most malignant form of skin cancer and had initially been floored by the news, but true to form, he had found his own way of looking at the situation.

'One fine day, over a beer, I made up my mind. One thing was that science had spoken. I had cancer – a bad and advanced kind, but I'm the one who decides how to live through that. That's my right – to decide how I'm going to live. I wouldn't want my kids or my wife to talk about there being a "pre-illness Michael" and a "post-illness Michael." And suddenly, I felt empowered and said, "I'm going to decide how I'm going to live," I got quite fired up.'

A line that Robinson regularly used in interviews also beautifully captured that mindset. 'Cancer – I hope later rather than sooner – has one shot: it might be able to kill me once, but it's not going to do it every day.'

The news hit the country hard. 'It was like everybody's uncle was dying,' says Lowe. 'It was like he was part of all of them.'

Robinson continued to work, travelling the country and the continent for commentaries and still driving the production of his radio and television shows forward. All while undergoing intense hospital treatment. 'It was pretty brutal, the treatment he went through,' says Lowe. 'I remember I sent him a message saying, "How are you getting on? What's happening?" His response was, "Thanks, Sid. I'm OK. I'm having a right old scrap. Things are going to be alright." And here's another one: "I'm fine. I've just renewed my contract for three more years, so *Movistar* seem to think that I'm going to be OK. I feel in great nick, a bit like Ben Stokes." And it just was always him, like, yeah, I'm here, but there was no pretending that it wasn't shit.'

As Europe confronted the outbreak of the COVID-19 pandemic in March 2020, Robinson was on commentary duty for one last time before football went on an imposed hiatus. Poetically, that assignment took him to Anfield for Liverpool's Champions League tie with Atlético Madrid. In a poignant moment captured on film, his long-time commentary partner Carlos Martínez is seen watching wistfully as Robinson sang along to 'You'll Never Walk Alone' just before kick-off.

While life across the planet went on hold, Robinson's cancer cruelly accelerated. Those close to him steeled themselves for the worst, but there was one last typical act of defiance. When one Spanish journalist erroneously reported his death, Robinson responded via social media. 'For all of you who are asking, I'm still fighting. Thank you all so much for your interest and your displays of affection. I hear you, like at Anfield: "You'll Never Walk Alone." Thank you from the bottom of my heart and much encouragement during confinement.'

A week later, on 28 April 2020 – 48 days after that emotional night at Anfield – Robinson died at his home in

Madrid, surrounded by his family, at the age of 61, bringing his brave struggle to an end.

* * *

Friends and colleagues of Robinson were forced to manage their grief while trapped behind closed doors.

'When he died,' says Lowe, 'I remember sitting here in this office, just sort of looking at the screen and thinking, "What do I do now?" Then thinking I want to write but then thinking I don't want to write – I don't want to do this. But then being pleased that I had written, partly because then Aimee, his daughter, contacted me, and you know what, if nothing else, it's worth it because of that. For her to know how much he mattered.'

The following day's newspapers each carried the news on their front pages and featured tributes from the likes of Andrés Iniesta, Sergio Ramos, Rafael Nadal and the Spanish Prime Minister, Pedro Sánchez.

Restrictions denied Robinson his deserved send-off. One of life's most social characters departed behind the crematorium curtains at a family-only ceremony. Some form of redress came six months later when the production team that he so adored produced *Good, Better, Best*, a documentary that charted his life from a Blackpool bed & breakfast to the television and radio studios of Madrid. The premiere finally allowed family and friends to meet, mourn and celebrate an extraordinary life.

A few years on, those closest to him feel his absence as keenly as ever.

'I miss him every day,' says Foster. 'I'm looking at a picture on my wall with me and him with a bottle of Champagne and two teacups. That was when we'd beaten Man City 4-0, and there's me and him celebrating with Champagne. I used to tell people that was half-time.

'I still have his number on my phone,' says Lister. 'I still talk about him in the future tense quite often. He was the biggest influence on my life. It was because of him I met so many people in Spain. I would never have got through those doors.'

'I miss him because, although I didn't speak to him every day,' says Lowe, 'he was the person that sort of made you think, "Right, there's someone there that I know, his judgment is sound, and I know that his view is right." So there is a kind of an inspirational element to him – a sense that he did things how I would like to do things.

'So he's sort of always there, in that he always symbolises that sense of "What is this for? What is the point of this?" And I think the point of it, Michael got, and Michael expressed it and communicated it. That thing that says, here's a story about football, but it's kind of not really about football – it's about the people, and it's about the warmth, and there's no cynicism.'

And there's a certain spirit that lives on in the restaurants of Madrid whenever someone catches a waiter's eye long after a meal and orders another gin and tonic.

The bill can always wait. There's another story to tell.

El Palco

The Directors

13.

Carmen: Celta Vigo's Wonder Woman

THE IRON gates of the Pazo Baión heaved violently back and forth. The hinges began to buckle, and the single, giant bolt came close to giving way to a surge of maternal rage.

Police made a vain attempt to make themselves heard over the metallic thumps and manic screams. The estate's security muscle appeared on the scene, only to be scolded into retreat by faces etched with years of suffering..

A woman with a red megaphone emerged to exert some control, settling the crowd to the confines of the approach road. With its 70 acres of gardens and vineyards, the medieval Galician manor had become a symbol in the fight against drugs. A struggle driven by mothers disgusted with seeing lives around them devastated while others prospered from the tonnes of narcotics that flowed in along the Atlantic coastline.

At the forefront was a woman whose own family had been destroyed by drugs. Carmen Avendaño had inspired a movement that grew from Vigo's working-class neighbourhoods – *las Madres Contra la Droga*. A motherly reaction to a scourge they had to rally together first to comprehend, then to confront.

Avendaño's intervention sparked a profound shift, piling pressure upon those in authority who had been complacent or complicit with Europe's most powerful drug cartels to finally take meaningful action. It would take years of unrelenting campaigning – surviving intimidation and attempts on her life – but it was Avendaño who would emerge victorious when Galicia's clans were eventually dismantled.

Years later, Avendaño would become a fixture on the board at Celta Vigo. A club that was once a plaything of the region's smugglers was finally represented by the woman who had defeated them.

***

'I remember going to the protest. My mother went, my grandmother too, and other mothers from the association who are no longer with us like Fina and Dora,' recalls Avendaño's youngest son, Rubén Cagiao. 'We arrived in front of the Pazo. Those mothers were desperate. Truly desperate. I remember seeing how they started shaking the gate, screaming, lost in their despair. They were really, really distressed.

'I was just watching, amazed by it all. My mother kept telling me not to worry that nothing was going to happen. She was always trying to calm them down, but even my grandmother, I remember seeing her grabbing the gate and shaking it, screaming, "This can't be!"

'I also remember taking the bus there, singing the whole way. They had songs prepared. I remember one – *"No somos locas ni terroristas, somos madres muy realistas"* ("We're not crazy or terrorists, we are mothers and realists"). They had their chants, and they sang all the way to the protest. Then we arrived – it was a scene that left a deep impression on me.'

That 1994 protest made enough of an imprint on Cagiao that he now continues his now retired mother's work as the president of Érguete. Created in Vigo in 1984, the organisation took its name from the Galician for 'rise up' and grew out of the early meetings between parents desperate to find support and information about the problem that was erupting around them.

'I grew up in a *barrio* called Lavadores. Back then, it was a very working-class neighbourhood. Lots of people worked at the Citroën factory and places like that. We had a strong sense of community – it was like a village where everyone knew each other. We had close relationships – my friends would come into my house, and I would go into theirs. That's how it was.

'So, I grew up and had a very happy childhood. In this kind of neighbourhood, with the relationships we had, it was a very happy upbringing. Then, of course, came the destruction of drugs.'

Cagiao's world changed dramatically when two of his four older brothers succumbed to addiction.

'I saw how it dragged down our family, the neighbourhood, everything. I always say that at eight, nine, ten years old, I lived through things that a child shouldn't have to experience. A kid at that age should be playing, but instead, we lived through my brothers' addictions, the addictions of our neighbours. Then, my mother's ferocious battle to find a solution and change society's mentality towards this massive issue emerged. That was what I experienced in my environment, my city.

'My brother Jaime, the second-oldest, was the first to have problems. He was a very intelligent guy; he was always a restless kid, a bit rebellious, and always the first to do things, and at 14, he started experimenting with drugs. Of course, back then, my parents didn't even know what that was.'

Drugs flooded the streets of 1980s Galicia at a terrifying speed. As Europe's main gateway for cocaine and a prolific importer of marijuana, both were readily available at bargain prices. Heroin rarely arrived via Galician shores, but established distribution networks and a young population accustomed to casual use meant the opiate ripped through the region at an even higher rate than the epidemic engulfing the rest of Spain.

'From the age of 14 or 15, my brother started using heroin,' remembers Cagiao. 'Then came the downward spiral – problems, thefts to be able to get drugs, etc. But it wasn't just him. It was all his friends of the same age. There are documentaries that call it 'The Lost Generation' because entire families lost that generation. It was completely wiped out. Many died.'

'The virus of drugs caused so much damage; it destroyed so much. That's what really marked all of us – that time, that era. The change, the lack of knowledge – there was a complete lack of understanding.'

Parents were suddenly confronted with an issue they knew absolutely nothing about, and they leaned on their existing networks for support, as Cagiao explains.

'When my parents moved to Lavadores, my mother found a neighbourhood with no sewage system, many deficiencies, transportation issues, and so on. She got to work and became the head of the Lavadores Residents' Association and was always someone who fought for the most disadvantaged, doing important work in the association like getting the sewage system installed and the neighbours organised. She always had that calling.'

Residents' meetings, usually devoted to matters of parking issues or refuse collection, began taking a far more disturbing tone as addiction tore through the neighbourhood and the city. More and more families were plummeting into chaos, and parents had nowhere to turn.

The first thing they had to do was educate themselves, seeking as much information as they possibly could. Much of the literature they acquired was in English, requiring translation to Spanish or Galician. What they read was harrowing.

Avendaño transitioned from the residents' association, establishing and becoming president of Érguete as the urgency of the situation became apparent. An early ethos was established that would eventually change the course of drug policy in Spain – addicts should be seen as victims who needed support.

'What was really happening with the drug addicts, the children of these mothers, was they were thrown in jail,' says Cagiao. 'They were prosecuted. They had no assistance and no access to lawyers who could defend them. The drug policy was that there was no drug policy.

'So, the association and my mother helped create the first drug policy. She established a legal and social support team to assist these young people, to guide them toward rehabilitation communities. That's when the association really started working, welcoming mothers who didn't understand what was happening to their children, explaining that they were not alone and that many families were going through the same thing.

'It wasn't about normalising drug use. It was about giving them tools to face the problem in a better way.'

Another key strand of the mothers' philosophy was that the stigma of dependence was something that should be carried by the suppliers, not the addicts.

'Something very important happened back then,' says Cagiao. 'The drug addicts were treated like the worst of the worst. I remember it clearly because I experienced it at school. When I was little, they would say to me, "Hey, your brother is a drug addict," as if it were something terrible, like he was a bad person.

'Meanwhile, the drug traffickers – the ones actually getting rich from selling and distributing drugs – were well regarded. Why? Because they provided jobs unloading drug shipments. They bought football teams; they invested a lot of money.

'I mean, I don't even know how to put it – drug traffickers were almost acclaimed because they knew how to make money. Here in Galicia, we've always been a very *caciquil* [a boss-led, patronage-based] society. So, when people saw these guys making lots of money, they would say, "Wow, they're so smart, they're so good at making money."

'I remember in my class, a lot of kids would say, "When I grow up, I want to be a drug trafficker," because they saw them driving fancy cars and living a comfortable life. That was the mentality, but little by little, as our brothers started dying, society began to rethink things.

'Of course, the mothers fought back. They launched a relentless campaign against the traffickers. They took to the streets.'

But, as Avendaño and her fraternity of *madres realistas* would find, challenging the clans was anything but simple in a corner of Spain where smuggling had a prestigious history.

* * *

With around a thousand miles of coastline made up of tiny islands and the mysterious, rugged inlets known as *rías*, Galicia has long been a perfect access point for anything people would rather the authorities not see.

A proud seafaring tradition meant that successive generations grew up with a meticulous command of the waters and coastline that set them several steps ahead of any officials inclined to pry. The logistical networks that kept Spain's fish markets stocked easily doubled as trade routes for whatever else needed to be dispensed across the country.

In the aftermath of the Civil War, smuggling emerged as a noble pursuit. As Spain's impoverished north-west corner cast envious glances across the border to its relatively affluent neighbour, Portugal, it was those who spent their days at sea that were able to procure essentials like penicillin and petrol as well as basic foodstuffs like cooking oil.

As the 1940s wore on and Europe suffered the shortages brought on by war, smuggling became even more prolific, with an increasing list of everyday items multiplying in value. Seaside communities became increasingly accustomed to the rhythms and routines of hauling contraband ashore, with rural workers able to supplement their wages with a few hours of well-paid work unloading boats in the *rías*.

As Spain's economy clambered to its feet, the demand for mundane items subsided, and tobacco quickly became the smugglers' staple. With Spain's tobacco industry controlled by Tabacalera, a state-organised monopoly, conditions were perfect for a boom in black market imports. Fishing crews began supplementing their income by bootlegging cheap cigarettes from Cuba and Portugal during the 1950s before more organised operators latched on to a practice that was lucrative, socially accepted and weakly legislated against.

The trade became structured and efficient, and consignments were handled slickly. Smaller boats were launched to meet larger vessels offshore, whisking crates of cigarettes back to warehouses and fish factories, where they would be parcelled up and dispatched.

Unsurprisingly, those at the top of the most prolific operations soon became wealthy, and a familiar pattern of patronage emerged. Church collection plates overflowed, sympathetic politicians earned generous backing, and local police took a suspiciously light-touch approach, conducting a few token raids for the benefit of the bigwigs in Madrid.

It was little surprise when football drew the attention of those flush with the spoils of bootlegging. Celso Lorenzo Villa was an eccentric former Republican military pilot who had been one of the first to cotton on to the profitability of tobacco. By 1959, his fame and fortune had made him president of Celta Vigo, where he named another of Galicia's smuggling godfathers, Vicente Otero Pérez – known as *Terito* – as his vice president.

Celso Lorenzo was known for flying over Balaidos in a propeller plane during games as the crowd below puffed away on cut-price cigarettes courtesy of their president. In a brief period that became known as *el Celta de Marlboro*, the club's dire finances were cured, but on-field success proved more elusive. Despite travelling to away games in a luxurious, ultramodern Dodge team bus – a gift from the president's connections in Havana – the team narrowly missed out on a promotion to *Primera* with successive play-off defeats.

The tobacco trade continued to be the golden goose for decades, ticking along efficiently and discreetly with the temperamental Galician climate more of an impediment than law enforcement. The clans entrenched their power bases, expertly laundered their profits and earned a global reputation as trusted partners.

The early 1980s saw the gangs fall in with international drug traffickers using their expertise and apparatus to transport boatloads of marijuana ashore, where it was stored, returned to its owners and filtered across Europe. Some were tentative at first but soon found they were moving huge quantities of cannabis for healthy commissions at little risk.

At one stage, so much marijuana was arriving that locals struggled to house it all. One farmer who obligingly rented out some barn space awoke one morning to find one of his pigs had eaten his way through an entire bundle of hashish and died a psychedelically premature death.

However, it was the arrival of a new generation of trafficker – younger, more ambitious and with contacts in Panama and Colombia – that would change the face of Galician smuggling, blowing away its conservative business model. The foremost of these was Sito Miñanco, a son and grandson of sailors, who had already begun exploring transatlantic trade links when his budding bootlegging career was interrupted by a six-month term in Madrid's notorious Carabanchel prison in 1983. By sheer chance, his spell there coincided with two of Colombia's most powerful drug barons, Jorge Luis Ochoa Vázquez of the Medellín Cartel and Gilberto Rodríguez Orejuela of the Cali Cartel.

Miñanco's release and return to Galicia supercharged the *rías*. Cocaine now flowed in, with smuggling crews old and new getting in on the act. Miñanco's audacity and innovative use of technology to coordinate shipments saw him rapidly accumulating power and wealth. Inevitable comparisons were drawn between Miñanco and Pablo Escobar, with similarities evident in both style of dress and a philanthropic streak that naturally extended to football.

Miñanco took control of the humble Club Juventud Cambados from his native village. His largesse powered the side from Spain's fifth tier to the verge of *Segunda*, where at their peak, they vied for promotion against the likes of Getafe and Leganés. Tales of lavish cash bonuses, off-season tours of

Central and South America and promotion parties attended by Panamanian dictator Manuel Noriega were fabled throughout the glory years. Eventually, Miñanco's attentions were drawn elsewhere, and the club slid back down the leagues.

Galicia's bootlegging scene had undergone a revolution, and by the mid-1980s, 80 per cent of Europe's cocaine supply was arriving via the region. Rowing boats and coded torchlight had been replaced by tuned-up speedboats and two-way radios, but the old routines were familiar. The clans remained a step ahead of police and prosecutors, who showed a marked reluctance to confront those making outrageous profits from Colombia's European expansion.

As towns and cities became awash with cheap cannabis and cocaine that had been siphoned off for the local market, a parallel boom in heroin wreaked havoc among Galicia's youth, and it seemed the only ones prepared to challenge the absurdity of young lives being shattered while gangsters cruised along as society's elite were Carmen Avendaño and her grassroots movement of distraught parents.

***

Having established pathways to education and rehabilitation, even striking a deal with local businesses to employ former addicts, Avendaño and Érguete took the fight to the suppliers.

In 1986, the mothers called a press conference in Vigo, attended by local media and politicians, at which they read out the names of 38 bars in the city at which drugs were being sold. A further meeting a few days later saw bar owners and police attending to see for themselves what was happening.

The group organised similar gatherings, including in the coastal areas where the clans operated a stronghold. Attendances were sparse at first, with crowds often made up of the cartels' foot soldiers sent along to keep a watchful eye, but the movement gained momentum and within two years of its formation, Érguete opened almost 40 local branches across the region.

The rallies and demonstrations of *las madres contra la droga* (the mothers against drugs) made for a compelling media narrative – a group of heartbroken mothers fearlessly taking the fight to drug gangs who initially responded with menace towards Avendaño.

'There were death threats,' says Cagiao. 'They even cut the brakes on her car. She also received direct threats from drug traffickers – phone calls, the usual kind of thing, but my mother is a person of strong character who always pushes forward. I think they never went beyond threats because she became too influential in society by then. They didn't dare to go any further.

'There were moments, especially during trials and protests in front of bars and places where drugs were being sold, there were some small confrontations, but at a certain point, the drug traffickers didn't dare say anything to the mothers anymore. I mean, how could you say anything to a woman whose son had died just a week ago?

'Even the police came to understand them. I remember my mother going to the courthouse, and the officers in the cells would open the doors for her so she could speak with the young lads inside.

'Politicians also started listening. They opened doors for my mother and, by extension, for the association. There was a shift, a huge change. In just a few years, the perception of these women went from "these crazy mothers" to people who were respected and taken seriously.'

One high-level door that opened was that of Manuel Fraga.

'Fraga had stepped down as the national leader of the Partido Popular and then ran for election in Galicia,' explains Cagiao. 'He won and became the President of Galicia. That's when he received my mother. My mother arrived with a group, and as soon as she started speaking, she laid everything out. She told him everything – problem after problem, issue after issue. She just went on and on.

'At one point, Fraga had his head down, and my mother thought, "He's not even paying attention, and here

I am, pouring everything out." So, being direct as she always is, she asked him, "*Señor Presidente*, are you even listening to me?"

'When he lifted his head, it became apparent that he had been crying – Fraga was crying.

'That moment really left an impact on my mother. She had been admonishing him, thinking he wasn't paying attention, but in reality, he was so moved that he had tears in his eyes.

'During that meeting, he told one of his advisors, "Take note of everything this woman is asking for. We need to address all of it."

'Then someone pointed out, "*Señor Presidente*, you do realise she's from the Socialist Party?"

'And Fraga, right there in front of everyone, responded, "Do we have people like her in our party? No. Well, do as I say. We'll address all of her requests."

'The truth is, my mother always had a great relationship with politicians, regardless of their party.'

Soon, the mothers had the ear of Madrid-based politicians from across the political spectrum. Prime Minister Felipe González met with them and offered funding. His opposition counterpart and successor, José María Aznar, also sat down with them, but it was the involvement of the crusading prosecutor, Baltasar Garzón, that finally led to the first large-scale effort to challenge Galicia's cartels.

The extent of the gangs' activities was deemed too complex an issue for local law enforcement to deal with, and the brief was handed to Garzón, who ordered a massive police deployment targeting leading traffickers codenamed *Operación Nécora* – Operation Velvet Crab.

Garzón's work naturally brought him into contact with Avendaño. Though hailing from two very different worlds, the pair struck up an unlikely friendship, as Cagiao recalls, 'I remember Garzón well. I remember one day, suddenly, a bunch of cars pulled up – guys in suits, all security personnel. I stood there at the door, watching.'

'Then, Garzón steps out of one of the cars, and he just says, "I've come to eat at your house." I have that memory of Garzón sitting there, eating, surrounded by a bunch of security officers – because, at that time, he was under serious threat.

'He was sat there in our house eating a tortilla that my father had made.'

Garzón orchestrated months of investigations based primarily on wiretaps and testimony from two informants until the time came to strike. The plan was to make dozens of simultaneous arrests on the morning of 12 June 1990. Crucially, the swoop was kept completely secret from Galician police and politicians who had a reputation for leaking planned raids to the clans. Even the legion of police officers seconded from Madrid to conduct the arrests had no idea where they were going until they were safely sat in vehicles heading northwards.

As dawn broke that summer morning, helicopters buzzed above the *rías* as some 350 police officers arrested 54 suspects. The eventual 'macro-trial' at Madrid's Casa de Campo, which began some three years later, saw 49 of those arrested face charges. The trial captured news headlines for months as clan heads faced cross-examination in full gaze of the mothers who had helped drag them there. For all of the spectacle, *Nécora* proved a disappointment. Clumsy detention protocols and inadmissible evidence allowed most of the main figures to sidestep the most serious charges with infuriating ease.

One of the main targets had been Laureano Oubiña, one of the old-school tobacco smugglers whose success had earned him the money to purchase the Pazo Baión. Oubiña had long been a target for the ire of Avendaño, who happily testified against him.

Oubiña turned up to the trial each day in clogs, defiantly batted away questions and was acquitted of drug trafficking charges. Sentenced to 12 years in prison for money laundering, he was given parole just months after the trial's conclusion, having spent four years on remand after being swooped upon in *Nécora*.

Oubiña's release triggered the outpouring of rage and assault on the gates of his estate as Avendaño and the other mothers reeled from *Nécora*'s unsatisfactory outcome.

Despite its shortcomings, Cagiao believes it was an important milestone in the fight against drugs, 'I always say the same thing: *Nécora*, led by Judge Garzón, gave visibility to the public's outrage against drug traffickers. It exposed the deep frustration that society had towards them.'

'*Nécora* was huge, but in the end, not many people were actually sentenced. It was more about the social impact and awareness than the legal outcomes. The operation itself was crucial, but the trial… the trial didn't result in many convictions. It was more about the public awakening it caused, which I believe was so important, because in the end, sentencing was complicated, it was very complex.

'Garzón, as a judge, was the one who changed everything. He changed history for the drug traffickers. He was the first to start it all.

'His operations didn't always achieve the desired results due to their difficulty, but he was the one responsible for leading those first major assignments.'

Indeed, eventually almost all of Galicia's leading figures were convicted. Sito Miñanco evaded *Nécora* but was arrested in Madrid in 1991 and sentenced to 20 years in prison for drug trafficking, tax evasion, and document forgery. After his release, he was caught again in 2001 when a police raid found him coordinating a shipment of 4,000kg of cocaine off the coast of French Guyana using satellite phones and nautical charts from a chalet on the outskirts of Madrid. He was handed down 16 years and a fine of €390m.

In 1999, Oubiña was sentenced to four years in jail for transporting marijuana, with further sentences for trafficking and money laundering lengthening his prison stay. Finally released in 2017, he remains outspoken, adamantly denies ever dealing with hard drugs and relishes taking pops at his nemesis, Avendaño.

'Her time will come,' Oubiña told radio station *Cadena Ser* upon his release. 'She hasn't suffered a family tragedy because of me and I didn't traffic the kind of drugs that caused it. She wants to keep the issue alive to get subsidies. There are many subsidies and a lot of competition for her role.'

* * *

With Galicia's clans serving time or effectively dismantled, life for Avendaño quietened down just enough for her to entertain other ideas. One intriguing invitation came shortly after the changing of the guard in the Celta Vigo boardroom in 2006 from the newly arrived club president.

'When Carlos Mouriño took control of Celta, my mother was already a well-known figure,' says Cagiao. 'By then, she had already founded and was leading Érguete. Mouriño said to her, "Look, I know you're not involved in football, but you have an important role – you're great at building things, and I need your support for Celta's foundation."

'With her experience from the foundation and the association, Mouriño wanted her to contribute, and she did – helping to create and run the Celta Foundation. That's how she became a board member, and she did that role for 13 or 14 years.'

In addition to running the club's charitable arm, Avendaño became involved in the club's day-to-day life.

'She wasn't just a board member in the traditional sense. She would go to matches, talk to the young players and the workers, and sign agreements with the staff; she was involved with everyone in the club. She was definitely very involved. I don't know how she managed it all. I really don't. She was still running the foundation [Érguete], and yet she still had time for the club.

'She wasn't just close to the players; she had a special connection with all the workers at Celta. She had a very special relationship with everyone because my mother has this charisma, this kindness, and this way of looking out for people.

'Even now, if I walk into the Celta store, the staff will say to me, "The one who fought the hardest for our salary increases, for better conditions, was your mother."'

In a boardroom where smugglers once called the shots, a woman who'd helped take down their heirs was now an influential figure.

A journalist once noted during an interview with *La Voz de Galicia* that Avendaño was the only woman on the Celta board. 'And the only person from the left, too,' she quipped. 'They're quite a conservative bunch.'

She confessed that she had once tried to resign. 'They wouldn't let me, and that's despite the fact that I always say what I think. Like when I was the only one who voted against the purchase of Balaídos from the council. A city cannot give up its public assets.'

A fixture at that stadium in February 2021 brought a poignant reminder of what Avendaño and the city's youth had gone through. Celta took the field for their game against Elche in black armbands. They stood for a moment of solemn silence to remember the life of Abel, one of Avendaño's sons who had struggled with addiction during the 1980s and had died at the young age of 50.

A Celta side featuring six local-born players provided a fitting tribute with a 3-1 win. The goals were scored by young men from those same *barrios* of Vigo that Avendaño fought valiantly to protect.

* * *

The iron gates of the Pazo Baión heaved open. Flinging them wide apart, beaming a huge smile was Avendaño – the first to stride through to jubilant applause from the crowd of dignitaries gathered behind her. In contrast to the scenes of distress at those gates 14 years earlier, this time, there were flowers, balloons and a string quartet playing music as videos of the mothers' fight against drug trafficking were played on a big screen.

Emilio Pérez Touriño, the President of Galicia, hailed a day that was 'full of symbolism, mixed emotions, joy for closing a chapter, but also remembrance of the suffering endured'.

The estate, once the emblem of the ostentatious success of Galicia's smugglers and drug traffickers, had been confiscated by the state in 1995, then later seized by Baltasar Garzón to settle a fine imposed on Laureano Oubiña and his wife. It was reinstated as a winery and became a tourist destination showcasing a particularly fine version of that more noble product of the *rías* – albariño wine. That 2008 ceremony commemorated its €15m sale to the wine group Condes de Albarei, who pledged five per cent of profits towards drug rehabilitation programmes and opened up a pathway for former addicts to work at the estate.

For Avendaño, it was a sweet moment in what her son describes as a 'very intense life'. A story that has drawn the attention of more than one screenwriter. A 2005 film, *Heroína*, was based on Avendaño's struggles – 'Friends would ask me, "Is everything in the movie true?" And I'd say, "Yes, everything. That's what we lived through,"' says Cagiao.

The Netflix adaptation of Nacho Carretero's book *Fariña* also features Avendaño as one of the main characters as it explores the changing face of trafficking in Galicia.

Approaching her 80th birthday, Avendaño takes a well-deserved back seat these days as the foundation she helped set up – still based in the same *barrio* of Lavadores – is guided along by Cagiao and the many others who followed in her trailblazing wake.

But she's not the type of personality that will be forgotten about any time soon. 'A fighter. A mother who fought. A person of deep convictions. Someone with a strong character who always knew exactly what she stood for. That's how I would describe my mother.'

14.

The Man Who Could Organise Anything

HE WAS the man who could organise anything. Always on top of every little detail – that's why they put him in charge of this.

He'd already changed the course of Spanish football history when he'd been dispatched to sign Alfredo Di Stéfano for Real Madrid from under the noses of Barcelona. He then played a part in adding the likes of Paco Gento, Raymond Kopa, José Santamaría and Ferenc Puskás to the squad.

Then, not content with helping create the greatest Real Madrid side of all time, he intervened at a crucial stage in the creation of the competition that would define them – the European Cup.

He'd revolutionised basketball in Spain, then Europe too, creating the Spanish league and the European Champions Cup, and, of course, he then revitalised Real Madrid's basketball team so successfully that they came to dominate both competitions.

So implicitly trusted was Raimundo Saporta by Santiago Bernabéu, he was essentially left on his own to run the club as the Real Madrid president grew older.

That's why he'd been given this job. After all, this was a man used to creating competitions from scratch – how hard could arranging one football tournament be?

THE MAN WHO COULD ORGANISE ANYTHING

But just weeks before Spain was about to welcome the world, Saporta was feeling the strain. So overwhelming were the demands that the phone in his apartment seemed to ring non-stop, the answering machine long since filled to capacity. The media speculated about his health, reporting trips to a clinic in Switzerland for medical checks.

Saporta persevered, admitting to extreme fatigue but otherwise dismissing what was being printed by the newspapers – 'The press has been very difficult to deal with.'

They could all agree on one thing – organising the 1982 World Cup was proving far more challenging than anyone had anticipated.

***

'I would say that he is a very complex figure. His whole life in sports, he was a unique figure,' says Miguel Ángel Lara, a journalist at *Marca* for almost 30 years and the newspaper's resident historian.

'Really, for me, more than sport – he is an example of diplomacy, a character shaped by the Cold War era. Everything surrounding Saporta is deeply political. He is incredible, even from his beginnings – his family background is really striking.'

The man tasked by Royal Decree with delivering a successful World Cup wasn't a natural part of Spanish footballing aristocracy. Indeed, he'd only become involved in the sport because he knew precisely nothing about it. And he didn't originate from Spain. In fact, Raimundo Saporta's background was so veiled in mystery it took a pair of intrepid historians to unpick it.

Official documents in Spain have always shown that Saporta was born in Paris on 16 December 1926. Saporta's standard line was that he was born in France to a Spanish father and a French mother and had moved to Madrid in the early 1940s.

But a 2015 investigation by Fernando Arrechea and Víctor Martínez Patón for the Spanish football history organisation

CIHEFE revealed a much more complex picture. The pair tracked down documentation at Saporta's former school in Paris that stated he was born in Constantinople (now Istanbul).

Saporta's parents were Sephardic Jews who had moved to Turkey after Greek forces had taken their native Thessaloniki in 1912. The couple established a family in Constantinople, with Saporta's brother Marcelo born there in 1923, followed by Raimundo three years later.

The Great Depression of 1929 triggered a move to Paris, where the family settled happily. The brothers attended the prestigious Lycée Carnot in the city's 17th arrondissement, where they would bump into future French President Jacques Chirac in the playground.

When German boots reached Parisian streets in the early part of the Second World War, the city became a precarious place for anyone suspected of being Jewish, and families began taking measures to conceal their ethnicity. CIHEFE found evidence that Saporta's later school records had been edited to remove any reference to Constantinople in an attempt to avoid Nazi scrutiny.

As the threat to the Jewish population in France grew critical, the family played their escape card. A 1924 mandate by Spain's ruling dictator, Miguel Primo de Rivera, gave Sephardic Jews the entitlement to automatic citizenship as an attempt to redress the shameful expulsion of Jews from Spain under the 1492 Alhambra Decree. Presciently, Saporta's parents had availed of the right before they'd even left Constantinople, meaning the family were Spanish citizens over a decade before setting foot on Spanish soil.

They arrived in Madrid in 1941, but tragedy struck just six months after beginning their new life. Saporta's father was hit fatally by a tram, leaving his wife Simona to raise her two teenage sons in their brand-new surroundings.

'Imagine,' says Lara, 'this woman alone in Spain in the 1940s and 1950s. He [Saporta] was very young at the time, carrying a mark because like it or not, the Jewish world was still a world apart. Even though Spain allowed them to stay, Spain was allied with Italy and Germany, making the situation quite complicated.'

In an uncertain political environment, the most prudent course of action was to blend in. References to Saporta's true place of birth were embellished, and the backstory of being the son of a French widow and a deceased Spanish father was set. That the family's surname sounded passably Spanish was an added advantage.

The heartbroken family had no choice but to press on and adapt to their alien surroundings, although they afforded themselves some familiarity with both sons enrolling in the *Lycée Français de Madrid*. The French school had a lively basketball scene that Saporta very much enjoyed. Realising his physical talents would never guarantee him a place on the squad, he began helping out in administrative roles and was named the team's official delegate.

Saporta's exceptional organisational talent soon turned heads at the Spanish Basketball Federation. The governing body's president, Colonel Jesús Querejeta Pavón, was so taken by the 19-year-old that he immediately sought to add him to the board, but he was frustrated by the federation's own rules, which stated directors must be at least 21 years old. Saporta worked in an unofficial role until being installed as vice president upon reaching the required age in 1947.

Saporta set about improving and restructuring Spanish basketball. By 1952, he was held in such regard that when Real Madrid president Santiago Bernabéu began searching for someone to organise a basketball tournament as part of the club's 50th anniversary celebrations, he received the same answer from whoever he asked – Raimundo Saporta.

With minimal fuss, Saporta arranged an impressive four-team tournament, including international opposition in the form of Racing Club of Paris, the Puerto Rican national team and a talented team of Suffolk-based American servicemen that called themselves the Lakenheath Pirates. In the final, Real Madrid rallied from a huge deficit to beat an excellent Puerto Rican team, described by *ABC* as 'possibly the finest team to have ever played basketball in Madrid'.

'Bernabéu was struck by how he managed everything and controlled expenses,' Lara explains. 'Because Bernabéu was obsessed with financial matters – not spending a single extra peseta. That was something deeply ingrained in him. He was extremely strict regarding economic management, to the point where he himself lived by financial constraints – something nowadays that is unimaginable for a club director. What Saporta did impressed him greatly, and from that moment on, he started gaining influence.'

Bernabéu immediately recruited Saporta – still only 25 – to his board. Legend has it that when Saporta politely pointed out that he knew absolutely nothing about football, Bernabéu shot back, 'That's why I want you, *chaval*. There are too many around who think they do.'

Saporta's creative problem-solving, attention to detail and linguistic abilities saw him quickly become Bernabéu's most trusted lieutenant. As a pair, they complemented each other perfectly.

'Bernabéu was famous for his character,' says Lara. 'For being very direct, Saporta was much more of a politician. He knew how to handle every situation, and he was the kind of person who always knew what to say, when to say it, and the most appropriate course of action.

'Bernabéu, on the other hand, wasn't like that. He was far more straightforward – he would tell you if he thought you were a fool or a cheat. Saporta wouldn't. He would find another way, he would approach you, give you a pat on the back – he was, in essence, a politician.

'Bernabéu was something else. He was a pure football executive, a lifelong *Madridista*, because he had grown up in Madrid since childhood. For Bernabéu, Real Madrid was everything – from turning off a light bulb to turning off a tap to closing a door, things like that mattered to him.

'Saporta, however, was different – he was the politician behind Bernabéu's strong personality.'

So immediately was trust established between the pair that Saporta was already entrusted with solving some of the club's most complicated issues within a year of his arrival. And it didn't get more convoluted – or epoch-defining – than the transfer of Alfredo Di Stéfano.

* * *

Di Stéfano's predicament was perplexing enough even before Spain's two biggest clubs became involved.

In the wake of a 1949 players' strike in Argentina aimed at earning professional status, Di Stéfano had walked away from River Plate to play for Millonarios of Bogotá in Colombia's highly lucrative but blacklisted league. An agreement with FIFA two years later paved the way for Colombia to rejoin FIFA on the proviso that all foreign players would be returned to their previous clubs by October 1954.

By late 1952, Di Stéfano had returned to Buenos Aires with a hefty chunk of wages that had been paid to him up front. In a strange netherworld where he was in dispute with River, who held his registration, and Millonarios, who he was contracted to, he contemplated retirement at just 26 years of age.

Di Stéfano had caught the eye of Spanish clubs during another of Real Madrid's anniversary celebrations, firing Millonarios to a 4-2 win over the hosts at Chamartín. It was Barcelona who moved first, visiting Buenos Aires to strike a deal with River, on the basis that they held the player's FIFA-approved rights. Madrid's response was to send Saporta to Colombia to agree a fee with Millonarios. True to character, Saporta also went to Argentina, where he negotiated a 'non-aggression' pact with River, with the Argentines agreeing not to oppose Madrid's claim to Di Stéfano should Barcelona's deal fall through.

The impasse was set, but while Di Stéfano seemed likely to join Barcelona, spending the summer of 1953 living in the city and training with the club, Madrid and Saporta weren't ready to give up, as Lara explains.

'By then, Di Stéfano had already played two or three matches for Barcelona, but he felt somewhat alone. He didn't feel integrated into the club. The team had left for a tour in South America, and he was left behind. Samitier, the sporting director, had just resigned. At that moment, Di Stéfano felt a bit abandoned in Spain, wondering, "What am I doing here? I came to a club that doesn't seem to care about me."

'That's when Saporta approached him, convinced him, and ultimately brought him to Real Madrid. He played a crucial role in every step of the process – travelling to South America, realising that Barcelona was ahead in negotiations, that they had already paid money and had convinced Di Stéfano.

'Saporta went to Barcelona, with Di Stéfano already playing there, and managed to completely turn the situation around. He convinced him – whether through money, persuasion or simply making him feel valued – but most importantly, Di Stéfano felt that Real Madrid was truly interested in him.

'He understood that Madrid really was there for him – and Saporta made that happen.'

The deadlock dragged on, and the two clubs eventually agreed to honour the outcome of a FIFA-led mediation process held that September. The verdict was bizarre. Di Stéfano was to alternate between Real Madrid and Barcelona for four years. Crucially, the first season would be at Madrid, with the player reverting to Barça the following term. The clubs had no alternative but to accept the resolution, but a fractious boardroom split in Barcelona saw the president resign and the club give up their rights to Di Stéfano to Madrid in exchange for a financial settlement.

Di Stéfano's arrival in Madrid proved to be seismic. Having only won *Primera* twice – and not for 21 years – the club immediately rectified that and went on to win 12 of the next

16 league titles. Yet it was continental success that would define them. The only issue was that the European Cup was yet to be conceived at the time Di Stéfano first pulled on a white jersey. Once again, Saporta would play a decisive role in resolving that.

With *L'Equipe* journalists Jacques Ferran and Gabriel Hanot seeking support for a European version of South America's Copa Libertadores, they initially approached Barcelona but were met with a distinct disinterest. A phone call to Saporta proved much more productive, with him and Bernabéu immediately recognising the idea's potential. *L'Equipe*'s Barcelona-based correspondent was immediately whisked to Madrid for talks.

A meeting in Paris was quickly called. There, Saporta's ambassadorial tone and command of multiple languages were to the fore. With Real Madrid's formal approval, political support, and desire to include Eastern European clubs, the European Cup was duly approved by UEFA.

An early conundrum came in just the second round of the competition, in December 1955, when Madrid were drawn against Partizan Belgrade. With an exchange of visas between Franco's right-wing Spain and Tito's communist Yugoslavia an impossibility, Saporta used his connections to secure players and staff free passage through obscure border posts without visas. A challenge to the competition's viability had been averted.

While Madrid embarked on a period of domestic and European domination – winning the first five editions of the European Cup – Saporta still found time to keep an avuncular eye on his players' lives.

'Where Paco Gento lived,' says Lara, 'that house was bought by Saporta, very close to the stadium. He found a house for Di Stéfano too, also near the ground, so that he would drive as little as possible and avoid using a car.'

When forward Ramón Grosso went to celebrate a successful season by buying himself a brand new SEAT 600, he was frustrated, as Lara recounts.

'Madrid had just won a European Cup, and Grosso decided he wanted to buy a car. But when he went to pay, he found that his account was blocked. He asked, "What's going on?" and they told him, "Talk to Saporta."

'So he spoke with Saporta, and Saporta simply told him, "A car isn't a good idea for you. It's too expensive."

'Later, Grosso went to buy an apartment, and the same thing happened – his account was blocked, but this time, they called Saporta and told him it was for a flat. He immediately unblocked the account.'

Justo Tejada, who won two league titles with both Barcelona and Real Madrid, once recalled to *Panenka* magazine, 'Barça is the club of my heart, but at Madrid, they looked after every little detail. You couldn't even forget your wife's birthday as a bouquet would show up with a card that said, "From the office of Raimundo Saporta."'

Similar stories abounded from Real Madrid's basketball section, where Saporta was known as *'Tío Rai'* ('Uncle Ray') – always on hand to resolve players' personal issues, ensuring they ate properly and that youngsters continued their studies.

In 1956, he established the first Spanish basketball league, which surprisingly turned a tidy profit in its first year. Naturally, Real Madrid won nine out of the first ten editions. Two years later, he was the leading architect behind the launch of the FIBA European Champions Cup, a competition that was initially dominated by teams from the Soviet Union. Real Madrid did, though, find their feet in the 1960s, and titles arrived – along with some delicate geopolitical issues.

Trips to the Soviet Union were prohibited by the regime and had to be negotiated by way of carefully picked stopovers. Though one trip to Moscow garnered Franco's blessing and a special assignment for Saporta, according to Lara.

'In Moscow, he met with *La Pasionaria*. She was the leader of the Communist Party during the Civil War and fled to Moscow. She was very close to Stalin and to the hardline faction of the Communist Party. He met with her because he had a mission. Franco wanted to know what life was like in Russia; if things were as harsh as people said. So, Saporta meets with Dolores Ibárruri, *La Pasionaria*, and when he returns, he tells Franco what he saw in Moscow.'

On another occasion, Saporta had to work his magic to help his president out of a tight spot after Bernabéu handed out one bauble too many on a basketball trip to face Maccabi Tel Aviv.

'It involved Bernabéu and Moshe Dayan, the Israeli general,' explains Lara. 'The club awarded him their gold and diamond insignia. This caused a huge scandal in Spain because there were no diplomatic relations with Israel at the time. Spain, under Franco, was much closer to the Arab world – Morocco, Egypt, etc, so, this became a major controversy.'

With Arab leaders in uproar, raising complaints to Spanish embassies, the Ministry of Foreign Affairs summoned Bernabéu to give an explanation.

'He refused to go,' says Lara. 'Instead, he sent Saporta and told him to say whatever he wanted. Bernabéu went to the beach in Alicante, and somehow, Saporta handled it. No one really knows exactly how, but he managed to explain things to the government, and the issue was resolved.'

Saporta had undoubtedly been influential in Real Madrid edging ahead of a fine Barcelona team, and the Di Stéfano transfer, in particular, would forever form a cornerstone in the story of their rivalry. Yet Saporta was never driven by red-blooded antagonism. He maintained strong friendships with figures from Barcelona and was at the heart of one of the most wholesome episodes in the clubs' shared history.

By the time László Kubala had become manager of Barcelona in 1961, he had been separated from his mother for over 12 years, having left her behind when he fled his native Budapest. Attempts to secure permission for her to visit Spain had been repeatedly rejected by Hungary's communist government. But Real Madrid took advantage of a European Cup preliminary round tie with Vasas to lobby the Hungarian

Football Federation and in turn the government to allow Kubala's mother a reunion with her son.

After Bernabéu's public request, Saporta worked assiduously as ever behind the scenes. When Anna Kubala arrived in Barcelona two days before Christmas, finally able to meet her three grandchildren, an overjoyed Kubala passed on his generous thanks to Bernabéu and Saporta via the assembled press.

That same year, Saporta officially became vice president and took increasing responsibility as the years passed. By the mid-1970s, Bernabéu's health was in decline, and he mainly resided in Alicante. His board procrastinated over finding a successor, and on 2 June 1978, just as the 1978 World Cup was getting underway in Argentina, Bernabéu died, still holding the presidency he'd been elected to in 1943.

Saporta stood in as president for an interim period. Many, including the board, presumed that, as a relatively young man, he would be Bernabéu's natural successor, but Saporta had no interest in the role, as he outlined some years later, 'Don Santiago once told me that I shouldn't accept the presidency after his death – and that's exactly what I did. Firstly, I had no personal ambition, and secondly, because he told me I would suffer greatly in the position.'

Instead, Saporta oversaw the choice of a new president and, in September 1978, bid farewell to the club he had been involved with for 26 years. On his final day, he packed up his belongings and said goodbye to club employees. Typically, he finalised a sponsorship deal for Real Madrid's reserve basketball team before walking away.

Just weeks later, he would be back in football – by royal command.

**

In London in the summer of 1966, FIFA confirmed their plans for three future tournaments. Spain stood aside for West Germany to host the 1974 edition, which meant they were automatically selected when the competition returned to European soil eight years later. Though by the time 1982 came around, the World Cup – and Spain – had radically changed.

In the mid-1960s, the notion of hosting a World Cup was almost quaint. The cosy 16-team affair lasted less than three weeks, was broadcast sporadically in sleepy black and white, and its 32 matches were mainly attended by curious locals. A decade and a half later, it was well on its way to becoming a global technicolour jamboree. FIFA had eagerly expanded the competition, meaning Spain would host the biggest tournament yet – a 24-team, month-long extravaganza requiring more host cities and accommodating more fans than ever before.

While the World Cup had evolved, Spain had changed immeasurably. Franco's death in 1975 led to a period of rapid but fragile transition. A new Spain aspired to become a modern democracy, but the process was complex and hindered by political distrust. On the periphery of the process, violence reached alarming levels, and the spectre of ETA hung heavily over the event.

It was that grim threat that inspired the title of writer Albert Ojeda's book about the tournament, *Cuero contra plomo – Leather against lead*. As Ojeda explains, the list of issues facing organisers was almost endless.

'It was, without a doubt, an organisational and logistical challenge on every level. To begin with, the stadiums were not up to the standards required. Then there was the political situation, which was unstable – or certainly complicated – because democracy had not yet fully taken root. There were major upheavals, such as the attempted coup in 1981. Additionally, an economic crisis was hitting the country hard. The effects of the 1973 oil crisis were still felt across Europe, particularly in Spain. It was a difficult context, with recession and high inflation. There were many factors that made organising the World Cup extremely difficult. Another major issue was the terrorist threat.'

Saporta took charge of the process in September 1978, King Juan Carlos's decree naming him president of the World Cup Organising Committee. After visiting the King at the Zarzuela Palace on the outskirts of Madrid, Saporta told reporters, 'His Majesty has shown great interest in all the details of the championship's organisation and has encouraged us to put in our maximum effort in our work so that the World Cup achieves the success we all desire.'

That chirpy tone did not last as Saporta was dragged down by a process like never before. Set against an already difficult backdrop, the unwelcome surprises seemed to keep coming. There was the discovery that Spain's entire television network had to be upgraded to broadcast the tournament at a cost of 17.5 billion pesetas. Then, the outbreak of the Falklands War potentially put holders Argentina up against England, Scotland, or Northern Ireland in a host country where public opinion was overwhelmingly against the UK's claim to the Falkland Islands.

At one stage, a row with the Socialist Party (PSOE) over the role of the host cities' municipal governments escalated to such an extent that Saporta offered his resignation, causing an almighty panic in the government, the Spanish federation and FIFA. His resignation was refused, and a compromise was reached.

Matters weren't helped by the fact that Saporta had finally found someone that he couldn't get along with, as Ojeda points out, 'He had an openly hostile relationship with another key figure on the organising committee, the president of the Spanish Football Federation, Pablo Porta. They had no chemistry and often clashed due to personal differences and struggles for prominence.'

Saporta drove on, solving problems as he always had, but the pressure had taken its toll, and things continued to go wrong – even at the draw.

Taking place shortly after Christmas in Madrid's Palacio de Congresos, the creative minds among the organising committee decided to theme the draw along the lines of Spain's Christmas lottery, using both the distinctive golden cages used to draw the numbers and the purple-sashed pupils of the San Ildefonso school.

The event quickly descended into farce, with the presiding FIFA delegates apparently forgetting their own fairly basic stipulations, drawing Belgium and then Scotland into the wrong groups. 'Quite extraordinary,' exclaimed Barry Davies in his inimitable fashion on the BBC's coverage. 'They went to great lengths to explain the procedure, but when it's come to the draw, they've not adopted their own plans.'

Even after correcting the errors, the draw dragged on interminably. FIFA officials, including Sepp Blatter, grew increasingly impatient with the time it was taking the schoolchildren to extract the balls and deliver them to their table. The farce degenerated further when the miniature two-piece Adidas Tango balls containing the teams' names began to break apart inside the cages. This led to the unedifying spectacle of fingers being poked into the machinery in an attempt to get them moving.

Saporta managed to strike an upbeat tone, 'Spain have a good chance to qualify for the second round. After that, we'll see. I think the tournament is guaranteed to be a financial success. On the field, we'll have to see, but whatever the outcome, we'll support the players.' But as the tournament drew closer, alarming reports emerged surrounding his health.

Just two months before the opening game, *El Pais* noted, 'For the first time, the once untouchable Saporta found himself overwhelmed. The mounting pressure led to a noticeable shift in Saporta's behaviour.

'Once a discreet and reserved figure, he began making bold public statements and frequently referencing the King as his "only boss", which reportedly started to irritate the Royal Household. Those close to him confirmed that he was undergoing medical treatment and taking medication to either calm him down or induce a state of euphoria – both of which were uncharacteristic of him.'

As Saporta's nerves jittered, ETA struck. The group blew up the eight-storey headquarters of Telefónica in central Madrid with 170kg of explosives, taking 20,000 lines and 700,000 telephones off the network in the capital on the same day Real Madrid hosted Barcelona in a decisive league match.

With ETA activity occupying the daily headlines, hopes they might leave the competition alone appeared misplaced. 'ETA had initially stated that they would not carry out attacks during the World Cup because, interestingly or rather strikingly, one of their members said, "We like football too,"' says Ojeda. 'But there were indications that led many to suspect that ETA, and possibly other far-left or even far-right extremist groups, might try to disrupt the tournament and cause chaos.'

An attack during the tournament felt inevitable, particularly after a *Guardia Civil* officer was shot dead by ETA in Gipuzkoa just as Argentina kicked off the World Cup against Belgium. The centrepiece of the opening ceremony at Camp Nou had been a giant human montage of a white dove of peace – an image that immediately felt forlornly optimistic.

As the competition progressed, Saporta's problems miraculously subsided. The Falklands War ended just a day into the tournament. ETA's guns didn't quite fall silent, but they never directly targeted the World Cup, nor were there any major operations. On the field, it proved to be an event that lived in the memory, serving up a combination of compelling football and skullduggery in equal measure in matches attended by over two million spectators. The only thing missing was a strong showing from the hosts, who were eliminated after winning just one of their five matches.

As Italy's Dino Zoff held the World Cup aloft in Madrid, stood just a few feet away in the stadium that bore his old mentor's name, Saporta could finally allow himself a sigh of relief. It had been a success.

Financially, the tournament even technically reported a profit with infrastructure debt either covered by lottery funding or creatively kicked down the road by accountants. Saporta – who refused to be paid for his work – was widely commended for his efforts. In their review of the year, *ABC* called the World Cup the biggest success of 1982, lauding Saporta as the 'mastermind behind the event'.

***

Ojeda believes the 1982 World Cup stands as an important moment in Spain's complex modern past, 'It's a memorable milestone, an extraordinary achievement that was highly significant for our history. It allowed Spain to show the world that the country was leaving behind the dictatorship, that it aspired to align itself with Western democracies, and that it had a modernising vision. And it gave the Spanish people an injection of excitement.

'Despite all the threats, dangers, and circumstances that made its organisation difficult, the World Cup turned out quite well. There were some less-than-ideal aspects, of course, but in general, it was a great success – pulling it off under such challenging conditions was truly an accomplishment.'

For Saporta, there was a legacy too. Despite delivering a successful World Cup, the stress left its mark, 'It seemed to leave some lasting effects on him,' says Ojeda. 'Both psychological and physical, particularly related to his heart. Carrying all that responsibility took a toll on him.'

Saporta took a break from football for a while, focusing on basketball and Spain's hosting of the 1986 FIBA World Championship, which he described as 'child's play' compared to its football equivalent. But before that tournament arrived, he was back at Real Madrid again after Ramón Mendoza became club president and looked to Saporta's experience, appointing him as vice president.

Saporta admitted that the 1982 World Cup 'did me a lot of damage' but pledged to serve with the same 'humility and dedication' as he had to Bernabéu. Though, as Lara describes, it was a hollower version of Saporta that returned to Chamartín, 'By that time, his role was more symbolic than truly active. He was no longer the energetic, hands-on Saporta of the 1960s and 1970s, but still, he was *Raimundo Saporta* – a legend, an iconic figure. Even if he wasn't as involved as before, having him close was still a great asset. His mere presence in a meeting would make people take notice. When Saporta was in the room, people would say, "Be careful. This man knows what he's talking about. He really understands what he's doing."'

A heart attack in 1987 slowed Saporta further, and he reduced his workload with the club until he resigned as vice president in 1991. He spent his later years still contributing to his first love, basketball, on the Spanish federation and FIBA boards.

On 1 February 1997, Saporta died of a kidney condition in a hospital in Madrid. He was survived by his childhood sweetheart, Arlette, another Sephardic Jew that had made the wartime move from Paris to Madrid. The then-president of Real Madrid, Lorenzo Sanz, paid tribute, 'The most important man in *Madridismo* after Bernabéu has left us. Saporta was a man to whom this club owes so much, and for that, we will give him the tribute he truly deserves.'

Barcelona vice president Joan Gaspart also paid his respects, 'I personally had a very special affection for him, as he always treated me with great kindness and openly shared his experiences as a director at Real Madrid.'

Spain's basketball head coach, Lolo Sainz, remarked that Saporta was 'so good that he leaves behind no enemies. I will be eternally grateful to him. At times, he may have seemed tough, but he was a person of great kindness.'

Real Madrid's glimmering remodelled stadium on the Paseo de la Castellana stands as the ultimate tribute to Santiago Bernabéu, but for younger generations, there is little to remind them of a man who, as Lara says, 'wasn't Bernabéu, but you

THE MAN WHO COULD ORGANISE ANYTHING

simply can't understand Real Madrid without Saporta. Real Madrid without Saporta just doesn't make sense.'

As Spain prepares itself to host the World Cup once more, it's perhaps worth taking a moment to remember the kid from Constantinople who became the man who could organise anything. The 1982 World Cup had tested him like nothing before, but he'd prevailed.

And did it all for free.

14.

You Will See Me at Atotxa Applauding la Real

THE WAY he saw it, he had four options – and he had ruled out the first three. He wouldn't pay, he wouldn't negotiate, he wouldn't flee.

He'd thought about barely anything else since the letter had arrived. The envelope bore the unmistakable stamp – a snake wound around an axe alongside the motto '*bietan jarrai*' – 'keep up both' – the serpent symbolising the political fight and the axe the armed struggle.

That axe had been sharpened of late. Spain had embarked on its nervous transition into a modern, Western democracy, but ETA's violent pursuit of Basque independence had turned bloodier than ever.

Such an onslaught required resources, and the most common ETA tactic was to look amongst their own, targeting businesses from small to large throughout the Basque Country, ordering the payment of a 'revolutionary tax'.

Maybe the only surprise was the demand hadn't arrived sooner. In many ways, he was the classic target, a successful businessman with a high profile and a man about town in the glimmering resort city of San Sebastián.

His mind flashed with images of those who'd refused. Suddenly disappearing for weeks on end, some ending up as the most appalling of newspaper headlines.

But the time for thinking was over – he'd made up his mind. The only thing left for him to do was tell them.

* * *

It was April 1980, spring was in the air, and Real Sociedad were top of *Primera* – within touching distance of a first-ever league title. Life was good, particularly for Juan Alcorta, who was winding down toward retirement, having skilfully reshaped some of Spain's most rustic trades into modern industries able to compete and export internationally. He'd accomplished those feats without ever coming close to a labour dispute with company employees – something he declared himself prouder of than any numbers on a balance sheet.

Born in 1921, Alcorta served on the Republican front line of the Civil War as a teenager before returning to San Sebastián to work in the family olive oil business. By his early 20s, he had become president of the regional wholesalers' association and soon realised the sector's potential to emerge from its homespun ways. He led a group of small manufacturers to merge their interests to create Koipe, which became a key part of the world's biggest olive oil supplier.

Alcorta then eyed Spain's fragmented, small-scale winemaking industry, which still predominantly supplied wine to bars and restaurants in barrels. Again, he brought producers together, with wineries across the Rioja region establishing a collective known as SAVIN. Rapid advances in manufacturing, marketing and distribution came at the perfect time to deliver bottles of smartly branded, good-quality wine to Spain's burgeoning number of supermarkets.

As president of SAVIN, Alcorta founded Bodegas Campo Viejo in 1967 and began producing the brand that became the best-selling Rioja in the world and a ubiquitous sight on shelves to this day. The winery in Logroño still bears its founder's name, as does a line of 'Alcorta' wines distinguished by words which pay homage to his character – daring, agile, bold, advanced, audacious, passionate and open.

Alcorta's commercial spirit also drove him to found Banco Industrial de Guipúzcoa, set up to support new companies across the region before becoming Bankoa years later.

Alcorta's acumen made him a natural choice to serve on the Real Sociedad board under their charismatic president, José Luis Orbegozo. Under Orbegozo's stewardship, the club had been transformed, and an almost entirely homegrown team had risen from also-rans to title contenders.

The goals that flew in at their seaside Atotxa stadium were hailed in a novel fashion by a tradition started by Alcorta's brother, Patxi. One of old San Sebastián's most eccentric characters, Patxi had a fascination with all things airborne, which at one stage extended to attempting to fly a donkey out to the island of Santa Clara powered only by a giant kite in an attempt to win a bet.

To allow fishermen in the Bay of Biscay to follow matches at sea, Patxi had struck upon the idea of launching fireworks after each goal – one if the away side had scored, two if *la Real* had. Local police, unimpressed, regularly fined him, but the tradition caught on, and the club officially adopted the custom in its new home in the south of the city.

Patxi was also known as the owner of 'Irutxulo', the bar that was the place to be in the Old Town popular with celebrities and sportsmen who would occasionally guest behind the bar. Revellers invariably left merry from the hospitality and good Basque wine – the lucky few with Patxi's trademark gift, a classic Basque *txapela* (beret), perched upon their heads.

With Real Sociedad top of the league, holding the slightest of edges over Real Madrid with just a few games of the season to play, the city was abuzz. For Juan Alcorta, life couldn't really get much better.

But then, the letter arrived.

* * *

For many across the Basque Country, checking the mail each morning was something of a macabre lottery. By the time ETA declared a ceasefire in 2011, it was estimated that as many as 10,000 Basque business people had been targeted by the group and asked to pay the 'revolutionary tax'. For ETA, with its far-left ideology, the business class was a legitimate target. Basque independence was just one strut of a political struggle which viewed the 'bourgeoisie' as 'oppressors of the working classes' who should be punished.

Though thousands received the letters, the effect on the recipient was usually to push them into a pensive solitude – weighing up their options in silence, often hiding the threat from their families, business partners and friends.

Some chose to move away, attempting to manage their operations from afar. Others hired bodyguards and mixed up their travel routines. Even submitting to the extortion and paying came with its risks.

Some who chose to pay had ended up in legal problems with judges who took a rather odd view of those who 'funded terrorism'.

While many chose simply to ignore the demand, the risk of non-compliance was very real. Throughout ETA's campaign of terror, 40 business people were murdered, and dozens more were kidnapped.

As Alcorta deliberated his best course of action, he would have been mindful of the case of another local businessman just a few years earlier. Ángel Berazadi, the managing director of a sewing machine company and a familiar figure on the local football scene as the president of CD Zarautz, failed to return to his home in San Sebastián after a day at the factory in March 1976.

The previous summer, he'd received a demand for the payment of 10m pesetas. Held in a farmhouse for almost three weeks, ETA demanded a sum of 200m pesetas – the equivalent of around €1.2m – for his release. With his family unable to raise such a sum, Berazadi's body was found dumped on a rural road two days after the deadline, blindfolded and with a set of rosary beads clutched between his hands.

Alcorta had weighed up his options and he'd chosen the last of them. The only thing left to do was end his silent suffering and send his response.

On the Tuesday morning of 29 April 1980, seven separate newspapers across the Basque Country carried a full-page, open letter from Alcorta to ETA.

> Like so many fellow citizens of the various classes and conditions, I have received the letter from ETA demanding, under threat of death, the payment of what they consider to be a 'revolutionary tax.'
>
> Before anything else, my first feeling was a deep bitterness. The bitterness of a person who feels that he is the victim of a grave injustice. But that is not the end of the anguish of this situation since that bitterness is aggravated by the impression of helplessness and defencelessness.
>
> I have thought long and hard before making a decision, and I have tried to do so with the utmost serenity, carefully weighing all the factors that I believed could have any influence on it.
>
> I'm revolted by the idea of having to pay to save my life, of giving in to the absolute fear of dying. I am not a hero, nor do I want to be one. I know that with this decision, I am putting the remaining years of my life at risk. But there is something in my conscience, in my way of being, that makes me prefer anything over giving in to a blackmail that is destroying my land, my people, and my community.
>
> We have always said that as Basques, we are not cowards. Among the negative qualities we may have (and we do have them), I believe cowardice is not one of them, and as a good Basque, I do not want to be a coward.

After directly quoting a paragraph from the letter he had received, which demanded a huge sum of money be paid via an intermediary in the south of France or face execution, Alcorta revealed his thought process and his final decision.

> The alternatives I have left are:
> First: Pay and continue living (for now).
> Second: Negotiate, plead, and try to obtain a discount through the 'intermediaries'.
> Third: Escape, flee.
> Fourth: Not to pay, not to negotiate, not to flee, and continue living (a lot or a little, I don't know) though certainly with some undeniable anguish.
> I have chosen the fourth. But I have decided to do something else. I have decided to make my attitude public, and to this end, I am writing to the newspapers. I think that in exchange for my delicate situation, I can provide a service to the Basque Country.
> I do not think this can be considered petulance on my part, nor am I trying to make a public matter out of a personal problem since it is well known that this situation has already affected thousands of Basques.'
> This has led me to realise that we are facing a public problem – one of extreme importance. I would say that ETA's actions constitute the most serious issue facing the Basque people, to whom I belong in every sense and whom I deeply love.
> And in the face of a problem of this magnitude, I believe that more is needed than the silence of the victims and the indifference of everyone else.

The letter drove on, urging Basque society to focus and take measures against ETA's extortions. Several paragraphs were devoted to the allegation that had clearly irked Alcorta that he was a 'bourgeoisie' – 'this alleged bourgeoisie does not seem to have gone to my head. I still have the same friends from 30 years ago, and my children live just like any of my employees.'

Alcorta concluded with a defiant flourish.

> ETA: I will continue to live as I have always lived. You will see me in the companies where I am responsible. You will see me at Atotxa applauding *la Real*. You will see me at a game of pelota. You will see me in some popular society having dinner, happy, with my friends, but perhaps with a gesture of sadness and tiredness that I didn't have until now. That you already have achieved.
>
> So, you will have no need to look for me, as you say in your letter. I intend to continue my normal life, which, unfortunately for me, will make it all too easy for you to find me.
>
> Allow me to say goodbye to you without hatred or rancour, in the hope that one day you will be part of an authentic people and that you will reveal your faces without fear.
>
> Despite my anguish, I still have faith in the future of the Basque people. I will continue to put stone upon stone in our shared foundation as long as I have my life, and if you take it away from me, may God forgive you.

Alcorta's bravery competed with news of the death of Alfred Hitchcock in the following day's newspaper headlines. An editorial in *La Vanguardia* declared that, 'The personal bravery of a Basque man, Don Juan Alcorta Maiz, restored much of the confidence lost along a dark path of crimes, cowardice, and surrender that has plagued the Basque Country.

'A strong and courageous voice has risen,' the column continued. 'The voice of a man who refuses to give up his humanity, of a Basque who resists the slow descent of his people into disaster, of a Spaniard who, without seeking to, has given his fellow citizens a lesson in civic heroism. This is the heroism that, out of moral integrity and dignity, is willing to sacrifice everything rather than turn life into a shameful and constant submission.'

Support poured in. A joint statement of solidarity signed by 248 people, 'all with Basque surnames and verifiably identified' was published in *El Diario Vasco*. The San Sebastián town council passed a motion pledging complete support to Alcorta and any others faced with extortion.

The president of the Basque government, Carlos Garaikoetxea, called Alcorta's stance 'consistent and coherent' and one he hoped would be 'contagious and serve as encouragement for those facing such difficult situations'.

Newspapers' letters pages teemed with support, and Alcorta personally reported receiving hundreds of letters from fellow Basques moved by the stand he'd taken.

True to his word, five days after announcing his intentions, Alcorta was at Atotxa applauding *la Real*. Sporting his trademark *txapela* and mackintosh jacket, he was pictured at the game in the company of the Basque parliament's leader of the Spanish Socialist Workers' Party (PSOE), Txiki Benegas. Perhaps another rejection of the bourgeoisie label that had so irritated Alcorta.

There was much to cheer too, as Real Sociedad eased to a 3-1 win over Malaga which put them top of the table, a point ahead of Real Madrid, with just two matches remaining. The team were undefeated and had conceded a miserly 18 goals in 32 games, and holding the head-to-head tiebreaker over Madrid, travelled to Seville knowing even a draw would keep destiny in their own hands in the final game of the season at home to a dysfunctional Atlético Madrid side.

But *la Real* faltered disastrously in Andalusia, losing 2-1 to a Sevilla team that played for half an hour with nine men. The defeat handed the league on a plate to Real Madrid, who duly took care of formalities to clinch the title in a drama-free final week.

It was a shattering blow – one still dwelt upon, but just like Juan Alcorta, this superb *la Real* side refused to go away. In the following 1980/81 season, they were again contenders, but once more, it looked like the title had eluded them. Only needing a draw away to Sporting in the season's final game, they let an early lead slip. When all seemed lost, Jesús María Zamora bludgeoned an 89th-minute equaliser through the pouring Gijón rain to the rapture of travelling fans and eruptions from bars all around San Sebastián's Old Town listening in on the radio.

The following season, they retained their title, and Spain leaned heavily on a talented generation at that summer's World Cup, as the hosts began the competition with five Real Sociedad players in the starting line-up. Zamora was joined by Periko Alonso, Jesús María Satrústegui and Roberto López Ufarte in a side captained by Luis Arconada.

Though the club supplied half the team, the city of San Sebastián had missed out on the tournament. With Atotxa not meeting FIFA requirements, president Orbegozo and his board planned to build a new stadium on land at Zubieta on the outskirts of town. But deep divisions within the city council regarding a municipal loan of 125m pesetas saw the proposal voted down. Orbegozo stepped down as president in 1983 having helped create the best Real Sociedad side of all time but feeling he'd failed after being unable to deliver the club a new home.

* * *

Juan Alcorta retired in the summer of 1982. Announcing his retirement to the boards of his companies, he was adamant that the blackmail attempt had no bearing on his decision. 'I had already decided to retire when I turned 60,' he told reporters. 'Last year, I reached that age. ETA's threats did not influence my decision to step down from these positions, just as they were not going to force me to work for the rest of my life.'

YOU WILL SEE ME AT ATOTXA APPLAUDING LA REAL

Asked if he had any plans to leave the Basque Country for his own safety, he replied unequivocally, 'I have no intention of leaving Euskadi; I will continue living here for the rest of my life, enjoying my retirement after working for more than 40 years.'

Again, true to his word, he lived out his days in San Sebastián, applauding *la Real*, though the club never managed to match the glory of those two league title wins with a brilliant team that came within a single goal of reaching a European Cup final.

On 12 December 2004, Alcorta died at the age of 83. By a strange quirk of fate, on the night of his death, another talented incarnation of his beloved Real Sociedad were in Madrid to face a malfunctioning Real Madrid side. With the teams level at a goal apiece in the 88th minute, the game was suspended due to a bomb threat. The Basque separatist newspaper *Gara* had received a warning call from ETA, who had been active in the capital around that time. The stadium was quickly evacuated, with fans greeted by the surreal sight of players – still in full kit – waiting around in the streets surrounding the Santiago Bernabéu.

Bizarrely, *la Real* had to return to Madrid a month later to complete the remaining six minutes of the match. Madrid – now with a different manager in charge – found a winner from the penalty spot in a frenetic sprint finish.

Alcorta was finally at peace. ETA, sadly, were still causing chaos.

16.

The Night Barcelona Shook

IT WAS perhaps appropriate that Ronaldinho announced his arrival in Barcelona with a sway of the hips in the early hours of the morning.

Receiving the ball from a Victor Valdés throw-out midway inside his own half, two twists took him dancing away from the Sevilla midfield before he arrowed a shot, which arched over the goalkeeper and shook the crossbar. The ball crashed downwards, seemingly well over the line, but the roof of the net bulged exquisitely to remove any doubt. Camp Nou broke into rapture.

It was a moment that would prove to be seismic, figuratively and literally, shaking the city's foundations and stirring a club from years of torpor.

It was a goal that heralded a new beginning – a goal that was scored at 1.26am.

***

'It was fun. It was an experience, it was something special – but also a real challenge because we were dealing with something we'd never faced before – a match that ended at two in the morning, and by two o'clock *on the dot*, we had to have the paper finished.'

Journalist Edu Polo was on duty for *Mundo Deportivo* for what was one of the most significant and surreal games in FC Barcelona's recent history.

It was September 2003, and it was Barça's first home game of the season. The fresh breeze of Joan Laporta's presidency had brought an air of optimism to Camp Nou. Laporta and his cadre of sure-footed young professionals cut a striking contrast to the shambling disaster of his predecessor, Joan Gaspart.

Gaspart's final season had started with the unpopular managerial reappointment of Louis van Gaal and a Copa del Rey elimination to third-tier Novelda. He resigned the presidency in February, with Barça positioned alarmingly in both the league table and on the balance sheet – two points from relegation and many millions in debt.

Laporta, helped by the endorsement of Johan Cruyff, swept to power in the election held in June. He and his fresh-faced team promised to dedicate 'the best years of our lives' to a club in desperate need of renewal.

'It was very necessary and very positive,' says Polo. 'They'd had Núñez as president since 1978, and then he was replaced by Gaspart, who had been his number two. So, really, everything had stayed the same. It was the same old cycle.

'Laporta came in. He was 40 years old at the time. Sandro Rosell, his vice president, was also 40. Everyone around him was young. It was when society as a whole was changing when the internet era was arriving. This was 2003. There was no WhatsApp, no iPhone, none of that yet. All of that came in during those first few years. So, Barça modernised in parallel with society – unlike a lot of other clubs who were stuck with presidents from another era.

'In that sense, Laporta and Barça were pioneers in that change, in that modernisation – which was much needed and worked out very well for the club.'

For all that promise, the Laporta era began with the breaking of a key electoral pledge. Though not one that anyone had ever truly believed, nor one that ever drew recrimination. Precisely the opposite. Midway through their campaign, Laporta and Rosell announced they had agreed a deal to sign David Beckham. What's more, they had a letter from Manchester United and a PowerPoint presentation to prove it.

It was a transfer that never had a chance of happening. It was one thing to have an agreement with a club but quite another to have reached one with a player. By that point, Beckham's transfer to Real Madrid was so set in stone that the blaze of publicity to the contrary didn't ruffle a feather in Madrid. Nevertheless, the Laporta campaign had grabbed significant airtime and an aura of credibility – they could go to the grandest clubs and negotiate for the biggest names.

Three days after Laporta's landslide victory, Manchester United announced to the London Stock Exchange that Beckham would be transferring to Real Madrid. That was soon forgotten by fans and media alike a few weeks later with the signing of Ronaldinho from Paris Saint-Germain, a player who would transform the club.

A new coach, Frank Rijkaard, arrived too. Although not the board's first choice, the Dutchman personified the club's new direction, combining Cruyffian DNA with a cool, modern style.

As club shops morphed into megastores and fusty offices became airy, co-working spaces, the surging spirit of regeneration was captured in a fascinating documentary – *Barça Confidencial*.

'It was the first "fly-on-the-wall" type documentary made here,' remembers Polo. 'Before that, this kind of thing didn't exist. It was a big success because it let us see things that the public never had access to – signings, cameras inside cars, meetings... all of that was really, really interesting.

'On top of that, with Laporta the way he is, it gave us some memorable quotes. I remember one when they signed Edgar Davids in December – he was there with the board members, and he let out an angry shout, the kind he still does today, yelling, "We've done it!" and then shouted, "They never learn – let them learn!" That phrase became a meme and followed Laporta through all the comedy shows that imitated him.'

THE NIGHT BARCELONA SHOOK

A vibrant energy was coursing through the club, but almost quaintly, as the start of the 2003/04 season approached, the new board found themselves engaged in one of La Liga's most enduring traditions – bickering over kick-off times.

* * *

After the opening weekend, the league had scheduled a midweek round of games that butted awkwardly against the forthcoming international break. Barça's fixture on Wednesday, 3 September fell, problematically, within the window in which club sides had to surrender players to their respective national teams.

The club had been previously stung when a Copa del Rey semi-final, second leg clashed with an international window in April 2000. After an almighty row, captain Pep Guardiola led a team of just ten players on to the field to face Atlético Madrid before informing the referee that they would not be playing. Barcelona were fined and expelled from the following season's cup, although eventually received a presidential pardon from the Spanish Football Federation when Ángel María Villar won re-election.

Fearing being shorn of many of their squad on the new board's gala night at Camp Nou, Barcelona made the request to their opponents, Sevilla, for the game to be switched to the Tuesday night. Sevilla refused, pointing out that such a change would give their players less than the mandatory minimum of 48 hours of recovery time after their Sunday night fixture at home to Atlético.

Barça's suggestion that Sevilla bring that game forward to the Saturday night, thus creating a 72-hour respite, was rejected by the Sevilla president, José María Del Nido. He stated that Sevilla were contractually obliged by the television company *Sogecable* to play in the Sunday night slot. Rosell called *Sogecable*, only to be told that wasn't the case.

Ever the lawyer, Laporta found the solution that gave Barça the outcome they sought while abiding by the very letter of the law.

'We have an expression in Spain,' says Polo, *"Hecha la ley, hecha la trampa"* ("Every law has a loophole"). We have to play on Wednesday? Fine. We'll play on Wednesday – but at 12:05 am. Legally, that's Wednesday.'

Sevilla were furious. 'Barcelona's attitude is disgraceful,' thundered Del Nido. 'They've thrown a tantrum like a bunch of little boys. They think the whole world revolves around them. If the match is played at midnight, it will be to the detriment of the entire competition.' Yet he was powerless to stop it.

Barcelona players seemed much more amenable to the time. 'No problem at all,' said midfielder Luis Enrique. 'I'd rather play at midnight than midday if just for the temperature. It'll be a lot cooler for us.'

With the bizarre kick-off time confirmed, there was plenty of work to do. Scheduling a game to finish around 2am threatened to embarrassingly deplete the attendance. That fear heightened when the city of Barcelona announced it could not extend the metro service beyond midnight at such short notice. *Audiovisual Sport*, the TV rights holders, didn't care much for continuing their own service into the small hours either and pulled their live coverage. Without some inventive thinking, there was a real risk the board's audacity could backfire.

The answer was to turn the game and the circumstances into an event and convince fans that they were golden ticket holders to a unique footballing occasion rather than being obligated to attend a game at an ungodly hour. It worked.

'Normally, playing a match at midnight is unthinkable,' says Polo. 'There were lots of doubts. Then again, it was still early September, still summer, really. So, people first took it as an offence to Barça – what had been done to them. Then, the idea of playing at midnight seemed so clever that it caught on. Sure, some older club members couldn't go, but they lent their season tickets to someone else – to their kids, a cousin, a friend. The atmosphere ended up being incredible. It far surpassed anything we had expected in the days leading up to it, more than any of us could have imagined.'

Gates were opened at 9.15pm, and a local production company, *El Terrat*, was commissioned to direct the pre-match festivities. Their tongue-in-cheek show, 'Insomniac Football', incorporated live video link-ups with club legends such as Ronald Koeman, Hristo Stoichkov, and various Catalan celebrities.

A further masterstroke was the idea to supply the entire crowd with a 'picnic' as they entered the stadium. It was supposedly themed on their Andalusian opponents, but in truth, the menu was more a result of what companies could supply at low cost and at short notice. Nevertheless, it was a hit and provided the crowd with a perfect boost of blood sugar at the time of night bodies were usually flagging. The first item on the menu even lent the occasion its eventual nickname, '*El Partido del Gazpacho*' (The Gazpacho Game).

The playing staff, too, were adapting their dietary habits for the night. On the morning of the game, in *Mundo Deportivo*, club doctor Lluís Thil had detailed the day's meal plans, including dietary supplements 'such as caffeine – and always within the legal limits'.

In the offices of that same publication, plans were being finalised on how to get coverage of a game that would finish at 2am on newsstands just a few hours later.

'It was a challenge,' laughs Polo. 'Back then, we didn't have a website like now. Nowadays, you write the match report and quickly publish it online. But the paper was print-only, so typically, you had some time and a bit of margin to play with. Not that night. Our print deadline was midnight, so it could reach the presses and the kiosks. Of course, by midnight, the match wouldn't even have started yet.

'So yeah, it was like, "Wow, we've got to adapt, we need to talk to the printer, delay production, have everything ready, leave the minimum number of pages blank, and be as fast as possible." At the time – well, even now – I had a bit of a reputation for being one of the fastest at closing pages. That's why I went to the stadium – because I was one of the quick ones. I don't remember exactly what I had to cover – I really don't – but I do remember that I had to finish writing almost as the match was ending, to be able to get everything in for the morning paper.'

'We were a team of ten or 12 people, each one in charge of a page, and we had to rush. So it was like, "Hey, some of these pages can be done in advance" – like the atmosphere in the stands. That kind of thing you can work on during the match, but of course, you don't know what's going to happen. You can't imagine that Ronaldinho's first goal will come the way it did.'

As kick-off approached, one of Laporta's smart, young marketing executives, Esteve Calzada, detailed the measures the club had taken to entice supporters to the game. With everything that had been put in place, he estimated an attendance of somewhere between 50,000 and 70,000.

As Tuesday ticked over to Wednesday, Calzada was proven wrong – there were 80,237 in Camp Nou.

* * *

Looking back, the team sheets of that night make for interesting reading. Both sides were at the very genesis of what would become golden eras. Although not everyone on the field would share in the success that followed, there are comedies, tragedies and curiosities everywhere you look.

Laporta's manoeuvring hadn't been enough to save Barça's five-strong Dutch contingent. Despite last-minute negotiations, the Dutch federation had been steadfast that the players reported for camp on Tuesday night. That left them shorn of Michael Reiziger and Giovanni van Bronckhorst in defence, Phillip Cocu's steady presence in midfield and the dynamism of Marc Overmars and Patrick Kluivert in attack.

Likewise, Javier Saviola returned to Buenos Aires to prepare for Argentina's game against Chile, leaving Barça very much stretched and reliant on youth players to fill out the squad.

Although the Turkish superstar Rüstü Reçber had recently arrived, 21-year-old Victor Valdés continued in goal, having taken over the position the previous season.

Carles Puyol was a rugged and established presence at right-back. The centre-back pairing of Rafa Márquez and Patrik Andersson was unique, as they never started a game together before or again. Márquez, making his debut, was on his way in, while Andersson was very much on the way out after an underwhelming couple of seasons.

Xavi was already a fixture in midfield, where he was partnered by Gerard López, whose dazzling form with Valencia had brought him to Barcelona but he was beginning to struggle with injuries.

Making a Camp Nou debut was the epitome of the flashy winger Ricardo Quaresma – a one-man mission to change the world's beliefs about how a football should be kicked. His performance on the night 'combined high-level technique with moments of surprising clumsiness', according to *Mundo Deportivo*. Quaresma would go on to score just one goal in Barça colours before falling out with Rijkaard and returning to Portugal.

Fellow newcomer Ronaldinho was faring much better, and Luis Enrique, entering his final season, brought an element of experience and fight.

With the absences at centre-forward, there was an opportunity for the 'pearl of the B team', Sergio García. 'A brilliant start for a youngster who promises so much. Quick and with an eye for goal – last night he just lacked a bit of luck,' gushed *Mundo Deportivo*. Sadly, García would never score for Barça, but he moved on to play for an excellent Zaragoza side and became part of the furniture at Espanyol. He would be a member of Spain's Euro 2008 winning squad too.

From the bench, another youth teamer was transitioning to the senior ranks. A 19-year-old Andrés Iniesta earned some token minutes as the hour hand approached two.

For their part, Sevilla were bedding in a young Daniel Alves at right-back. In the heart of the defence, the side was led by the notorious Pablo Alfaro and his heir apparent, the equally uncompromising Javi Navarro, who would go on to lift two UEFA Cups as captain as the club began their remarkable domination of the competition.

Further forward, a formidably sized defensive midfielder was being inventively repurposed as an attacker. Julio Baptista had scored just ten goals in four seasons with his native São Paulo, yet Sevilla coach Joaquín Caparrós had seen something that led him to experiment with him in a more attacking role. Baptista ended his first season in Spain as La Liga's second-top scorer with 20 goals.

Completing the Sevilla forward line were two free spirits of the game. Europe's top clubs were keenly eyeing José Antonio Reyes, already with over 60 first-team appearances. This game arrived between his 20th birthday and his first full cap for Spain. The peroxide-blond Uruguayan, Darío Silva, lined up alongside him. Shockingly, despite their talent and verve, both would ultimately be remembered for the car crashes that cost Silva his leg and Reyes his life.

The two combined for the opening goal. Silva was brought down by Valdés, with Reyes converting from the penalty spot after only ten minutes. That set up a full-blooded game in which Reyes was superb. Tempers flared on several occasions – not least with the spectacular sight of an enraged Luis Enrique taking on both Alfaro and Navarro after a tangle in the Sevilla penalty area.

Barça were groggy and struggled for fluency. 'The strangest thing wasn't the kick-off time,' began *Mundo Deportivo*'s match report, 'but seeing Barça without any Dutch players. It was more than just an improvised team – it was stripped of its essence, almost unrecognisable from the start.'

Just when it seemed the night's novelty was giving way to a much more familiar frustration, Ronaldinho intervened.

While Polo holds no recollection of what he frantically typed in the 34 minutes between Ronaldinho's reverberant leveller and the deferred print deadline, page six of the edition that hit the city's *quioscos* hours later bears testimony to the work he did on his night shift.

'Ronaldinho was signed to be the leader of this new Barça,' wrote Polo, 'and he carried the team on his back last night and tried everything to turn the game around.

'The number ten didn't just show off his technique – he brought out his passion and character. He clashed with half the Sevilla team and tracked back to defend in his own area whenever he lost the ball or was dispossessed, often due to fouls that referee Megía Dávila ignored.

'After suffering multiple fouls – some of which weren't even called – Megía showed him a yellow card for his first foul. Little by little, his frustration grew, and with it came more dribbles, changes of pace, and spectacular touches.

'Just for the move that led to the equaliser, it was worth playing at midnight – and worth more than 80,000 fans staying up late to attend a football match. He left two Sevilla defenders behind with a change of pace and a feint, then unleashed a powerful shot from 22 metres out that flew into the tiny gap between the crossbar and Notario's hands.

'The crowd erupted for the stunning goal by their new idol, and white handkerchiefs waved in the stands of Camp Nou. The fans bowed to Ronaldinho, while those in the *palco* held their heads in disbelief. No one could quite believe the goal he had just scored.'

There were handshakes between the two boards as the game ended 1-1. The pre-match war of words seemingly forgotten, 'We received exquisite treatment from the Barça board,' Del Nido told the press. 'The skill of both presidents ensured that the issue of the match time wasn't brought up.' He was though at pains to state that the return fixture, 'Will be played at a more orthodox and traditional football time.'

With copy filed, Polo's night still wasn't done. He rushed off to attend Rijkaard's post-match press conference, where there was agreement between all concerned that questions should be kept to a minimum, although not everybody seemed to get the message.

'I finished my page as fast as I could and ran to Rijkaard's press conference. That night we all said, "Look, the radio's live, sure, but…" Nothing from the post-match made it into the paper, it was saved for the next day. I remember us all saying, "Look, it's 2:30am, three questions, and we're out. No need for any more."

'Then I remember a colleague from a Catalan radio station who raised his hand just when we all thought it was over. "Frank, one more question. Now that you've been in Barcelona for two months, getting to know the city, the food, the culture… what has surprised you the most?" Even Rijkaard himself calmly said, "Look, if you want, you can ask me this on Friday."

'I clearly remember all the journalists going, "Come on, Jordi, man… what kind of question is that at 2.30 in the morning? Seriously, let's go home."'

With that – players, fans, staff and press disappeared into the Barcelona night.

***

If there were some bleary eyes at schools, offices and factories the next day, those sluggishly slogging through their Wednesday could at least console themselves with having witnessed Ronaldinho's first Barcelona goal. It was a moment that came to symbolise a new Barcelona that would go on to unprecedented domestic and European success. Though, as ever, there's an element of revisionism at play.

Barça toiled for long parts of that first season. A defeat at home to league leaders Real Madrid in December saw them slump to 13th. Humiliating defeats in Málaga and Santander left Rijkaard's future on a knife-edge.

'That team struggled,' says Polo. 'They really struggled. It didn't start to come together until December when Davids arrived, and Rijkaard changed the system. It took a lot of time. So, on the one hand, there was a lot of excitement – Ronaldinho, Rijkaard, everything that was happening – but on the other, it was tough going. Football-wise, there were a lot of doubts.'

The rookie board held their nerve and were rewarded with a 17-game unbeaten run, including a cathartic win at the Santiago Bernabéu. Barça finished second to Rafa Benítez's Valencia, while Madrid endured a miserable second half of the season as the *galáctico* project began to fray.

The foundation had been laid for the titles that followed. The disastrous recruitment of the previous regime was gradually unpicked with the arrival of the likes of Samuel Eto'o and Deco. La Masia was bearing fruit, too, with the emergence of Iniesta. Meanwhile, a diminutive Argentine was making eye-catching progress with 31 goals in 21 games for the *Juvenil A* team.

Looking back, that one night and one moment that would go down as marking a new chapter. 'It's one of the most remembered nights,' says Polo. 'The match itself, a 1-1 draw with Sevilla, is nothing special, but it has that element the first goal by Ronaldinho – which means it's always remembered.

'Then there's the brilliance of that "gazpacho game" after midnight. It's something people will always recall. I told my 12-year-old son about it once, and he didn't believe me, but when I explained it, he thought it was hilarious. People remember it, and it has a place in Barça's history that it definitely wouldn't have had any other way.'

Ronaldinho's intoxicating dance through the night air shook an arena that has struggled to recreate an atmosphere quite like that ever since.

It shook a city too. Literally.

'Two days later, a really good study came out about the noise levels in Barcelona,' says Polo. 'Of course, Barça had never played that late before; the city is usually asleep at that hour. Then, you had a goal, not just any goal, but one like that, and quite late in the game. The roar from Camp Nou – more than 80,000 fans at that hour of the morning – registered with the monitoring machines. It was an impact the city never experienced before at that time of night. It was like a small earthquake.'

In the hills surrounding the city, some 4.5km north of the stadium, stands the Observatori Fabra. On the night shift, at precisely 1.26am and 28 seconds, the seismometer recorded just over a minute of tremor in the city. The epicentre had been Camp Nou.

Thanks to the arrival of Ronaldinho, Barcelona would become the epicentre of world football for some years to come.

La Grada

The Fans

17.

The Derby Like No Other

HE JUST smiled.

His team were 3-0 down to their greatest rivals, and all around him, the stadium bounced. Backs turned to the pitch, arms slung across shoulders, blue and white shirts of various vintages heaved joyfully up and down, side to side.

He stood among them, arms folded – a lone figure in red and white, revealed as the home fans briefly parted. He looked left, then right, calmly taking in the mayhem. Then he looked straight ahead – and just smiled.

The moment zipped across timelines around the world – instantly relatable, a perfect antidote to football's usual fractious animosity. And it was a very 21st-century snapshot of one of football's grandest rivalries, fiercely contested on the field for over a century but free from rancour beyond it.

There's no flak jacket or riot shield required when a matchday crowd packs San Sebastián's Old Town or drifts slowly north along Bilbao's Pozas, mingling in bars and restaurants ahead of a derby that really is like no other. Where fans sit together, display their colours and ride the highs and lows of the game without fear or hostility.

It's an occasion underpinned by a shared culture and identity – where the revelry buzzes with something more profound. And where, even when your team is being played off the park, sometimes – like Jon Azanza – you just have to smile.

THE DERBY LIKE NO OTHER

* * *

'Honestly – I didn't see the cameraman at first,' says Azanza, whose image flashed across the globe. 'I was just watching everyone jumping around, and suddenly I looked forward and saw the camera guy standing there, pointing the camera right at me. And when I looked at him, he smiled – because, of course, he could see what he was recording on his screen. So I started laughing when I saw him, and that's exactly the moment he caught me on camera. One for the memories.'

It was the first Basque Derby of the 2023/24 season, and Azanza's team, Athletic Club, had travelled to Guipúzcoa to play Real Sociedad. A friend who supported *la Real* offered Azanza a spare ticket in the most vocal and boisterous section of the home end – the Grada Aitor Zabaleta.

Despite being an away fan in the home end at one of Spain's biggest derbies, Azanza had no hesitation in digging his 2014/15 Athletic shirt out of the wardrobe and heading along. He'd never been to Anoeta before and was keen to see it. He took a stroll around outside before kick-off as he waited to meet a friend, taking it all in.

'You could feel it,' remembers Azanza, 'people getting ready for the match because it's always special. And in San Sebastián, for Real Sociedad fans, it's a big day. Where the hardcore fans usually gather near the ground, there were flares, lots of excitement, lots of celebration. I went to grab a drink somewhere quieter.'

Eventually, Azanza headed to the stadium. 'It was packed, but, when I got in, people were acting totally normal. Someone else was wearing an Athletic jersey, but it was just like walking into a shop – very calm. I'm not going to lie, the atmosphere got louder when *la Real* scored their goals.'

Athletic created chances on the night, but their hosts were more clinical, Robin Le Normand thrashing them ahead after half an hour, with Takefusa Kubo doubling the lead just minutes into the second half. The buzzes from Azanza's pocket hinted that the cameraman stationed in front of the stand had already taken an interest in him.

'Friends were messaging me, "Hey Jon, we saw you during the first goal," and "You popped up again during the second," and "Jon, there you are again!" And after the third goal, they were like, "Jon, you're a machine! We don't know what you're doing, but you've made our day!"'

That third goal came on 67 minutes when Real Sociedad's captain, Mikel Oyarzabal, went through on goal and easily rounded Unai Simón to put the game beyond any doubt. When the immediate celebrations died down, the home fans went to their favourite mode of marking a goal.

'They turned their backs and started doing the "Poznan". And I was like, "Well, I'm OK. If we come back, great. If not, oh well."'

As the entire stand bounced, Azanza just stood there. There was no hostility towards him. Indeed, the blue-and-white-sleeved arm of his friend clung onto him for balance as she celebrated. Then the cameraman caught those few seconds that went viral – quickly clipped up and shared by television companies and fan accounts across every social media platform.

'I soon knew a lot of people had seen it because I started getting WhatsApp messages. A friend sent me a Twitter link, but I didn't realise it had blown up until the next day, when people kept sending me stuff – Twitter, Instagram, all kinds of media. I thought, "Wow! What has happened?"'

The next day, a routine Sunday, started normally, but it didn't take too long for eager media researchers to identify the man in the Athletic shirt.

'I slept just like any other day,' says Azanza. 'Then I went with my mother to visit my uncles, and while we were having a drink at a bar, I started getting messages on Instagram. One said, "Hi Jon, I create content on social media, and I'd love to meet you this afternoon. Would it be possible to shoot a short video?" I didn't reply – I was like, "What is this? What's going on?"'

'A friend then messaged me, "Hey Jon, my colleagues at *Gol TV* would like to do a live interview with you tonight." Then I started getting more messages on Instagram, Twitter, and LinkedIn, and people adding me.'

'There came a moment when I thought, "You know what? I'm going to say yes to everyone – to anyone who wants to interview or talk to me – because I don't want to make it an exclusive for just one outlet." After all, this is about spreading a message, and the derby is like – well, it's not exactly a friendly match, but it can be seen in that spirit. And that's when I realised, "This is going to make a mark."'

Those first few days were a whirlwind. 'Between Sunday night and Wednesday – so in three days – I did about 30 interviews.'

'*Gol TV* was the first. I think it was 9pm or 10pm [on Sunday night], and it was enjoyable. It didn't feel strange even though it was live because I couldn't see the whole audience. So, it felt more just like a one-on-one conversation. I felt very comfortable and thought, "Hey, maybe something good can come out of this."'

Despite never having been interviewed for anything before, Azanza cut a relaxed and likeable figure – almost like the sort of guy who can still find joy even when his team are 3-0 down.

'Since the situation was so unexpected, I didn't really know how to react, but I didn't get nervous. I thought, "Why would I be nervous? This has never happened to me before." I did get a bit overwhelmed trying to respond to everyone – some people I just couldn't get back to because I'm only human, but it all felt quite natural, and I actually learnt a bit from the experience.'

At the time, Azanza was studying for his master's degree in engineering, juggling academic demands with sudden media attention.

'I was in class, and there were moments when I would step out to take calls and answer questions. Sometimes, I'd even leave the building entirely because a journalist would come by to do an interview. They'd show up to take photos and talk to me. It was pretty extraordinary.'

Those who dug a little deeper into his story found a surprising musical footnote. Azanza was a bandmate of Athletic forward Asier Villalibre. The two played together in Sakatu, an electric version of a traditional Basque marching band or '*txaranga*'. Villalibre was, of course, on trumpet – the same one he famously played after Athletic's 2021 Super Cup win – while Azanza played the *trikitixa*, a miniature Basque accordion.

'It's a music group that could play on a stage,' Azanza explains, 'but the stage is actually the street. It's made up of musicians, and a cart carries the sound equipment – the speakers, the mixing desk. During festivals, if there's a two-hour concert, the group moves along a route, stopping at different points to play songs. There's no division between the stage and the audience – it's all mixed together. So you're playing, and maybe someone from the crowd comes up and hugs you while you're still playing. It's more… immersive, I'd say.'

Azanza's stoic smile had been shared across the world, becoming a very modern symbol of one of Spain's most traditional rivalries.

* * *

Athletic and Real Sociedad have been playing each other since 1909 and can lay claim to being La Liga's oldest derby. The two sides drew 1-1 on the opening day of the inaugural *Primera* season in February 1929. But while most derbies around the world have become increasingly fierce and bitter, the Basque Derby has taken a different path. History and politics have drawn the two fanbases closer, even during times when relations at institutional level have been strained.

That very first meeting took place in the quarter-final of the Copa del Rey with Real Sociedad competing as 'Club Ciclista' taking a 4-2 win in a game noted by *ABC* for its physicality. 'The players' intensity yesterday was a bit excessive; there were frequent collisions, and several of them fell to the ground unconscious, although they were able to come to thanks to the care they received immediately.

'One would hope that in the remaining matches, these regrettable incidents – so justifiably condemned by spectators yesterday – are not repeated.'

Two decades later, in that first-ever league meeting, played at *la Real*'s old Atotxa stadium, the same publication noted 'the Bilbao side receiving an excellent welcome from an impeccably behaved crowd'. That despite observing the home side had been 'notably disadvantaged' by the referee.

After the bombing of Guernica during the Spanish Civil War – a city situated between Bilbao and San Sebastián – Spain plunged into the dark decades of Franco's regime. The rivalry continued, but the repression of Basque language and culture shaped a dynamic where there was far more that united the two clubs than divided them.

It was perhaps telling that the regime-friendly *ABC* failed to mention one of the most impactful moments in the clubs' shared history in its match report of their league fixture at Atotxa in December 1976. The country was a year removed from Franco's death, but reform had been slow, and a ban was still in place on the Basque flag, the '*ikurriña*'.

The two squads had already agreed to pay tribute to Real Sociedad midfielder Gaztelu, who was celebrating ten years with the club, when the idea of a more symbolic gesture took shape. It was *la Real*'s José Antonio de la Hoz Uranga who arranged for an *ikurriña* sewn together by his sister to be smuggled into the stadium. With unanimous support from both teams, captains Inaxio Kortabarria and José Ángel Iribar led the players out, proudly holding the flag between them in front of a packed, already buoyant crowd. In the now-iconic photograph of the scene, the non-playing Uranga is just visible – identified only by his flared jeans as he supports the flag at its centre.

'That is the moment,' says Athletic fan and radio journalist Beñat Gutiérrez, 'when we talk about how this rivalry has an element of shared background or identity. That's the moment that explains it best.

'Real Sociedad fans, Athletic fans, Real Sociedad players, and Athletic players share the fact that they chose not only to display their identity together but also to take a risk together – because what they did was risky. At the time, it wasn't legal. Their act was a form of pressure for the legalisation of Basque symbols, like the Basque flag.

'When you look at that generation of players, you can see that some later went on to have political careers or at least moments in their lives where they clearly expressed their political beliefs. What happened then was very special – unprecedented, even. I don't think we'll ever witness something of such political significance again.

'Iribar and Kortabarria were the faces of that moment, but many other players took part as well. Some even had to sneak the *ikurriña* into the dressing room in the first place. That was a powerful gesture.

'If you define the rivalry only by signing each other's players or by the fight to win a trophy, you're missing part of the picture. You also need to understand how both clubs have represented a shared Basque identity – one that, in many ways, has been suppressed or targeted. That common struggle has forged a sense of unity among many fans on both sides.'

Guardia Civil officers on duty at the game chose not to intervene, and the game played out in a festival atmosphere, lifted further by a 5-0 home win. Just over a month later, the *ikurriña* was officially legalised. The version sewn by Uranga's sister was preserved and framed by the club and was proudly displayed at a derby 34 years later – played on the anniversary of that day in 1976 when a politically conscious group of players made a brave and historic gesture.

Athletic's captain that day, José Ángel Iribar, has since become a towering figure in the club's history. A statue of him now stands outside the new San Mamés, and at 82, he still accompanies the team on their European travels.

'Right now,' says Gutiérrez, 'he represents all the values Athletic Club wants to transmit to the world. He's the ideal example – a man who's been free from scandal or controversy throughout his career.

'Outside the Basque Country, some people might criticise him for having briefly been a member of the national board of a left-wing party – at the time, associated with Batasuna [a party with links to ETA]. That's something people often see as controversial in the rest of Spain, but inside the Basque Country, Iribar is largely free of controversy.

'He represents many positive values – he's calm, well-spoken, and highly respected. He also serves as a living link to one of Athletic Club's most glorious eras. He's also been deeply involved in the club's public relations for years – attending events, engaging with supporters' groups and more. At this point, he *is* Athletic.

'And there's another interesting aspect – he's from Guipúzcoa. That reinforces the idea that Athletic represents all of the Basque Country – not just Vizcaya. The club and its fans often highlight that. Some people, especially in Guipúzcoa, might not agree, and I understand their frustration.'

Gutiérrez's final point hints that while these two clubs share history, identity and one of football's healthiest rivalries, there are still some things they can disagree agreeably upon.

* * *

'Unique in the world.'

It's a phrase Athletic Club often uses to describe itself – an expression of pride in its history and, above all, its *Cantera* recruitment policy. Since 1912, the club has chosen to field only players native to the Basque Country, a philosophy that now extends to players that have received their footballing education in the region.

Curiously, the concept began as a reaction to an attempt by Real Sociedad to have their neighbours thrown out of the 1911 Copa del Rey for fielding two Englishmen who *la Real* alleged had not been resident in Spain for the mandatory six months before a preliminary round tie against Fortuna Vigo.

Real Sociedad withdrew in protest, while Athletic went on to win the tournament before adopting their now-famous strategy in an attempt to quell further dissent. More than a century later, that globally admired policy has not only endured but flourished. It has helped Athletic remain in La Liga since its inception and fill a trophy cabinet that includes eight league titles and more than 20 Copa del Rey victories.

For many years, their great rivals Real Sociedad followed a similar path – until 1989, when Liverpool striker John Aldridge became the first foreign player signed by the club. The policy was relaxed further in 2002 when Sergio Boris became the first Spaniard from outside the Basque Country to join the team in over 30 years. Even so, *la Real*'s academy at Zubieta continues to rival Athletic's Lezama in producing high-quality footballers from the region.

Yet it's Athletic's focus on youth that draws coos of admiration and occasionally rubs Real Sociedad fans up the wrong way, as lifelong *realista* and avowed Basque nationalist Unai Lamariano Larrea explains.

'I'm going to be clear here that I want Athletic to win, both in La Liga and European competition, but I will say that their philosophy is a bit of a cheat. Because with Athletic... well, like someone whose father was in Bilbao for one day as a tourist and their kid was born in a hotel there – apparently that means they're eligible. So, there's a lot of joking around about that philosophy. I'm on board with the philosophy – that Athletic only wants to play with Basques – but I don't think it's completely true. Maybe it's 70 per cent true, but the other 30 per cent, it's like someone's dad just happened to pass through the area.'

With two clubs so intensely focused on developing homegrown talent, inevitably there have been tensions when one sees the other as fishing in their waters. Relations were most notably strained in the summer of 1995 when Athletic flexed their financial muscle to lure *la Real*'s gifted 17-year-old forward, Joseba Etxeberria, to Bilbao. The move enraged the Real Sociedad board to the extent that they broke off institutional ties and inserted specific 'anti-Athletic' buy-out clauses into player contracts.

Further spats followed, such as in 2005 when Athletic moved for right-back Iban Zubiaurre, and an ugly dispute ensued. 'Real Sociedad claimed that he still had a valid contract with them,' Gutiérrez explains, 'including a clause that extended it for another year. It turned into a legal mess, and the player spent a long time unable to play because he was with Athletic but not registered in the league. It basically ruined his career. Now he's a car mechanic.'

Gutiérrez notes that recent boards have proved adept at avoiding disputes or resolving them quickly and amicably. Iñigo Martínez's 2018 mid-season move to Athletic briefly threatened to reignite tensions. Even then, any unease in the boardroom didn't translate to animosity among fans who instead trade good-natured jokes, some – as in any rivalry worth its salt – based on some well-worn stereotypes.

'In San Sebastián, they have the beaches, beautiful buildings, and the people there are seen as very elegant,' says Gutiérrez. 'Just look at Xabi Alonso or Xabi Prieto – those guys could be considered the most handsome men in the Basque Country!

'On the other side, in Guipúzcoa, the stereotype about people from Bilbao, or Vizcaya in general, is that we are incredibly arrogant. That we exaggerate all our achievements, act like we're always doing more than we really are and try to make everything seem massive and important.'

Lamariano concurs – and provides some colourful examples, 'A guy from Bilbao always has to be "a big shot".

If he's had sex once, he'll say he's had sex eight times. If he owns one house, he'll claim he owns 20. If he's had one glass of wine, he'll say he's had 30. That's the stereotype of someone from Bilbao. The people from San Sebastián are seen as more posh, more refined, and more moneyed. I think those are the two classic caricatures.'

'There are some underlying political dynamics,' says Gutiérrez. 'Bilbao has often been seen as the main city of the Basque Country, even though it's not the official capital [Vitoria]. Some people in Guipúzcoa perceive Bilbao as being privileged by the Basque government. Bilbao is also the headquarters of the Basque Nationalist Party, which has been the dominant political force historically. So all of that comes into play, especially when games get intense.'

And they do get intense. Despite the off-field bonhomie, the game itself is never an easy assignment for a referee. 'The players get along very well with each other, but Basque football has always been very physical, very intense, very much about going in hard. There's a kind of sportsmanship, there's no dirty play, but they go all out,' says Lamariano.

* * *

While encounters between Athletic Club and Real Sociedad continue to go against the grain as a derby and an occasion, Lamariano holds some concerns that it might not always be that way, 'My son is a Real Sociedad *socio* – he's 23 years old. He doesn't experience the derby the same way as I do. I want Athletic to win because they carry the *ikurriña*. They stand for a Basque nation, a Basque state, but I notice that our kids are increasingly anti-Athletic.

'When I was young, there was a much more intense political conflict than now. Basque teams playing away in the Spanish league always got a poor reception. There was more solidarity back then. Our children don't experience it like we did. So, I think the nature of the derby is starting to change a bit.'

'Those of us who hope it stays the same are united by these things, but there are people who are starting to see Athletic as the enemy. My son is fiercely pro-independence, but when it comes to Athletic, I do nothing but argue with him. So I can see that a new generation is coming that perhaps doesn't understand that photo of Iribar and Kortabarria with the *ikurriña* and that fight, that struggle.'

For now, the game remains special and an occasion where you're more likely to witness poetry than a punch-up, as Gutiérrez explains.

'You have events that go beyond football. One really interesting collaboration during the derby has been something called *bertsolaritza*, which is a traditional form of improvised Basque poetry. The *bertsolaris* are given a topic and must compose something on the spot, following strict metric rules. Recently, they've brought in *bertsolaris* to support each team and had them perform a kind of competition. It's a really cool way to highlight how culture plays into the game.

'There's also this tradition where fans of both clubs walk to the match together in what's called a *kalejira* – a kind of parade. On a more informal level, it's also common to see fans from both sides mixing because, at the end of the day, the Basque Country is small – there are people from Guipúzcoa working in Bilbao and vice-versa. Families and friends are often split between the two teams.

'So you'll see groups of young people where most are Real Sociedad fans, but there's one guy in an Athletic jersey – and the same the other way around. What's funny is that the one person wearing the rival shirt is usually the most invested in the match. They're the one who *needs* to win.'

One of Spain's grandest rivalries continues to defy the typical derby-day impulse toward spite and acrimony. There remains a distinct joy to the occasion – something rooted in a deeper sense of connection. Even if you're that one fan in a different shirt, and the match couldn't be going any worse, as Jon Azanza showed – there's always a reason to just smile.

18.

They Tell Me Yellow is Cursed

A GROUP of mafiosos bursts onto the stage of a packed theatre, lower and aim their guns – '*Ra-ta-ta-ta-ta, ra-ta-ta-ta-ta.*'

The audience collapses in heaps of laughter and whoops of '*Olé*'. When the act reaches its crescendo, the crowd applauds wildly, swept away by the sentiment of the song – the defiant joy of the underdog, expressed, as ever, with a dash of *Gaditano* humour.

The judges are less enthused. As *La Familia Pepperoni*, a troupe of 1920s gangsters – all striped suits, fedoras, and spats – exits stage left, the jury hands down an underwhelming score. For some of them, it's no surprise. They were never sold on the tune to begin with.

But the song would take on a life of its own, echoing around the city's streets, squares, and the terraces of a football club trapped in the purgatory of *Segunda B*. An irresistible momentum built, and when mobsters became monks, and the group returned to the same stage two years later, it was the audience that sang to them – in glorious *a capella* – imploring one more rendition.

Me han dicho que el amarillo	*They tell me that yellow*
Está maldito pa' los artistas	*Is cursed for los artistas*
Y este color, sin embargo	*Yet, this colour*
Es gloria bendita para los cadistas	*Is blessed glory for los cadistas*

THEY TELL ME YELLOW IS CURSED

Soon, it would be adopted by the club and the fans it paid homage to, usurping the staid official anthem as the *himno* that welcomed the players of Cádiz onto the field each fortnight as they belatedly climbed up the leagues – only to tumble back down again.

It was a song that blended three essential elements of this irreverent city – community, club, and carnival – and the work of one of Cádiz's most beloved characters, Manolo Santander.

* * *

In a country where it sometimes seems no one can ever agree on anything, there's something all Spaniards subscribe to – Cádiz is different.

'I think it has a lot to do with the fact that, in a way, we are an island,' says Pedro M. Espinosa, a chief editor at *Diario de Cádiz*. 'We are connected to the European continent by a tiny strip of land 80 or 90 metres wide, and the city is entirely insular. I think this shapes people's outlook on life, leading them to adopt a certain philosophy – instead of taking things very seriously, they take things with a laugh. There are very funny people here with incredibly quick and sharp wit. There's even a language barrier – sometimes even Spaniards struggle to understand us. For someone who speaks Spanish, it can still be difficult to catch the nuances of a carnival act or local slang.

'I can't really give a scientific explanation. It's something passed down from father to son. I'd say it has a lot to do with the mix of flamenco, carnival, the sea, the sun. Here, we're not used to many days of rain, so when it suddenly rains for five days straight in Cádiz, you walk down the street, and everyone's in a terrible mood just because of the weather. Right now, it's early February, and I was sitting at a bar on the beach yesterday wearing just a t-shirt.'

Espinosa's colleague, carnival historian and lyricist José Manuel Sánchez Reyes, notes a historical context, 'Cádiz is a city that's been really battered. By politics, by the passage of time, by history. Cádiz only experienced wealth during two centuries when it was a key city in American trade – we're talking about the 17th and 18th centuries. After that, it's been hit hard, always struggling with high unemployment. Its geographical position also limits its opportunities for growth, in terms of industry and land, as we're like a little island.

'I'm like many *Gaditanos*, very sceptical because we've seen so many things come and go, so many promises. It's a city that just never quite takes off, but we have one virtue – we take things differently. That's how we survive. We sing, we laugh, we take life with humour, because otherwise, we'd have... well, we'd have already thrown ourselves off the blocks, as we say around here – we'd have thrown ourselves into the sea.

'Carnival helps with that too – when February comes, we get to say all the things we don't like. It helps us get through life in this very peculiar city. We have a way of living that's unlike anywhere else. In Cádiz, you don't need to be a millionaire to be happy. That's the truth. Just a little job and your own little things. It's an ideal place to live in. That also affects the character of the people.

'Even in winter, the weather is good. So here, life really happens in the street. People talking, surrounded by beaches – it's unique. In other places, you have to get in the car and drive to the beach. Here, you step out, and you're on the beach. It's right there at the edge of the pavement. That's a blessing.'

Teeming with characters and a playful approach to life, naturally, the city's football club also reflects the nature of this idiosyncratic little peninsula. Cádiz Club de Fútbol has spent as many years in Spain's third-tier as it has in *Primera*, and almost half its history has been played out bobbing along in *Segunda*, but the reputation of its supporters has earned a place in the heart of Spain's footballing public.

Espinosa covered the team for years as a reporter and encapsulated the club and the fans beautifully in his book *Eso no estaba en mi libro del Cádiz CF* (*That wasn't in my book about Cádiz CF*). He uses a particular term to describe the mischievous sense of fun the city is famed for.

'There's a word used to define it: *guasa*.

'Cádiz is a team that's very *guasón* [full of *guasa*] and whose fans have a lot of *retranca* [dry, ironic wit]. They have a very jokey nature when it comes to watching matches or giving players nicknames. Football is lived here in a very unique way.

'For example, the famous chant *"¡Gol! ¡Gol! Hemos venido a emborracharnos. El resultado nos da igual"* ("Goal! Goal! We came to get drunk. We don't care about the result") was invented here. It became really well-known across stadiums all over Spain.'

The most famous antics of Cádiz supporters are well told. Mention their fans around Spain, and you'll likely hear the same anecdotes. But like any good yarn, there's a beauty in the retelling.

'One is from a dreadful season in *Segunda* when the team only won four matches, and fans stopped going to the stadium out of boredom.

'There's a famous scene of a group of fans following a linesman along the sideline, mimicking his every move. Groups of 20 or 30 people would form a line and mirror his run up and down the sideline of the stand, where the old Olympic tower used to be. That image became very popular in Spain. It was like a ticking time bomb – they followed the linesman as if their lives depended on it.

'If the linesman turned, they'd all do the same. It was surreal. In truth, it was a little pathetic for those of us who cared deeply about Cádiz because it showed how people had started to see the whole thing as a joke. The match would go on, but fans weren't really watching – they were just there for the laughs.

'There was a banner that became really famous, too: "*árbitro guapetón*" ("handsome referee") – which is still displayed in the stadium today. In other stadiums, the referees get all sorts of insults, but here he gets told how good-looking he is.'

One of the club's most famous and hilarious victories arrived in the form of a 3-1 defeat. When Real Madrid came to town in December 2015 for a Copa del Rey tie against a Cádiz side two divisions below them, a routine win looked on the cards when the seldom-used Denis Cheryshev opened the scoring after just three minutes.

'Then a rumour started spreading in the stadium,' says Espinosa, 'that Cheryshev was carrying a suspension from his time at Villarreal and shouldn't be playing. Things started to snowball. The commentators on the radio also mentioned it, and suddenly, from the south stand, the chant went up: "¡*Cheryshev no puede jugar!*" ("Cheryshev can't play!").

'Everyone was singing it. The mood in the stadium turned into a party, and the faces on the Real Madrid bench were priceless.'

As a bewildered Rafael Benítez and the Madrid delegation realised the gravity of their mistake, the Estadio Ramón de Carranza was in gales of laughter, rolling out songs like, 'Benítez check Twitter, Benítez, check Twitter' and 'Cheryshev, I love you'. Two more Madrid goals made no difference as Cádiz were handed an administrative 3-0 win, and Madrid disqualified from the competition.

The fans' countrywide fame is due in no small part to the work of Michael Robinson, who, despite having no connections, fell deeply in love with the club and the city.

'Robinson helped Cádiz a lot during a time when no one remembered us. He kept the club alive through his *El Día Después* programme. He always found a reason to feature Cádiz in some segment of the show. That's why they offered him the role of advisor on the board. He was wonderful. I had the chance to meet him, talk with him, and hear him telling stories with that thick accent of his.

'The way he'd talk about football, like the 1984 European Cup Final in Rome, was a true delight for those of us who love football and grew up in that beautiful, romantic era of the game. I've always been a fan of English football. I used to trade VHS tapes with an Italian friend of mine, and suddenly, I found myself chatting with Robinson!

'He used to say he was from Cádiz – that someone from Cádiz had been left behind from a wreck of the Spanish Armada, and he'd ended up with *Gaditano* blood. That was the only way to explain his profound love for the city. He came here every chance he got – he'd head out to the villages and have the time of his life. It was a joy to see him and listen to him.'

Those doldrum years of the mid-1990s and early 2000s were all the more painful for having followed the club's most glorious era. From 1981 to 1993, the club spent ten of 12 seasons in the top flight. Fittingly for the city and the fans, that sustained success was more a result of the sheer talent of a motley crew of renegades than polished professionalism.

There was a buccaneering right-back, Juan José, who was known as 'Sandokan' due to his similarities to a fictional pirate. Alongside him was the balding, moustachioed Carmelo Navarro, nicknamed the 'Beckenbauer of the Bay'. Supplying the goals was the chain-smoking centre-forward Pepe Mejías.

And then there was a tousle-haired attacking midfielder from El Salvador named Jorge Alberto González Barillas, more simply known as 'Mágico'.

No one holds a more revered place in the lore of the club than Mágico González. On the field, he was a sublime talent – a sashaying anthology of flicks, twists and dinks. He was once declared a finer talent than Diego Maradona by none other than… Diego Maradona, who also ranked him above Pelé for good measure. Off the field, Mágico's reputation for nightlife, female company and strumming his guitar on the beach when he should have been training only served to further beatify his status. Utter his name to 100 *Gaditanos*, and you'll likely be told 100 different tales in return.

Espinosa holds fond memories of that time covering the team for his newspaper, 'Back then, we were practically inside the dressing room. Press conferences with the Cádiz manager were held in a small office right next to the players' dressing room, and we would talk to them as they walked around in towels, singing, joking – it was all very relaxed.

'You'd run into figures like Mágico and even big-time talents like Kiko Narváez, who went on to become a Spain international, all the time. That kind of contact with players is unimaginable now.'

One particular vintage of the team even had a stab at becoming a carnival band. 'They actually performed in Seville, at the Lope de Vega Theatre, during the 1981/82 season.

'After training, the players would stay behind in the dressing room. They had a bass drum and two or three guitars, and they would sing *pasodobles* and *cuplés*. They ended up taking the act to Seville, performed it, and caused a huge stir.

'They went against the orders of the club president, who tried to stop them. Mané, the captain, told him to take whatever disciplinary measures he wanted; they had given their word to perform at a charity gala.

'Even under the threat of punishment, they went anyway. They didn't care.'

* * *

The spirit of Cádiz is distilled into its purest form in the *barrio* of La Viña, an old fishing neighbourhood packed into a few streets at the south-western end of the peninsula next to La Caleta beach. Its narrow, palm-dotted streets and whitewashed facades are evocative of Latin America. So much so that the area has served as a body double for Havana in a host of movies.

The neighbourhood is famed for its strong sense of community and as the home of a whimsical cast of characters that wouldn't be out of place in a Louis de Bernières novel.

There was La Uchi, a cheeky, pugnacious girl who never really grew up. Seen every day zipping around the streets and alleys of the *barrio* on the bicycle she'd had since childhood in an FC Barcelona tracksuit, often imitating the siren of a police car. La Uchi unwittingly found global fame in 2016 when she startled Rick Stein into an incredulous 'Bloody hell!' as she burst into a bar calling out for the waiter as the celebrity chef was shooting a piece for the BBC about white anchovies.

La Uchi famously never tolerated any slight of her beloved Barça, but another La Viña personality was legendary for his loyalty to his local club. They called him Macarty, a man short of stature but big of heart.

'There was a time when no one anywhere in the world really wore football shirts,' says Espinosa. 'If you look at old images of the Chamartín stadium in Madrid, for example, people are dressed in suits and ties. But Macarty would go to football matches in the 1960s wearing a wool cap – even in the heat – and a yellow Cádiz shirt with the club crest, which he would buy at a shop on Calle San Francisco called Casa Rural Portugal. He'd buy the badge and the shirt there and go off to the stadium. People thought he was crazy.

'There's a really beautiful carnival song dedicated to him. It tells the story of how people thought this man was mad simply for loving Cádiz CF so deeply. Every cent he earned was to follow the team. He even flew with the squad on away trips. It was a passion that bordered on obsession.

'To earn a living, he delivered coffee from a local café to stalls in the central market, and later, he made money by selling clandestine lottery tickets, a practice that was common in Cádiz during the 1980s. That was his job. And everything he earned, absolutely everything, was spent on following Cádiz.'

That Macarty and La Uchi are immortalised in carnival songs is natural in a neighbourhood that is the spiritual home of the city's biggest annual event. It's the streets of La Viña that buzz all day and long into the night, with groups of musicians roaming the streets, playing impromptu sets during the 11 days of silliness and mayhem that engulf the city each February.

And it's the *barrio* that's most renowned for producing those performers, including the most famous of them all, Manolo Santander, whose most treasured composition is belted out before kick-off each time Cádiz play at home. Although he didn't come from a family with a musical tradition, growing up in La Viña, where carnival is a way of life, meant Santander was soon hooked. By the age of 18, he had won his first carnival gold medal, beginning a four-decade love affair with the competition and the crowds that pack the city's Gran Teatro Falla each year.

Seeing a carnival group roving through the streets, delivering their lyrical punchlines, seems like a freewheeling, carefree pursuit. But beneath it all, and especially when it comes to the annual Official Competition of Carnival Groups of Cádiz (known as COAC), there are rules and structure aplenty.

'Carnival is a very serious kind of fun, as we say round here,' laughs Sánchez Reyes, who collaborated as a songwriter with Santander and is well-placed to provide a rough guide to the competition's components.

'Since the mid-1970s, four official types of Carnival groups have existed. The *cuarteto* which was created in the 1970s. It's the most difficult one because it has to be funny all the time. Four or five people perform with nothing but themselves in front of the audience. In fact, very few groups compete in it. This year, for example, there are only five *cuartetos*, because it's so hard to pull off. It's more like theatre.

'There's the *coro*, which has the most members – between 35 and 45 – and its main musical piece is the tango, which is one of the fundamental pieces of the Cádiz Carnival – one of the most genuine expressions we have.

'Then there's the *comparsa*, which has 15 members and is the most serious style. It's based on emotion, criticism and feeling.

'Then, the *chirigota*, which has a maximum of 12 members and is the most outlandish and humorous in style. There are many sub-styles within it. For example, we do a kind of classic *chirigota* where the *pasodoble* is serious, but the rest is comedy. Then there are other groups that are funny from beginning to end.

'We, in particular, continue the style of Manolo Santander – that of the old traditional *chirigoteros* of Cádiz.

'If a group makes it to the final, they must perform four times – preliminaries, quarter-finals, semi-finals, and the final. It's like the Champions League. In all four rounds, the *chirigota*, for example, repeats two pieces: the presentation and the *popurrí*. These are known as the "fixed parts", and they generally stay the same.

'What must be brand new – this is mandatory according to the rules – are the *cuplés* [a short, satirical song] and the *pasodobles* [a longer song with no chorus]. They have to be completely new in each performance.

'In the final, the rules allow you to repeat one *pasodoble* and one *cuplé*, but almost no one does it because the more new lyrics you bring, the better your chances with the judges. And repeating pieces in the final is seen as a sign of weakness – like you don't have enough strong material.'

What sets the Cádiz carnival apart is the satirical tone that drives the acts, as Sánchez Reyes explains: 'There was a journalist at *Diario de Cádiz*, named Bartolomé Llompart, who coined the phrase, "Carnival is sung journalism". In each competition, the groups review events that have happened during the year in a critical tone, a humorous tone, or some mix of both. So we get the chance for one month to say out loud all the outrageous things you can't say anywhere else. To criticise whatever you want, to make fun of whoever you want – it's a real opportunity. That helps us, in a way, to escape reality a bit.'

With a thematic refresh for each annual competition involving dreaming up and designing elaborate costumes and tours around the country for the most successful groups, the life of a *chirigotero* is a year-round endeavour. It was this cycle of inspiration, creation, and performance that Santander was devoted to, from his first success as a teenager in 1981 to his final, poignantly triumphant appearance in 2019.

It's a legacy that is continued by his son, who quite literally continues the name, only distinguishable by the use of the diminutive 'Manolín'.

'I'm marked for life! I mean, my name is Manolo Santander. So people look at me and say, "You're his son, right?" But it's a source of pride. It's an incredible honour to carry his name and to do the things he used to do. I'm glad he passed those things down to me because I love them, too. He's going to be remembered forever. For someone to become immortal like that, to live on in people's minds – it's amazing.'

Manolín isn't doing too badly himself. A gold medallist with his *chirigota* in 2022, followed by a silver a year later; after a break, he was back in 2025 and winning again, this time in the *comparsa* category alongside some childhood friends from La Viña and an act that paid a classy homage to his father's most famous work – *'Me han dicho que el amarillo'* ('They tell me that yellow').

For the endless toil to impress the judges, it's a curiosity that a song that went down badly with the jury and didn't even enthuse Santander's bandmates has become so all-conquering.

'My dad was a huge Cádiz CF fan, totally devoted to the team,' recalls Manolín. 'So he often wrote a song for them, and the one he did that year, back in 1998, was when it all started.

'Back then, Cádiz were in *Segunda B*, the third tier of Spanish football. Hardly anyone went to the games, but he always had a special place in his heart for the team. So he wrote the song for the carnival competition and just to cheer them on.

'He sang that *pasodoble* because he wanted to. They sang it on the first day of the contest, and the jury rated it poorly and gave it a low score. But they made it to the final of the competition, where you are allowed to repeat a piece – and he chose to repeat that one, even though the rest of the group were against the idea. And well, it turns out that thanks to singing it again, it grew and grew and grew... all the way until today.'

That year, Santander and his *chirigota* were themed on a prohibition-era mafia family – *La Familia Pepperoni*. They took to the stage dolled up as gangsters, Santander himself as the *capo* in a bright white suit and comedy cigar. The refrain of '*Ra-ta-ta-ta-ta, ra-ta-ta-ta-ta*' as they playfully lowered their mock Tommy guns has become a cherished element of the song.

Referencing the club's famous yellow colours, the *pasodoble* builds as a stirring tribute to a fanbase that remains devoted and admired despite never expecting to win a thing, leading to the rousingly defiant sign-off.

Por eso viva mi Cádiz,   So long live my Cádiz,
Vivan los cadistas,   Long live los cadistas
Vivan sus cojones.   Long live their cojones.

While the COAC judges were indifferent, in the streets, the song gained an energy of its own. Soon, it was being sung on matchdays at the Carranza, introduced by the ultras of the *Brigada Amarilla*, then spreading throughout the stadium. Two years later, when carnival rolled around, and Santander and his merry men were competing again, this time styled as an order of Franciscan monks – *Los de Capuchinos* – something very special happened.

Towards the end of their semi-final performance, the group performed a *pasodoble* that thanked Cádiz fans for embracing their song. As the song finished and the band stood, heads bowed, waiting to begin the next number, the audience began an impromptu rendition of '*Me han dicho que el amarillo*'.

'That was a unique moment,' says Manolín. 'Really unusual. He sang a *pasodoble* to thank the fans and the crowd... the crowd sang back to them. It was historic.'

The *chirigota* stood there, clearly moved, trying to resist the temptation to join in before joyfully succumbing, risking the wrath of the jurors. 'Technically, since they started singing with the audience, they had performed one song too many. They could have been penalised or disqualified, but they got away with it.'

Los de Capuchinos progressed and won gold, but it was that semi-final moment which became emblematic. 'The people had made it their own,' says Sánchez Reyes. 'That's something Manolo always took pride in – that *pasodoble* no longer belonged to him, it belonged to the people. And that's the best thing that can happen to a writer in the Cádiz Carnival – for their song to become immortal.'

The club sensed the way the wind was blowing and soon officially installed Santander's *pasodoble* as the anthem the players took the field to. The team gathered momentum, finally breaking out of *Segunda B* after an excruciating run of failed promotion attempts.

With Cádiz at last back in the professional ranks, Santander became the face of the club when he fronted their annual TV advertising campaign, selling season tickets and memberships for several years. 'He was the most *Cadista* carnival performer; he was known as a big fan of the club,' recalls Manolín. 'So they started doing these campaigns with these low-budget ads. Instead of hiring someone to make an ad, people from here made them. It was cool, a real fun experience.'

The gloriously homespun skits featured Santander as a patient in hospital with 'yellow fever', a chef in a spoof cooking programme and embroiled in a dramatic confrontation with Darth Vader that won him over to the 'yellow side'.

Cádiz reached *Primera* in 2005, 12 years after their last appearance, but as quickly as they climbed, they tumbled back again, collapsing into *Segunda B*, plagued by ownership issues. A new board eventually brought improvement and recognition for Santander. In 2015, he received an award from the club with his lyrics inscribed on the wall of the trophy room.

Santander continued creating and performing, competing each year until his final carnival in 2019.

'That was tough,' says Manolín. 'He was diagnosed with cancer and was undergoing treatment, but he got worse and started losing weight – you know, all the things that happen to people with that horrible illness. But he found the courage and strength to put together a group – a really great one. They were dressed like octopuses and like *Pirates of the Caribbean*. He said it gave him life. Every day, he would go to rehearsals, he would sing, write, read – all of that helped.'

Santander's final *chirigota* – *'La maldición de la lapa negra'* ('The curse of the black limpet'), would provide one of the most emotional moments in carnival history courtesy of a *pasodoble* penned by Sánchez Reyes.

'He was sick,' says Sánchez Reyes. 'Everyone knew it – and even during some of the *Lapa Negra* performances, he had chemo in the morning and in the evening, he was performing at the theatre. A completely counterproductive thing, the doctors warned him, but he wasn't going to abandon his *chirigota*.

'So here was the thing – we were still missing one *pasodoble* for that competition. I had written one about him. So when he asked me, "Do you have anything?" I said, "Yes. I'll sing it at rehearsal tonight." He asked, "What's it about?" I said, "It's for you."

'He gave me a strange look because he hated being the centre of attention. He was humble, he didn't like the spotlight.

'So that night, I sang this *pasodoble* about his illness. I never mentioned it directly, but it spoke about the strength he was showing. Everyone there got quite emotional. Then he said, "I wouldn't have written this, but, if a friend has written it for me, then we'll rehearse it."

'So that was the song we performed in the final. That was the grand final of *La Lapa Negra*, and it was one of the most beautiful moments we've ever experienced at that theatre. It was late at night – we sang to him – and the entire place rose to its feet, knowing that Manolo was sick. Standing in the middle, Manolo removed his hat and bowed his head. I mean, I'm telling you this now, and I still get goosebumps.'

La Lapa Negra took gold, propelled by a song that said so much about Santander's illness without mentioning it at all. 'I called it *"una cosita"* (a little thing) because here in Cádiz, we always say that – "It's a little thing." That word *cancer* terrifies me – and I'm very superstitious about these things. In Cádiz, a lot of people don't call it that. They just say, "A little thing came up."'

The performance brought a huge outpouring of support, says Manolín, 'The people really rallied around him. The day after, people brought us gifts, things to lift him up and encourage him. If love alone could've saved him, he would've lived. In the end, it wasn't enough.'

His health deteriorated further until on 3 September 2019, just months after that triumphant final performance, Manolo Santander died at the age of 56.

'He won, and he left,' says his son, Manolín. 'He said goodbye in style, that guy.'

***

'The father of our *himno* has left us. His legacy will forever remain in the *"Me han dicho que el amarillo"* that proudly plays in our home, your home forever, Manolo.'

The club led the tributes to Santander. In their first home game after his death, the steps that climb from changing rooms to pitch were emblazoned with his lyrics. A huge tifo with his image was unfurled across the *fondo sur*. A minute's silence was impeccably observed with the anthem softly played by piano. A more raucous rendition got the game underway, and one last celebratory version greeted the full-time whistle after a 2-0 win.

Manolín, along with his mother and sister, were guests of honour, 'It was incredible. It was the most powerful minute of silence I've ever seen. Everyone was silent – completely silent. People were crying. The fans were crying. Paying tribute to him like that… it was something overwhelming.

'They gave us gifts – they placed a huge floral arrangement, which they never usually do, on the centre spot. They framed a jersey for us – the club went all in. And the fans did, too.'

Cádiz ended the season winning promotion back to *Primera*, where this time they managed a stay of four seasons. Their top-flight status even earned "*Me han dicho que el amarillo*" a place in teenagers' bedrooms across the world when EA Sports included it in *FIFA 23*.

'The club called me,' smiles Manolín. 'They said *FIFA* wanted to include it, and they asked if we could make it happen. I said, "Of course!" Imagine – anywhere in the world, you play a match as Cádiz, and my father's song comes on. How amazing is that?'

The same year Santander was immortalised in the world's most popular video game, he was remembered in his humble *barrio* of La Viña. Just yards from where he lived, one of the neighbourhood's main squares was renamed in his honour.

'It's in an iconic *plaza*, actually. There's a playground there that I go to with my daughter,' says Manolín. 'One day, when my daughter understands, I can say, "Look, this place is named after your grandfather." And in a few years, they're going to lay down grass and turn it into a proper park. It's going to be wonderful.'

Manolín attends every Cádiz home game, a season ticket holder along with his mother and sister, cheering on the team and getting a fortnightly tug of the heartstrings.

'That song was born in my house. So it's something I'm really proud of.

'It's something huge. People who never met my father are going to know him. My daughter will know him. My grandchildren will know him. It will be passed down from generation to generation, even though he's no longer alive. That's something really special. Very few people achieve that.

'I had the privilege of witnessing it and living it. It's an honour to hear it. It's emotional because it reminds you of him – and then you see little kids singing his words. It's really beautiful.'

ONCE UPON A TIME IN LA LIGA

Me han dicho que el amarillo (Spanish)

Me han dicho que el amarillo
está maldito pa' los artistas,
y ese color, sin embargo,
es gloria bendita para los cadistas.

Que aunque reciben a cambio
todo un calvario de decepciones,
de amarillo se pintan la cara,
amarillo son sus corazones.

Han dado su vida y sus gargantas,
siguiendo a donde haga falta
al Cádiz de sus amores,

Ra-ta-ta-ta-ta, ra-ta-ta-ta-ta,
Benditos sean los que llenan de esperanza,
Ra-ta-ta-ta-ta, ra-ta-ta-ta-ta,
Cada rincón, cada escalón de mi Carranza.

Sin importarles que nunca,
vayan a ser campeones
han conseguido el respeto,
de toda España, por estos colores.

Por eso viva mi Cádiz,
vivan los cadistas,
vivan sus cojones.

THEY TELL ME YELLOW IS CURSED

Me han dicho que el amarillo (English)

They tell me that yellow,
Is cursed for *los artistas*,
Yet, this colour,
Is blessed glory for *los cadistas*.

And though in return,
They endure a torment of disappointments,
It's yellow they paint their faces,
Yellow are their hearts.

They've given their lives and their voices,
Following wherever needed,
The Cádiz that they love,

Ra-ta-ta-ta-ta, ra-ta-ta-ta-ta,
Blessed are those who fill with hope,
Ra-ta-ta-ta-ta, ra-ta-ta-ta-ta,
Every corner, every step of my Carranza.

Without caring that ever,
Will they be champions,
They've earned the respect,
Of all of Spain, for these colours.

So long live my Cádiz,
Long live *los cadistas*
Long live their *cojones*.

Acknowledgements

IF TRUTH be told, I avoided committing to this book for longer than I should have. I feared it would be a solitary pursuit. As so often happens, I couldn't have been more wrong. It's been genuinely life-affirming to speak with all those who shared their memories. They entrusted me with their stories, and I only hope I've done them justice.

So, my sincerest thanks to everyone quoted within – without exception, it was a joy to speak with you. *Sois unos cracks.*

A special thank you to those who went the extra mile: Sergio Manzanera, Jesús Beltrán, Emilio Nadal, Oriol Jové, Antoni Daimiel, Santi Segurola, Rubén Cagiao, Pedro M. Espinosa and Manolín Santander.

I'm grateful to José Manuel Holgado of Racing Santander and David Tolo of Espanyol for sharing photos, and to Dan Parry, Luis Arconada Lamsfus and Jane Ledsom for their help arranging interviews.

Thanks to the staff at the National Archives at Kew, especially Paul Johnson, for their valuable assistance.

Thanks to Jane Camillin at Pitch Publishing, with special thanks to Paul for fielding my often-daft questions. Thanks also to Duncan Olner for his work on the cover, Dean Rockett for proofreading, and Graham Hales for his typesetting expertise.

A huge thank you to Sid Lowe for his foreword, a brilliant interview, and valuable counsel.

Ewan Flynn's friendship, advice, and tireless proofreading were indispensable. Graham Hunter's (expletive-laden)

ACKNOWLEDGEMENTS

motivational boosts and Colin Millar's timely support and perspective also meant a great deal.

I'll always be grateful to Jonathan Wilson at *The Blizzard* – the first editor to commission me – for giving me the space to explore the lives of Andrés Montes and the Hotel Corona de Aragón fire as they developed into chapters. Similarly, thank you to Daniel Gray and Ally Palmer at *Nutmeg* for the opportunities that helped me build towards this.

Phil Kitromilides and Alex Kirkland of *The Spanish Football Podcast*, along with *La Liga TV*'s Tim Lee encouraged and shared my writing in its tentative early days. And I owe a debt of gratitude to everyone who helped make *Fútbol es la leche* an unexpected success back when Spanish football on social media felt like a community – before someone broke the machine.

As ever, thanks to Tony Bloom, who gave me opportunity and set me on the path to this fascination with Spanish football. To Nick Marple, Juan Martin, Martin Bennedbaek, Kabir Viroomal, Rhys Blake, Dan Staff-Brett and Neil Nally for the long lunches, Copa del Rey finals, European nights and Mondays at Leganés. We're overdue another trip.

To Alec Bowers and Matt Lunn – always keen to ask how things were coming along – encouragement that meant a great deal, especially when mine wavered. And thanks to Cathryn Summerhayes for her words of wisdom on laps of the park.

Love and thanks to my mum, Sheila, and my sister, Helen. Our small but hardy family unit. Always there, no matter what life throws up.

To my wife's family – Joseph, Bríd, John, Tara, and Joe – thank you for your support.

Finally, to those to whom this book is dedicated. Without my wife, Sinéad, not a single line of this – or anything – would have been written. I'll never take your love, patience, and guidance for granted.

To my son, Malachy, and my daughter, Róisín – I promise I'll be spending less time staring at a computer screen, but I hope our trips across Spain and encounters with giant shellfish continue for many years to come.

And to my oldest and closest friend, Shane O'Connor. I remember the night over a couple of pints of the black stuff when I told you I'd dipped a toe into football writing.

'You'll be good at that. Proud of you, mate,' you replied.

Just weeks later, after a day watching Luton Town together, you were cruelly taken from us, leaving a huge hole in so many lives.

I hope I have made you proud, mate.